EIGHT
MILES
from the
FRONT
GATE

Nancy and Ted Paup Ranching Heritage Series
Paul H. Carlson & M. Scott Sosebee, series editors

EIGHT MILES

MILES

from the

FRONT

GATE

My Life on the
Y.O. Ranch with
Charles Schreiner III

Norma Schreiner

TEXAS A&M UNIVERSITY PRESS

College Station

∞ This paper meets the requirements of ANSI/NISO Z39.48-1992
(Permanence of Paper).
Binding materials have been chosen for durability.

LIBRARY OF CONGRESS CATALOGING-IN-PUBLICATION DATA

Names: Schreiner, Norma, 1944– author
Title: Eight miles from the front gate : my life on the Y.O. Ranch with
     Charles Schreiner III / Norma Schreiner.
Other titles: Nancy and Ted Paup '74 ranching heritage series
Description: College Station : Texas A&M University Press, [2025] | Series:
     Nancy and Ted Paup ranching heritage series | Includes bibliographical
     references and index.
Identifiers: LCCN 2025014372 (print) | LCCN 2025014373 (ebook) |
     ISBN 9781648433283 cloth | ISBN 9781648433290 ebook
Subjects: LCSH: Schreiner, Charles, III, 1927-2001 | Schreiner, Norma,
     1944—Homes and haunts—Texas—Y.O. Ranch | Ranchers—Texas—Texas
     Hill Country—Biography | Ranchers' spouses—Texas—Texas Hill
     Country—Biography | Ranch life—Texas—Y.O. Ranch | Big game
     ranching—Texas—Y.O. Ranch | LCGFT: Biographies
Classification: LCC SF194.2.S3 S37 2025 (print) | LCC SF194.2.S3 (ebook)
     | DDC 636/.01092—dc23/eng/20250602
LC record available at https://lccn.loc.gov/2025014372
LC ebook record available at https://lccn.loc.gov/2025014373

This book is lovingly dedicated to
all creatures great and small
that were part of the Y.O. Ranch
when it was owned by the Schreiners.

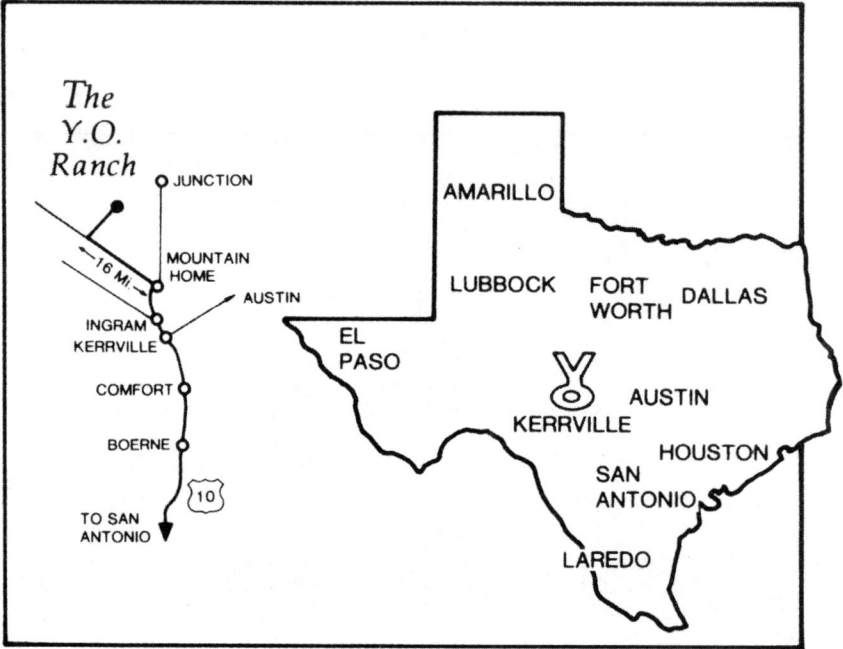

The Y.O. Ranch

JUNCTION

MOUNTAIN HOME

16 Mi.

AUSTIN

INGRAM
KERRVILLE

COMFORT

BOERNE

10

TO SAN
ANTONIO

AMARILLO

LUBBOCK   FORT   DALLAS
            WORTH

EL
PASO

Y
O
KERRVILLE   AUSTIN

HOUSTON

SAN
ANTONIO

LAREDO

"The past is never dead.

It's not even past."

WILLIAM FAULKNER

Contents

Acknowledgments

No book is written and published without the help and support of many people, and I am grateful to all of them. There are five people without whom this memoir would not have been birthed or printed. In alphabetical order they are:

Lydia Kualapai—a friend whose course in creative writing jump-started the first chapters that became this memoir. She was also the reader for the initial chapters and gave me the encouragement to keep going for another three hundred-plus pages.

Ted Paup—he enthusiastically recommended the manuscript be part of the Ranching Heritage Series that he and his wife, Nancy, are sponsoring at Texas A&M University Press.

Harold Prasatik—my first reader, tireless editor (who remains amazed at my aversion to commas), critic who pulled no punches on what needed changing, and my beloved fiancé in perpetuity. He also provided comic relief, champagne, encouragement, and nightly meals for his cooking-averse author.

Charles Schreiner IV—a constant and valuable resource for providing information about the Y.O. Ranch, photographs, names, dates, and other important and obscure information. He is currently writing his memoir of the Y.O., and I hope to be of equal assistance to him.

Chase Untermeyer—we met when he was in the Texas legislature and I was lobbyist for the Equal Rights Amendment. Chase is responsible for making me aware of the Ranching Heritage Series and sending my manuscript to Ted Paup. Words are insufficient to thank him for making my childhood dream of becoming a published author a reality.

I must also thank my first readers, all of whom made valuable suggestions that I took to heart to improve the manuscript: Kathy Crowley, Fritzi Harry, Gil Hartman, Valeria Perez, Frannie Roberts, Charlene Stacy, and Chase Untermeyer. And, Bill Head, who literally read the manuscript and recommended changes as he lay dying. Throughout the forty years of our friendship, Bill kept reminding me to write my memoir about the Y.O. The last time I saw him, his bed was covered with pages of my manuscript that he carefully reviewed with me.

My appreciation to Ron Dorsey, Joe Herring, Tiffany Schreiner, Charles Schreiner IV, and Wendy Watriss. They all gave permission to use their photographs, which greatly enhance my narrative. I also appreciate Digital

Pro Labs in San Antonio, especially Shirley, for the excellent job they did in reproducing the photographs in this book.

To my friends, who were kind enough to inquire about and show an interest in the book throughout the years it was being written, I express my heartfelt appreciation. One friend in particular, Marsha Maurer, who is also a writer, was an empathizing listener and encourager as I went through the birthing process.

My sincerest gratitude and appreciation to Thom Lemmons, editor in chief at Texas A&M University Press, for his patience in fielding my inquiries and guiding me in preparing the manuscript for publication. Abagail Chartier was my co-editor and a joy to work with. She not only kept me informed about the book's progress but was enthusiastic in her support of it. Matt Joyce, my copy editor, helped me solve quandaries about capitalization as well as making suggestions on wording that improved the book. I was fortunate to have such a dedicated and talented group working with me.

In keeping with the long tradition of writers having cats, I must thank all the cats who shared this endeavor with me: Fracker, Julius, Rumi, Odette, and Baca. They encouraged me by sitting in front of the computer screen, walking across the keyboard, lying on the keyboard, and dropping toys at my feet to so I would have a diversion.

Though my parents are dead, I thank them for instilling in me a love of reading and words, which led to my lifetime desire to write a book. Actually, this is my second book. My first book was written when I was ten years old. It was a mystery titled The Secret of the Old Fireplace. Written in pencil on lined notebook paper, it was a knockoff of the Nancy Drew books to which I was addicted. My longing and thinking about writing a book continued throughout my life, finally coming to fruition in *Eight Miles from the Front Gate*.

Without Charles Schreiner III, I never would have had this story to tell. If I had it to do over again, I'd still get on that plane to Guadalajara and move to the Y.O. Ranch. I am also grateful to Charlie Three's four sons, living and dead, who welcomed me into their family and treated me with kindness, consideration, and respect during the time I was with their father and in the years since.

Now that my childhood dream has come true, my heartfelt thanks go to you, my readers, who have purchased, borrowed, absconded with, or been given this book and invested your time in reading it.

EIGHT

MILES

from the

FRONT

GATE

CHAPTER 1

"More tears are shed

over answered prayers

than unanswered ones."

SAINT TERESA

Answered Prayers

TRAVELING AT OVER EIGHTY MILES an hour we come over a rise in the road. Up ahead on the right is a twenty-foot-tall sign made from cedar posts with "Y.O. Ranch" across the top.* Hanging between the posts is the ranch brand, a "Y" perched atop an oval shaped "O." Beneath it, arrows point down a caliche road.

We turn onto it and within minutes arrive at an unremarkable gate with signs declaring membership in the Texas and Southwestern Cattle Raisers Association, Texas Longhorn Breeders Association, and the Texas Sheep and Goat Raisers Association. As Charlie gets out to open the gate, I marvel that I am about to get a personal tour of one of Texas' historic ranches by its owner, Charles Schreiner III.

As a child in the 1950s, I yearned to live on a ranch. Cowboys and cowgirls dominated the movies and television and were mimicked in dress, manners, and games by my brothers, our friends, and me. I prayed the Lord would see fit to perform a miracle and turn my minister father into a rancher, a miracle that was as likely to occur as his answering my other prayer to turn my recently arrived baby brother into a much longed for sister. To comfort myself, I imagined my bicycle was a sleek black steed named Bluebonnet. Bending over the handlebars I whispered into her ear as I pedaled her into a gallop.

---

* Y.O. is pronounced as the individual letters "Y" and "O," not as "yo." It is written as Y.O. with no space after the period following the "Y."

My parents are to blame for my horse fetish, which remains to this day. When I was three, they placed me on the back of a horse at Kiddie Wonderland Park in Houston, Texas. It was necessary to drive by the park whenever we went to Houston to visit my grandparents. If we were on a tight schedule, it was my mother's job to divert my attention as we passed. Often she succeeded, but not always. My horse of choice was a spotted Shetland pony named Spunky. It was his job to plod around the dirt track at a glacial speed. I never left his back without pitching a fit that involved clinging to the reins and kicking and screaming at the top of my lungs.

My father would lift me from the saddle as my mother untwined the reins from my tiny fingers. One day my maternal grandfather, D. A. Binford, decided to take me to ride Spunky until I was sated in hopes it would squelch my equestrian yearnings. After two hours of circling the track at a snail's pace, my grandfather's patience was depleted. I was removed from Spunky's back in the usual manner and screamed all the way home. My tantrum led my grandfather to assess me as the most "headstrong child" he ever saw, which was saying a mouthful given my mother was his daughter. That trait would remain with me and be confirmed, not always in positive ways, by the men in my life.

When Charlie returns to the car, I point to a small building inside the gate with a sign saying "Game Warden." I ask Charlie, "Does the ranch have its own game warden?"

"Only during hunting season. Hunters arrive and leave at all hours and somebody has to check them in and out."

As we start down the caliche road, on the right I see a sign declaring, "Headquarters 8 Miles." Charlie slows his speed in deference to the road's ruts, loose rocks, and cavities that could have been created by cannon balls. The road stretches flat before us, bordered by rock-strewn pastures of stunted live oak trees, agarita bushes, and prickly pear cactus all wearing shrouds of gray dust. When I look behind us, the landscape has vanished in a cloud of dust.

"Now I understand why your car is always dirty," I say.

Charlie drove a station wagon whose exterior and interior were well-worn and perpetually covered in dust. Because driving was his preferred method of travel, the car had aged quickly. The original red interior was now a faded rust with scratches and gashes from whatever sharp objects had been placed on or dragged across it. Jammed between the windshield and dashboard were numerous notebooks and itinerant pieces of paper containing "to do" lists, phone numbers, and information on his many projects. A shotgun was wedged between the headrests of the front seat. The back of the station wagon could contain a mounted deer head, an antique Louis XV chair, a chain saw, or all of these objects. It was not the type of car one expected the owner of a large ranch to drive.

"Why don't you drive a newer model car?" I ask.

"When I first started running the ranch, my mother sent me to buy some sheep. I had a brand-new Buick I thought befit my new position as ranch manager. I pulled up to this ole boy's house and we start talking. He kept eyeing my car. The next thing I knew the price of those sheep doubled. I learned more from that experience than any business course I took."

"I understand that, but why don't you at least pave the road?"

"It's eight miles and costs $10,000 a mile, so what do you think? Besides, it adds to the ambiance. Like my hat." Charlie lifted his bedraggled straw cowboy hat. "When people from the city come here, it lets them know they're on a real Texas working ranch."

As we drive, Charlie points out various animals standing beside the road or bolting across it as the car spooks them. Some are familiar, like the native whitetail deer, but many, like the axis deer, blackbuck antelope, and scimitar horn oryx, I've never seen. We pass a high fenced pen with several eland, which Charlie tells me are the largest member of the antelope family and could weigh over two thousand pounds. Each time we cross a cattle guard we enter a new pasture with a sign designating its name: Gilmer, West Feed, Blackbuck, and South Home—a litany that would become as familiar to me as the Lord's Prayer.

"How many acres is the Y.O.?" I ask.

"Before I tell you, I'm going to teach you a basic rule of ranch etiquette. You never ask someone how many acres they own. It's the same as me asking you how much money you have in the bank."

"I'm sorry. Never mind."

"It isn't exactly a secret. Whenever an article is written about the ranch it always leads with its size. Fifty thousand acres. Used to be sixty thousand but we've had to sell some to pay the goddamned estate taxes to Uncle Sam after mother died."

It is as difficult for me to grasp how large that is as to unravel the twists of fate putting me on this rutted caliche road with Charles Schreiner III. What I could not know on this Indian summer afternoon was memories of that first drive would haunt me each time I drove this road for the next forty years.

CHAPTER 2

"Those who flee temptation

generally leave a forwarding address."

LANE OLINGHOUSE

Just a Sheep and Goat Rancher

CHARLIE WAS THE KIND OF MAN who could charm the rattles off a snake or be as menacing as one. The difference was the rattlesnake usually warned his victim before striking. To the world Charlie presented the facade of humble good ole boy who owned "a little sheep and goat ranch." From his appearance, you would never suspect he was scion of one of the historic and prominent ranching families of Texas.

His usual attire was sand-colored jeans, a red-and-white-checked Western shirt with pearl-snap buttons, and a misshapen sweat-stained cowboy hat, straw in summer and felt in winter. Only those familiar with such accessories would identify the hatband as horsehair and the wiry black object jutting from it as a turkey beard, which Charlie placed there after killing its owner. He was shod with black custom-made cowboy boots, worn but highly polished. Looking closely, one saw Charlie branded his clothing as well as himself. His ranch brand was embroidered on his shirt pocket, engraved on his belt buckle, and set in diamonds on a large gold ring worn significantly on the third finger of his left hand. This was his attire on the day we met.

It was the summer of 1977. I was at the Texas Capitol researching voting patterns for the political campaign for which I was working. I decided to drop by the office of one of my favorite house members, Jim Nugent. Since the Texas legislature wasn't in session, I didn't expect him to be there,

Charles Schreiner III, 1977.

but I could visit his staff and perhaps pick up valuable political gossip. But Nugent was in, and before his staff could announce me, he was bellowing, "Norma, come in here. There's someone I want you to meet." As I walked into Nugent's office, his visitor rose from his chair and removed his bedraggled cowboy hat. "How charming," I thought. Few men I knew stood to acknowledge a woman's entrance much less remove their hats.

"Norma, this is Charlie Schreiner," Nugent said. "Charlie owns a little sheep and goat ranch in my district. Charlie, this is one of my favorite lobbyists, Norma Cude. Norma lobbied for the Equal Rights Amendment during the session and did a damn good job of making sure we didn't have to vote on rescinding it." Nugent turned in my direction. "Charlie was one of my biggest adversaries until one day I decided it was time for us to work together. I flew out to his ranch, we talked things over, and he's been supporting me ever since."

Charlie grinned and extended his hand. "I admired Jim going to the trouble to visit me in person. We still have things we don't agree on, but unlike some decisions I've made, I've never regretted that one."

As Charlie spoke, I noticed he was ever so subtly appraising me while keeping a firm grip on my hand. His blue-gray eyes twinkled, and his salt-and-pepper mustache twitched mischievously. I took a seat across from Charlie as he and Nugent resumed their conversation. Nugent was asking

Photo of the author, 1977.

Charlie about a recent trip to Mexico. With Charlie's attention directed to Nugent, I studied the rancher more closely. He was attractive though somewhat paunchy. As they talked, Charlie worried his hat in his hands, hands that were gnarled and scarred and obviously not immune to hard work. Charlie removed a red bandana from his hip pocket and began cleaning his glasses. From time to time, he would glance at me with a shy smile. There was a presence to him, as well as a devilishness. Something about his demeanor told me he was not your average sheep and goat rancher.

"Remind me how long it takes to get from your front gate to that new house you're building," Nugent said.

"About thirty minutes but if it's rained it can take almost an hour."

"How many miles is it?" Nugent asked.

"Eight, give or take."

"How many head of cattle are you running now?"

"Around seven hundred crossbreeds and four hundred longhorns."

"Still running sheep and goats?"

"Yes, sir. About four thousand Rambouillet sheep and 2,500 Angora goats."

I wondered how large Charlie's ranch was to support so many animals. Should I ask? I was getting the feeling Nugent was asking these questions for my benefit. During our acquaintance, I'd never known him to do anything without an objective. He was one of the most powerful members of the Texas legislature and a master of guile. As one of the Texas political elite he had access to both the speaker of the house and the governor. As chairman of the House Rules Committee, he determined which bills went to the House floor for debate. Because Nugent wrote the rules, he knew them as well as my minister father knew the Bible. They were, in fact, Nugent's Bible, and he probably held the record for having bills killed on a point of order, thus his nickname, "The Snake." Whenever he rose to speak, hisses would erupt on the House floor from his opponents. Because of my friendship with him, a friend nicknamed me "The Snake Charmer."

"How's that menagerie you've got? Added any new ones lately?" Nugent asked.

"We're thinking about getting some buffalo. Problem is they're hell on fences, so we'll have to put them in a pasture with special fencing. A couple of zebras were struck by lightning last week but they're good

Photo of the author with
James E. (Jim) Nugent.

at propagating. I was hoping they were the ones biting the tails off the elands, but no such luck. The axis and blackbuck are so prolific it's hard to keep them under control. Thank goodness we can hunt them year-round."

Zebras. Elands. Hunting. I wondered, "Could it be?" A friend occasionally worked on a ranch in the Texas Hill Country that had exotic animals and hunting. At parties he entertained us with stories about the ranch and its animals.

I interrupted the conversation. "Do you own the Y.O. Ranch?"

Charlie looked at me in surprise. "How do you know about the Y.O.?"

"I have a friend who's worked there."

"Who would that be?"

"Rusty Cox."

Charlie looked astonished. "How in the hell do you know Rusty? Please don't tell me you're one of Rusty's lady friends." Rusty had a well-deserved reputation as a ladies' man, leaving in his wake a trail of broken hearts and wrecked homes.

"We went to high school together in Houston," I replied.

"Let's get one thing straight right now," Charlie said. "Rusty has done a good many things on the Y.O. but working is not among them. Yes, we've paid him. But I have never gotten a full day's work out of him."

I laughed. "Work isn't Rusty's strong suit."

"No, it isn't. But the ladies are, and you still haven't told me if you're one of Rusty's lady friends."

I smiled. "I consider myself a lady and I am one of his friends, so draw your own conclusions."

Charlie chuckled. "You're good at not answering questions."

"I consider that an answer."

"Let me try another one. Do you like to travel?"

"It depends on where I'm going and who I'm going with. Right now I'm going back to my office." As I rose to leave, Charlie also rose. Shaking my hand, he asked if he could call me sometime. I handed him my card, certain I would never hear from him again.

Several weeks later my phone rang at five thirty in the morning. An unfamiliar voice said, "Morning, ma'am. This is Charles Schreiner III. Jim Nugent introduced us a few weeks back. I remember you saying you like to travel, and I was wondering if you'd be interested in going to Guadalajara next weekend. I'm going down there to get some things for my new house. You'll be well chaperoned. My son and his wife are going, you'll have your own room, and I promise to be on my best behavior."

Groggy from sleep, I mumbled, "I hardly know you. Why would I go to Mexico with you?"

"Because I think you're the cutest thing I ever saw and I want to get to know you. Where better to do it than old Mexico? I'm flying down on Wednesday, and you have a ticket for Friday's afternoon flight on Mexicana. Just go to the ticket counter and give them your name. I'll meet you at the Guadalajara airport. See you then. Adios." He hung up.

Amazed at Charlie's audacity, I put down the phone. What made him think I wouldn't take umbrage at such a proposal? Many women would, but if I accepted his invitation it wouldn't be the first time I ran off with a man I didn't know.

CHAPTER 3

▚▚▚▚▚▚▚▚▚▚▚

"She has never rebelled yet,

but if hard driven she will rebel one day . . ."

CHARLOTTE BRONTE

▚▚▚▚▚▚▚▚▚▚▚

Twists of Fate

HANGING UP THE PHONE, I lay in bed thinking how strange it was that after years of hearing Rusty's stories about the Y.O. Ranch I would meet its owner in the Texas Capitol. It would never have occurred had I not been hired as the Texas lobbyist for the Equal Rights Amendment, and that happened because of events set in motion the summer of 1966.

I was taking a US government class at South Texas Junior College in Houston and the instructor made the course so interesting, dynamic, and relevant I was considering changing my major from English to political science. One evening he introduced a guest speaker, whose name I didn't recognize, saying he was a businessman in Houston. The speaker, a youthful-looking man, immediately took off his coat and loosened his tie. He sat down on the edge of the desk and rolled up the sleeves of his blue oxford cloth shirt. His relaxed demeanor put the class at ease and aroused our curiosity. He began talking about the uniqueness of our democracy, the importance of public service, and giving back to your community and country. He stressed how the most important role we played as citizens is to vote, and he hoped we would all do so in November. He spoke from his heart and exuded a love for our country and a duty to it that inspired the same in me. Concluding his remarks, the speaker said he was trying to practice what he was preaching and was running for Congress in November.

After class, I joined the queue to speak to our guest. Shaking his hand,

Photo of the author with Representative Brad Wright on the floor of Texas House of Representatives during hearing on rescinding Texas's ratification of the Equal Rights Amendment, 1977.

I thanked him, and, not very eloquently, stammered words to the effect that what he said was meaningful and gave me much to ponder. He smiled his charming smile and thanked me, saying my words made his endeavors worthwhile. I changed my major and received a bachelor's and master's degree in political science. My master's thesis was on the Texas Women's Political Caucus, which led to my being hired for my first job in politics—lobbying for the Equal Rights Amendment. Through lobbying I made connections that led to my current job, the advance person in a political campaign for the US Senate. The campaign manager told me I was the first woman in Texas and possibly in the US to do advance work. The guest speaker who set off that chain reaction became the forty-first president of the United States, George Herbert Walker Bush.

The woman I became was as far removed from the girl who spoke to the future president as is a penguin from a peacock. Coming of age in the late 1950s and early 1960s, the social mores in place were a holdover from the previous half century. There was a great deal of repression regarding a woman's role in society and her sexual freedom. If a woman did not succeed in nabbing a husband by the time she finished college, the acceptable career choices were office work, nursing, and teaching. Once a woman married and started a family, she was expected to become a full-time wife and mother, enjoy every minute of it, and never doubt whether she was finding fulfillment in this role. Being strong-willed and independent was encouraged by my parents who told me I could do anything I set my mind to. It never occurred to them that I might apply that adage against them.

It was assumed from my birth I would attend my father's alma mater, Baylor University. As a child, I had a cap and a sweater in Baylor's colors, green and gold, with the bear mascot prominently displayed. I loved wearing them and telling people I would be going there. But the summer I graduated from high school, I decided to attend the University of Texas (UT) instead. Several of my friends were going there, and no one I knew was going to Baylor. When I told my parents, my father did not become visibly upset but told me I would be on my own to pay for my education. I defiantly told him I would do just that.

My next decision was breaking up with Ron, the young man I dated throughout high school. Unbeknownst to me, Ron had confided to my mother he planned to give me an engagement ring at the end of the summer. My mother told me if I wanted to date other boys, I must continue seeing Ron once a week or be grounded. These two events only added to the increasing friction between my parents as their twenty-year marriage was disintegrating.

Amid this turmoil, my father invited to dinner his college roommate's son, J. B., who was in Houston visiting relatives. He attended Baylor before dropping out to join the Air Force, and my father was hopeful J. B. could persuade me to change my mind. Much to my father's pleasure and my mother's displeasure, after dinner J. B. asked me to show him around Houston. I was happy to oblige. He was nice-looking, resembling a young Mickey Mantle, and being good Baptists we ended up in a bar where we exchanged stories. J. B. told me he was expelled from Baylor after being caught in bed with his girlfriend in her dorm room. To escape the wrath of his parents and keep from being drafted, he joined the Air Force. He was leaving in several weeks for a two-year assignment in Japan.

When I told J. B. about my father's mandate, he said, "You've got no business going to Baylor. It's where fun goes to die." Why J. B. suggested what he did I will never know. It never occurred to me to ask, and in the brief time we were together he never told me. Now I realize it had to be something as powerful as what was motivating me. It was midnight when we returned to my house. J. B. waited in the car and I slipped into the house, packed my makeup, and left a note on my pillow saying, "J. B. and I have decided to get married."

My elopement with J. B. stunned my family and friends. It led my mother to have her first taste of alcohol (bourbon straight up), my boy-friend Ron to run his hand through a window and spend the night in the emergency room, and my friends to assume I was pregnant. Everyone was certain I had gone batshit crazy. I hadn't.

In my household there were two sacred books. I cannot remember when I first became aware of either. Both were always there, and I can quote freely from either. *Gone with the Wind* was my mother's Bible, and she quoted it as readily as my father quoted the holy scriptures. Whenever my family faced problems, be they financial, personal, or spiritual, my father always quoted Matthew 5, verses 11 and 12: "Blessed are ye, when men shall revile you, and persecute you, and shall say all manner of evil against you falsely, for my sake. Rejoice, and be exceeding glad: for great is your reward in heaven." My mother's guiding mandate in hard times was Scarlett O'Hara's mantra, "I'll think about it tomorrow."

The summer I married J. B. I reread for the second or third time *Gone with the Wind*. I took to heart Scarlett's flaunting of conventions, her refusal to be daunted by dire circumstances, and her willingness to take whatever action necessary to survive on her terms. Scarlett married the first time to escape the constraints of living at home and be closer to Ashley Wilkes, the man she thought she loved. If it worked for Scarlett, it could work for me.

When J. B. proposed we marry, he explained that as his wife I would be his dependent and receive a monthly check from the government while he was in Japan. The allotment would cover my expenses to attend the University of Texas. He was willing to do this if I agreed to divorce him after a year. I agreed, and by the grace of God did not become pregnant because we used no contraception. Two weeks after we married, J. B. left for Japan, and I enrolled at the University of Texas. We never saw each other again.

The following summer I divorced him. The day our divorce was granted, I burned our marriage license and all photographs of and letters from him. Each of us got on with our lives. I never considered J. B. my husband. Ours was a business deal. J. B. provided me the financial means to attend the University of Texas for a year, and I never revealed why I married him. Until now.

J. B. and our marriage became a distant memory, never mentioned again by my family. J. B.'s father and my father remained friends, though surely their children's actions tested their friendship. In 1994 I was visit-ing my father and he told me J. B. had recently died of cancer. He was only fifty-two. "I'm sorry," I said, and I truly was. My marriage to J. B. showed me I could break the rules and survive.

Trying to decide whether to accept Charlie's invitation to join him in Guadalajara, I remembered his twinkling eyes and roguish grin. I found myself smiling. The next Saturday was my birthday and going to Guadalajara with a man who intrigued me certainly beat eating cake and ice cream while watching an old movie on TV with my cat. If I would run off and marry a man I didn't know when I was eighteen, why wouldn't I spend a weekend in Mexico with another man I didn't know when I turned thirty-three? Regardless of how it turned out, it would be a good story, and Texans love good stories. Little did I know how many stories would emerge from my leap-before-you-look decision.

CHAPTER 4

"If you obey all the rules, you miss all the fun."

KATHERINE HEPBURN

South of the Border

FLYING TO GUADALAJARA, I remembered the trips my family often made to Mexico in the early 1950s when my father was a minister in Freer, Texas. It was an easy day trip to the Mexican border city of Nuevo Laredo and going there allowed my family to exchange the dusty wind-blown grayness of Freer for the exotic sights, sounds, and smells of Mexico.

Freer sits on the back porch of the famous King Ranch and shares with it an abundance of oil fields. I remember the pump jacks surrounding the town running continuously and the flares at night as natural gas was burned off the wells. Besides its oil fields, South Texas is also known for its machine politics. Duval County, where Freer is located, is headquarters for that machine.

Begun in the late 1800s by Archie Parr, the machine was an election-deciding force in Texas politics for many years. It gained notoriety in national politics under Archie's son George with the infamous "Ballot Box 13" incident in 1948 when Lyndon Baines Johnson was running for the US Senate. After several days of counting votes, LBJ won by eighty-seven votes, all of which were cast in box thirteen. Johnson's opponent cried foul, and when the box's voting lists were examined, it was discovered that voters rose from their graves to vote in alphabetical order for LBJ. When the ballot box was brought into court, the voting list had mysteriously disappeared. Johnson was declared the winner and started down the road leading to the White House.

My parents were not supporters of LBJ. Growing up I often heard the story of Ballot Box 13, but it was not until I was grown that my father told me another part of the story tying my parents to George Parr and his machine. Baptist preachers do not make a lot of money and my family was perpetually short of cash. While living in Freer, my parents borrowed money from the Parr-owned Texas State Bank. A dilemma arose when my parents were asked to serve as election judges for the Democratic primary in 1950. Apparently those in power thought having the Baptist minister and his wife certifying the election would provide an aspect of moral authority.

Knowing the power of the Parr machine and owing money to the Parr bank, my parents agreed to serve. But knowing the shenanigans occurring two years before, they feared the ethical dilemma they might face when certifying the election results. As my parents did whenever facing a crisis, they prayed asking the Lord for guidance. Three days before the primary their prayers were answered when my brother and I came down with measles. This gave them an excuse to gracefully bow out of their civic duty. A month later when my father went to the bank to make the monthly payment on his loan, he was told the balance was paid in full by an anonymous benefactor. The Lord works in mysterious ways, his wonders to perform.

My reveries were interrupted as the plane landed in Guadalajara. As it came to a stop and stairs were rolled up to the door, my heart began pounding. I made my way to the door and heard a shrill whistle. Looking in its direction, I saw Charlie's red-and-white-checked shirt and bedraggled hat. He was grinning broadly and waving. I reciprocated his grin and made my way across the tarmac.

"You came," he exclaimed, taking my luggage. "I wasn't sure you would."

"And I wasn't sure you'd be here."

"I may be a lot of things but not stupid enough to stand up a beautiful blond. What made you decide to come?"

"My curiosity got the better of me and tomorrow is my birthday. I thought this would be a good way to celebrate."

"We'll make it a birthday to remember," Charlie said as he steered me to a taxi.

When I told Charlie this was my first trip to Guadalajara, he spent the drive giving me a brief history of the city. Founded by the Spanish in the 1500s, it had five different locations before moving to its current site in

Left to right: Charles Schreiner III, Mary Helen Schreiner, and Charles Schreiner IV, in Guadalajara, Mexico, August 6, 1977.

southwestern Mexico and had become the second largest city in Mexico. In 1811 the city played a prominent role in the Mexican war for independence from Spain and again in the 1844 revolt against President Santa Anna, whose army defeated the defenders of the Alamo in 1836.

We arrived at the hotel, and Charlie escorted me to my room and said he would pick me up at seven for dinner. There was a bouquet of flowers sitting on the desk with Charlie's business card for the Y.O. Ranch. In a combination of cursive and printing were the words, "Looking forward to getting to know you, CSIII." Charlie showed up promptly at seven to escort me to the hotel restaurant. There he guided me to a table where a handsome young couple was sitting. The man rose and Charlie whispered in my ear, "You're about to meet your chaperones." He introduced me to his son Charles Schreiner IV and his wife, Mary Helen. He also told me that to avoid confusion, I should call him "Charlie Three" or "Three" and his son "Charlie Four" or "Four."

Charlie Four was seven years younger than I and had been a legislative aide to Jim Nugent while majoring in political science at the University of Texas. Four told me the most difficult part of the job was keeping up with Nugent's long strides as he walked through the Capitol. When I said his father and I met in Nugent's office an immediate bond formed. After receiving his bachelor's degree, Four attended the Range Management School at Texas Christian University (TCU). It was started in the 1950s with support from the Texas and Southwestern Cattle Raisers Association to create an educational program to address the needs of the ranching business. Charlie Four took over management of the Y.O. after completing the program. He was good humored, sardonic, and loved giving his father a hard time about his previous wives, the new house he was building, his frequent absences from the ranch, and his ability to begin projects but not complete them.

Four's wife, Mary Helen, told me of her concerns about repairs and renovations needed on the ranch, the camp for young people that Four was spearheading, and her preference for the ranch's photo safari rather than its hunting operation. Conversation vacillated between events on the ranch and questions about me. My chaperones relished that my political views differed from Three's and that I did not hesitate to express them.

After dinner Three escorted me to my room, gave me a chaste kiss on the cheek, and told me he would pick me up for breakfast at eight the next morning. Lying in bed, I replayed the dinner conversation and thought about all the questions it raised. How many times had Charlie Three been married? What was the house he was building like? What did Y.O. stand for? My fears of enduring a weekend with a boring oaf vanished. Charlie was charming, funny, intelligent, and a man of his word. I was sleeping alone in my own room, and Charlie Four and Mary Helen were charming chaperons. The phone rang as I was dropping off to sleep. Three's distinctive baritone with its underlying chuckle purred into my ear. "Happy birthday, missy. May all your birthday wishes come true." Before I could reply, he hung up.

The next morning there was a knock on my door promptly at eight o'clock. Opening it, I was greeted by Charlie in a blue-and-white-checked shirt.

"My goodness," I said, feigning incredulity, "I almost didn't recognize you without your red-and-white shirt. I was beginning to think it was the only one you owned."

Charlie blushed. "You'll be happy to know I have six so I don't wear the same one every day. I ordered some blue ones for variety. Are you ready for breakfast, madam?"

"Indeed I am."

After breakfast, the four of us squeezed into a taxi to visit Guadalajara's market in the heart of the city. Driving through the streets, I commented on the abundance of statues of Mexican generals and statesmen.

"That's why it's such a poor country," Three said. "The first thing a politician does when he gets in power is spend money erecting statues of himself."

"How do you know that?" I asked skeptically.

"He knows everything," Four said. "And if he doesn't, he makes it up."

We drove past a large plaza fronting a cathedral with gold-tiled spires. Charlie Three told me it was the Guadalupe Cathedral built in the late 1600s. Standing around the plaza, patiently awaiting passengers, were horse-drawn carriages adorned with brightly colored paper-mache flowers. Ordering the driver to stop, Three got out and began taking pictures. Four snorted in disgust. "Why are you taking pictures of horses? We've got horses at the ranch and you never take their pictures."

"Our horses aren't scenic. These are," his father replied.

Once we were at the market, Three pointed to the sandals I was wearing and said they were the same design as those worn by the Aztecs hundreds of years before.

"Is there anything you don't know the history of?" I asked.

"You. But I intend to learn it."

There were vendors selling clothing, shoes, baskets, pottery, jewelry, and live chickens and rabbits. Three kept trying to purchase items for me justifying them as birthday gifts, and I kept refusing. We stopped at a booth where a man was fashioning bracelets and rings from brass. Buyers would tell him the name or initials they wanted the jewelry to display and with a small saw he would cut the letters into the ring or bracelet. Both Charlie and I were intrigued by his craftsmanship. Charlie began speaking with the man in Spanish and purchased rings for Charlie Four and Mary Helen. I wanted to purchase one and asked Charlie to tell him to make one with "Norma." Before I could pay, Charlie purchased it. "It's a birthday gift," he said, smiling as he placed the ring on my finger.

We left Charlie Four and Mary Helen at the market and took a taxi to shops specializing in architectural antiques and furniture. Charlie purchased several benches and a pair of twenty-foot-tall antique doors for his new home. An oxcart with four-foot wooden wheels stood outside one shop. Grass grew up to the hubs of its wheels, and a vine wound tendrils around the cart's tongue. Three inspected the cart carefully, all the while explaining the finer points of determining if it was an antique or reproduction. A piece could be aged by skillfully applying chisels, hammers, and even termites to make it appear old. "I don't mind paying for an antique, but I sure as hell don't want to pay antique prices for something made a month ago," he said.

Charlie Three with his newly acquired ox cart in Guadalajara, Mexico, August 6, 1977.

A well-dressed man appeared, and he and Charlie begin bargaining in Spanish. As they talked, they walked around the cart. Charlie pointed to various parts, shaking his head with displeasure. Several times he took my arm to leave only to be called back by the shop owner. Finally the two shook hands, and Charlie took out his checkbook.

"How will you get this home?" I asked.

"I'll send Donnie or Tony down with the trailer. I'm also marking everything I buy to make sure I get the one I bought."

It was the first but by no means last time I found myself marveling at how nonchalantly Charlie purchased items few would have the space for much less the resources to acquire and ship.

"Bargaining makes me hungry," Charlie said. "Let's get some lunch."

Soon we were in a taxi meandering through a warren of narrow streets.

We arrived at a secluded quaint stucco building. Taking my hand Charlie led me down a narrow passageway that emerged into a tree-shaded patio with multicolored tile tables. In the center stood a fountain with pots of blooming geraniums and bougainvillea around it. Within minutes of sitting down we were served margaritas. Mariachis started playing and Charlie began tapping his foot and nodding his head in time to the music. Soon he was singing along. Seeing his enthusiasm, the mariachis moved to our table and Charlie joined in their serenade. Though I did not understand Spanish, it was no less enchanting. Charlie asked them to play "Adelita."

"Do you know it?" he asked. I shook my head no. "It's a *corrido*, or folk song, that tells a story. It's the most famous one from the Mexican Revolution. There are different interpretations of who Adelita was. I prefer the one that she was a woman soldier who refused to be oppressed." Charlie stood up and began singing along with the mariachis. The song concluded with a flourish and the mariachis applauded as Charlie bowed. Sitting down he said, "I want that played at my funeral. The final line is perfect, 'I beg you, do not mourn for me.'"

The mariachis were joined by four beautiful dancers in vivid costumes of fuchsia, orange, blue, and yellow. As we watched, Charlie leaned over and said, "Imagine you're a gringo cowboy, coming to town after months on the trail. You're filthy and stink and haven't seen a woman in months. You clean up, go to the cantina, and suddenly there's music and these beautiful women with their stunning dark eyes dressed in magnificent colors. How could you not fall in love with one of them?"

"Why, Mr. Schreiner, you're quite the romantic, aren't you? Who would have thought?"

"There's a lot about me you'll find surprising once you get to know me."

"That is something I definitely want to do," I replied smiling. I took his hand, the one on which he wore the gold and diamond ring, and begin tracing the diamonds forming the Y atop the O. "This is quite a ring for a sheep and goat herder."

Charlie smiled and took my hand. A thrill went through me. "I had it made after Myrtle, my mother, died. I used the stones from a pin my father gave her when I was born."

"When did she die?"

"Five years ago."

"How?"

"Heart attack probably. She was staying with a friend who found her in

Myrtle Barton Schreiner, circa 1920s.   Walter Richard Schreiner Sr., date unknown.

the bathroom. I was in Alaska bear hunting. It took a while for me to get word. Myrtle was one hell of a woman. I was only six when my father died. Even though she knew nothing about ranching, she took over the ranch and managed it successfully."

"Did you call her Myrtle?"

Charlie laughed. "When I turned eighteen, she told me from then on the only time I was to call her 'Mother' was when it was just the two of us. She said she didn't want people to know she had a son my age."

I was immediately fascinated by this woman and wanted to know more. "Where did she meet your father?"

"In New York City. They were married in the Little Church Around the Corner."

"Was she from New York?"

"Goodness no! She was born in Blooming Grove, Texas."

"Do you remember your father?"

"Only from pictures and stories I've heard."

"Did he grow up on the ranch?"

"No. He started managing it after he got out of law school. It was ten years before his father gave it to him. But I don't want to talk about me. I know all about me. I want to learn about you. Nugent said you were a lobbyist. How did you get that job?"

"I wrote my master's thesis on the Texas Women's Political Caucus."

Charlie held up his hand. "Stop. Do you have a master's degree? In what?"

"Political science."

"Now I'm really impressed. Are you still lobbying?"

"No. I'm doing advance work for a campaign."

"I have no idea what that means."

"Whenever the candidate is speaking at an event or traveling, it's my job to ensure everything goes smoothly. Like making sure there's media coverage of his events and the right people are invited. If he's giving a speech I have to check everything is set up and in working order before he arrives. I also try to keep him on schedule, but I seldom succeed."

"And you like doing this?" Charlie asked incredulously.

"I love it, even though it means long days, usually extending into the wee hours of the morning."

"I still find it hard to believe you're a women's libber. You don't look or act like one."

"I didn't know there was a particular way we were supposed to look or act."

"For one thing you're pretty and for another you have a sense of humor."

"So, women who support equal rights are ugly and humorless?"

"Most of those I see on television are."

"Believe it or not, women's libbers come in all shapes, sizes, ages, colors, and even sexes. There are a lot of men who support women's rights, and from what you've told me about your mother, I can't believe you aren't one of them. She was the epitome of a liberated woman."

"Mother did what she had to do. I bet if you asked her, she'd say she'd rather have had a husband taking care of her."

I looked at him skeptically. "I bet she'd say she wouldn't trade the experience of running the ranch for anything. I can't imagine not working and I bet she couldn't either."

"Are you telling me you'd rather work than have a man take care of you?"

"It isn't just about working. It's about being able to choose what you want to do and having a purpose. Women face a lot of discrimination if they choose a nontraditional role like a doctor or lawyer or even running for political office."

"So, you'd rather be down in the trenches with the men than up on a pedestal?"

"The reason men put women on a pedestal is to get them out of the way." This was a line I used repeatedly when lobbying and this conversation was beginning to remind me of exchanges with members of the Texas legislature. I smiled. "The problem with being on a pedestal is what happens if you're knocked off? What if your husband leaves you and you've never worked and have no money, and everything is in his name?"

"My first wife never worked and when we divorced she did very well, and I'm still paying for it."

"Most women aren't that lucky." I smiled. "Can we not talk about politics? Can we just agree we have different opinions on certain subjects?"

"Yes ma'am, we can. Tell me, are you having a good time?"

"Yes, I am! This is a birthday I will always remember."

Charlie smiled, raised his margarita, and said, "To agreeing to disagree!" He looked at his watch. "We better get back to the hotel. I know how you ladies like to freshen up and change for dinner."

At dinner the conversation was consumed by the day's activities, the purchases made, and the sights seen. Four was giving Three a hard time about sending the cattle trailer to Mexico to retrieve his purchases. "You are aware the ranch needs that trailer to haul livestock," Four said. "I don't want it stuck in Mexico when I need to ship cattle."

"That won't happen and if it does, I'll pay out of my own pocket to rent another one," Three replied.

"You seem to forget your pocket is also the ranch's pocket."

After dinner Four and Mary Helen excused themselves and Charlie and I went to the bar. Charlie ordered champagne and after the waiter filled our glasses, Charlie raised his and said, "*Feliz Cumpleanos*! I know it's impolite to ask a lady her age but I'm curious. How old are you?"

"Thirty-three today."

"Good. Only a seventeen-year difference. The same as my mother and father and nowhere near my last wife."

I raised my eyebrows. "How old was she?"

"Considerably younger. I refer to her as my menopausal wife because I was forty-eight and she was twenty."

I did not want to pry, so rather than asking him why on earth would he marry someone so young, I asked, "Have you ever considered dating women your age?"

"Yes, and I'll tell you why I don't. Most of them look their age and act ten years older. They've lost their *joie de vivre*, and all they want to talk about is their grandchildren. To put it bluntly, they're boring. Why would I be with someone like that when I can be with you?"

"So, you'll stick around until I get gray hair and wrinkles and then you'll find someone new?"

"You're an interesting woman now and something tells me you'll be one forty years from now.

I decided to change the subject. "Tell me about the house you're building."

"Not much to tell. I never would have done it except the Casa Grande burned down and I needed a place to live that had a fireproof gun room.

"The Casa Grande?"

"The house my father built after grandfather gave him the Y.O. When he brought my mother to the ranch, the house had no electricity, and on cold mornings turkeys roosted on the roof to stay warm. I often wonder what mother thought moving there from New York City."

"What caused the fire?"

"Who knows? Probably electrical. There was no sense calling the volunteer fire department because by the time they arrived, the house would be gone. Fortunately, it occurred during the day, so the employees were able to help get things out. My main concern was saving my gun collection. Only a few were lost. Since I needed a new house, I wanted one with a gun room that was fireproof. I was planning to keep the house small, but I kept having ideas and realized it would be a way to use some of the architectural antiques I've collected. Next thing I knew, it was almost eight thousand square feet and only one bedroom!" Charlie laughed quietly.

"How can you have that much space and only one bedroom?"

"I got carried away."

He took a napkin and began sketching the house, indicating locations of the various rooms.

"Who designed it for you?"

"I designed it. It's being built by ranch labor, which means whatever the ranch needs takes precedent. I started it two years ago and with luck it'll be finished in another two years." He raised his glass. "Here's to at least thirty-three more years and my sharing some of them with you."

He reached into his pocket, pulled out a small box, and handed it to me.

"What's this? I thought the ring was my birthday present."

"It is, but when I saw this it reminded me of you."

I opened the box. Inside was a lovely filigree butterfly necklace. "I love it!" I exclaimed placing it around my neck.

Charlie took my hand and kissed it. "I'm jealous of that butterfly. I wish I were that close to you."

I leaned over and whispered in his ear, "Let's adjourn to my room so we can make that happen."

CHAPTER 5

"And when you look at me

with those stars in your eyes,

I could waltz across Texas with you."

ERNEST TUBB

Waltzing across Texas

RETURNING TO THE FRANTIC WORLD of a political campaign, I found myself consumed by its activities. The next weekend the Texas Women's Political Caucus was having its annual convention in El Paso, and my candidate was speaking to the members. I was going there on Thursday to advance the trip. In the midst of making these preparations, Charlie called and asked me to attend a party on Saturday night in Van Horn, Texas. When I told Charlie of the conflict, he saw no problem. By Texas standards, Van Horn is a suburb of El Paso, being only ninety miles to the east. I would be finished with my responsibilities by mid-afternoon on Saturday and the party was Saturday night. There was another guest coming from El Paso, and I could ride with her and fly back to Kerrville on Sunday with Charlie.

The week passed in a blur as I juggled phone calls setting up the coming trip and talking with Charlie. I found myself going from a call arranging the candidate's schedule to one from a wooing Charlie. It made for a schizophrenic existence because I was never sure which persona to assume from minute to minute. I arrived in El Paso and began eighteen-hour days making the necessary arrangements. Charlie discovered he could always reach me at five thirty in the morning, and though it fit his schedule, it made for a semi-lucid conversation with me.

On Saturday afternoon, my ride picked me up at the hotel and we were off at ninety miles an hour across the Chihuahuan Desert heading east to Van Horn. My driver, whose name I do not remember, was an attractive brunette who was the date of the man giving the party. She told me he inherited oil royalties from his parents giving him a monthly income of $50,000. He was throwing the party to celebrate his thirtieth birthday and his recently acquired ten thousand-acre ranch in the shadow of the Baylor Mountains outside of Van Horn.

Arriving at our destination, it was obvious no expense was spared in bringing civilization to the isolated setting. Several hundred guests circulated among tents serving food and alcohol. The largest tent contained a dance floor and band. The strains of "San Antonio Rose" greeted me as I stepped from the car. Suddenly I was wrapped in a bear hug and there was Charlie, dressed no differently than the day Nugent introduced us. Taking my arm, he led me to the tent where guests in various interpretations of Western attire danced. Charlie took me into his arms and guided us onto the dance floor. As we danced, he made introductions to every couple we passed including our host, a mustached portly man wearing sunglasses. Minutes later we bumped into a young couple and Charlie put his arm around the man, drawing him and his partner into a circle with us. "Norma, I want you to meet my son Walter." I extended my hand and was warmly greeted by a good-looking man with a mustache who in no way resembled his father. The music was too loud to exchange anything but smiles. As we danced away, I expressed surprise at learning Charlie had another son.

"You've still got two more to meet, Gus and Louie," he said. "They're both at the University of Texas so it may be a while before that happens." The band begin playing, "Waltz Across Texas." Charlie held me close and whispered, "That's what I'm going to do with you, missy. You and I are going to waltz across Texas, from north to south and east to west. But right now, I'm waltzing you to the hotel and to bed."

As we lay in bed, I took Charlie's hand on which he wore his Y.O. ring. "What does Y.O. stand for?"

Charlie put his arm under my head and drew me closer. "Do you know about the Sutton-Taylor Feud?"

"Never heard of it."

Charlie reared back, a look of feigned shock on his face. "I don't believe it! It was the bloodiest and longest feud in Texas History. I won't bore you with the gory details, but it started right after the Civil War and went on for over ten years."

"And just what does it have to do with the Y.O.?"

"In 1880 Grandfather bought the Y.O. Ranch and cattle from a J. W. Taylor in Mason, Texas. Mr. Taylor previously lived in Goliad County where he bought the cattle from Mr. Y. O. Coleman. The thinking is Taylor moved to the Hill Country sometime in the 1870s to escape the feud. Grandfather didn't want to go to the trouble of rebranding the cattle, so he also bought the brand. I'm sure grandfather never dreamed we'd still be running cattle one hundred years later. Ranching wasn't Grandfather's major business. He got into it after his store and bank were successful."

"Did you know your grandfather?"

"No. He died in 1927, a few weeks after I was born. My dad was in his forties when he married Myrtle, so by the time I was born, Grandfather was almost ninety. It was strange growing up because my first cousins were old enough to be my parents."

"How did your grandfather end up in Kerrville?"

Charlie looked at me skeptically, "Do you really want to hear all this? I can think of better ways to spend our time."

"I wouldn't be asking if I weren't interested. It doesn't mean we won't do something else after you've told me." I smiled and kissed him on the cheek.

"That's a hell of an incentive," Charlie said. "Grandfather was born in Alsace-Lorraine, but his family immigrated to Texas when he was fourteen. They landed at Indianola in 1852 and then took a mule-drawn wagon to San Antonio. Eighteen days later, Grandfather's father died."

"From what?"

"Who knows. Some members of the family say it was a rattlesnake bite, but it could have been anything. He was only fifty-two."

"How did the family survive after that?"

"We don't really know. Probably Grandfather and his three brothers did whatever work they could find to support their mother and sister. We do know Grandfather enlisted in the Texas Rangers in 1854 when he was just sixteen. But then his mother died in 1857, and the family scattered. One of Grandfather's brothers got gold fever and went to California and then Central America, where he died. Another moved to San Antonio and died there. One stayed in the Hill Country as did their sister, Emilie, who married Caspar Real, who was also from Alsace. Grandfather quit the Rangers, moved to Kerr County, and went into the ranching business with Real. They sold beef and supplies to Camp Verde. I assume you know about Camp Verde."

"It's where the army had camels."

"Indeed it was. I'm impressed and will be more so if you know how that came to be?"

"It was the idea of Jefferson Davis who was secretary of war at the time. He figured if camels could be pack animals in the desert, why not in Texas? The only problem was the camels scared the bejesus out of the horses and made mules look docile."

"How do you know all this?"

"I read. A lot. And, as a sixth-generation Texan, my mother saw to it my brothers and I learned our Texas history early and often."

"I have to say you have the best stocked mind of any woman I've ever met."

"Thank you. Please continue."

"In 1861, Grandfather married Lena Enderle and they moved to a ranch he'd bought on Turtle Creek. When the Civil War broke out, Grandfather joined the Confederate Army and fought with General Walker's Greyhounds until the war ended."

"This is a silly question, but something tells me you'll know the answer. Why were they called the Greyhounds?"

"Because they were able to move long distances on foot."

"Is that where he became a captain?"

"No. He was a private the entire war. It wasn't until 1875 that the governor appointed him a captain of the Kerrville Mounted Rifles. It was a local militia formed in counties throughout Texas to fight Indians.

"After the war ended Grandfather came back to Texas, and on Christmas Eve in 1869 he opened his one room general store in Kerrville, which eventually became Schreiner's Department Store. A few years later he opened a bank and started acquiring land. He ended up with six hundred thousand acres where he ran mostly longhorns but also some Herefords. Later he added sheep and goats. He and his brother-in-law were among the first to bring sheep into the Hill Country, which is ironic because in other parts of the country there was so much conflict between the cattle and sheep factions. That wasn't the case in Texas. We're still running both and have thrown in goats as well. Many a year the sheep and goats support our cattle operation."

"I always knew the King Ranch was a million acres but, I hate to admit, I'd never heard of your grandfather."

"That's because his main business was never ranching. It was his store and the bank. He admitted the store was his first love. Once they were old enough, he let his sons take care of the ranches. The store provided the money to buy land, which was about twenty-five cents an acre, and the bank loaned money to small ranchers with their land as collateral. If they couldn't make their payments, then the bank took the land.

"You're a Texan. You know it's more romantic to be a rancher than a merchant. And, unlike a lot of big Texas ranches, Grandfather's six hundred thousand acres weren't contiguous. Ranching and being a cowboy may be more romantic, but you're a lot more liable to go broke, which grandfather discovered in 1896 when his ranching operation went belly-up."

Charlie began kissing me and after a romantic interlude I said, "What caused your grandfather to go belly-up?"

"I swear, missy. You don't let a man off easy do you?"

I smiled. "Not if I'm interested in what he's saying."

"You're the first woman who's ever taken an interest, but I'm happy to oblige. In 1873, Grandfather and two partners leased land from the Kiowa and Comanche Indians in Oklahoma to graze cattle. Only problem was when the lease was up, the Indians wouldn't let them on the land to round up their cattle. Seems the chiefs had spent the money rather than dividing it among the tribe members. Grandfather's partners went broke. He said the only reason he didn't was because of his store."

"I assume your father inherited the ranch when your grandfather died."

"Nope. He got it before then. Starting in 1913, Grandfather begin dividing his estate among his eight children, and Walter, my father, was given the Y.O. and another ranch, totaling around seventy thousand acres."

I started to ask another question, but Charlie had drifted off to sleep. I lay there thinking about my attraction to him and the differences between his world and mine. Charlie was old enough to be my father and had accomplished many things in life, whereas I was just beginning a career. His worldview centered around the Great Depression and World War II. Mine took root in the 1960s when Vietnam, social upheaval, and rock 'n' roll prevailed. He was an only child who came from wealth. I was the oldest of three children in a family where money was always scarce. He inherited the Y.O. when he was only six and it would always dominate his life. Could I, or any woman, hold their own in competition with the ranch? In spite of these differences, he was the most fascinating man I'd ever met, and I couldn't resist the twinkle in his eye and boyish charm, never mind he was a raconteur par excellence with his many and varied

Captain Charles Armand Schreiner, front row center, on his eightieth birthday, February 22, 1918, with his five sons. Back row, left to right: Charles Jr., Aime Charles (A. C.), and Walter (Charlie Three's father); front row, left to right: Gustave Fritz and Louis Albert flank their father. From the collection of Joe Herring Jr.

stories. Intuition told me he was equally attracted to me. I decided to enjoy the good times and not worry about what came next.

The next morning, we boarded buses chartered by our host to take us to the Van Horn airport, where a small air force of private planes was awaiting passengers. Some of the planes belonged to guests, and others, like the Learjet we boarded, were chartered by our host to ferry guests to and from the party. As I climbed aboard, I noticed straw Stetsons with an assortment of hat bands stacked across the back row of seats. When Charlie and I entered, the men rose to greet us. As we made our way down the aisle, Charlie introduced me to the occupants, all of whom were Y.O. Ranch employees and their wives. Charlie and I took seats across from Walter and his date and Charlie began asking his son questions about an upcoming longhorn sale in Oklahoma.

As Walter and Charlie talked, I studied my traveling companions. Weathered, tanned faces and muscular arms attested to men who worked outdoors using their bodies in their work. Most of their hands were missing parts or all of fingers. Many were bowlegged from years spent on horseback and most limped when they walked, the result of a mishap with a cow, horse, or both. My only experience with cowboys and ranches was what I saw in movies and on television. I had never been around cattle and though I loved horses, after my young riding days on Spunky, my exposure to horses was acquired in a hit and miss fashion at riding stables and on horses belonging to friends.

My first heroes were cowboys, and I was still a sucker for any male on horseback. Charlie said there was nothing more romantic than a horseback figure. I countered saying, "Or a pilot." I knew this from having been a flight attendant. Though at opposite ends of the romantic spectrum, each represented a character of daring, solitude, confidence, and danger that proved catnip to many women. I was no exception.

CHAPTER 6

"Other states were carved or born,

Texas grew from hide and horn."

BERTA HART NANCE

Of Hides and Horns

BEFORE MEETING CHARLES SCHREINER III, the only longhorn I had seen was Bevo, the steer that's the mascot of the University of Texas. Because of Bevo, I had my first personal experience with a Texas Ranger, who threatened to arrest me for cattle rustling.

I was attending UT in the fall of 1963 when the football team was on its way to its first national championship under the revered coach Darrell Royal. At two thirty one November morning my phone rang. When I answered, I heard the voice of my high school boyfriend, Ron Zappe. Ron was a student at Texas A&M, the biggest rival of the University of Texas.

"Hey, Teasip," said Ron, using the Aggies' derogatory name for UT students. "We've got your cow."

All I could manage in response was, "What?"

"We've got your cow."

"You're kidding."

"No. I have a broken foot to prove it. He stepped on it when we were loading him in the trailer. Thought you'd like to know so you can spread the word." He hung up.

By now my roommate was awake and I repeated what Ron said. She knew someone who was a Silver Spur, the men's service organization that took care of Bevo. She called her friend, told him about Ron's phone call, and suggested he might want to check on Bevo. Having done our duty, we went back to sleep. As I was dressing for class that morning, the house mother appeared at the door to tell me there was a Texas Ranger waiting to see me about my being involved in cattle rustling. She was obviously concerned and escorted me to the lobby. The Ranger was provoking much attention from the girls passing him on their way to class. Like all Rangers, he wore a white Stetson, which he was ceremoniously holding as he nodded to each young lady who walked by, causing a chorus of giggles and batting of eyes. The house mother escorted us into her office where the officer introduced himself, confirmed my identity, and asked for the name of the person who called me to report Bevo's theft.

"He's really missing?" I exclaimed.

"Yes ma'am, he is, and we've been called in to find him." He asked again for the name of the person who called me, what he said, and if I knew where to reach him.

I repeated the phone conversation with Ron but refused to give the officer his name. I loved the University of Texas, but I was not about to rat out a friend, especially Ron. I had inflicted enough pain on him with my elopement the previous year. Ron would go on to found Zapp's Chips and we would remain friends for the next forty-seven years until he died in 2010. At his funeral, the story of his cattle rustling escapade was proudly revealed to the mourners.

In a brusque voice, the officer told me cattle rustling was a serious crime in Texas and, unless I cooperated, I would be considered an accessory and charges would be filed against me. I held firm in my refusal. The Ranger took his leave saying he would give me time to think about my decision and be back that afternoon. To make a long story short, forty-eight hours after Bevo was "rustled," he was returned unharmed. No cattle rustling charges were brought, and UT defeated A&M on Thanksgiving Day and went on to win its first national championship by defeating Navy 28–6 in the Cotton Bowl.

Fourteen years later I would get the equivalent of a PhD in longhorns from the founder of the Texas Longhorn Breeders Association of America (TLBAA), Charles Schreiner III. Charlie invited me to attend the Texas Longhorn Breeders annual convention and also purchased membership in the association for me. This may seem a strange gift but, as with most things he did, there was an ulterior motive. As a member, I could attend the convention and vote for the slate of candidates Charlie wanted on the board of directors.

The convention was held at the historic Menger Hotel in San Antonio, Texas. The Menger sits on ground that was once part of the Mission San

Antonio de Valero, a.k.a., the Alamo. The hotel is almost as much of a San Antonio institution as the Alamo, getting recognition in several well-known songs including Gary P. Nunn's, "You Ask Me What I Like About Texas." I remembered staying at the hotel when my family would visit San Antonio while living in Freer. Staying there with Charlie was a very different experience. As we walked through the lobby, Charlie told me the hotel's history. William Menger built the hotel in 1859 adjacent to a brewery he owned. The original limestone hotel contained forty rooms and throughout the years additional wings were added, each representing the architecture of its era. Charlie preferred staying in the original portion, usually in a suite previously leased by his mother, or one used by Capt. Richard King, founder of the King Ranch.

The hotel's manager greeted us personally when we checked in, and as we walked to our room, every person we passed, from housekeepers to guests, greeted Charlie by name. On the way, Charlie detoured through the Menger Bar. Charlie was a great admirer of Theodore Roosevelt and wanted to show me where T. R. recruited the Rough Riders for the Spanish-American War. San Antonio was a logical place to do this since Fort Sam Houston is located there, and at that time, approximately 1898, it was the largest city in Texas.

According to Charlie, as part of his recruiting pitch, T. R. would buy a drink, or two, or more, for the potential Rough Rider. Many a recruit sobered up to find themselves at Fort Sam Houston attending basic training. Charlie told me one of the Menger's ghosts is reported to be T. R., who sits in a corner of the bar having a drink. Another prominent Menger ghost is Capt. Richard King, who died in his eponymously named suite in 1885. The suite was furnished with several original pieces from King's era, including a four-poster canopy bed. Any time Charlie and I stayed there, Charlie would comment the mattress was probably used by King given its poor condition.

At the association's welcoming dinner that evening, I met many of the longhorn breeders but the most notable was Happy Shahan. Happy owned the ranch on which John Wayne built the set for his 1960 film, *The Alamo*. It was the first movie set built in Texas and led to Shahan being declared the "Father of the Texas Movie Industry." After dinner, Charlie and I walked through the original lobby of the hotel with its marble columns, stained-glass skylight, original Western paintings, and antique furniture. We walked out to the patio, which was surrounded by the original rooms of the hotel. As we sipped drinks, Charlie entertained me with more stories about the hotel. At one time there was a large, fenced pool that was home to several alligators. The rumor of how this came to be was a guest who skipped out on his bill left the first one, and over time, others were added. Barbed wire made its debut outside the Menger in Alamo Plaza in 1876. Two enterprising salesmen staying at the hotel came up with the idea. One of these was John Gates, who would become a founder of Texaco Oil. Gates and his associate built a large corral enclosed by four strands of barbed wire. A herd of longhorns was driven into the pen as bystanders yelled catcalls about the idiocy of such an act. To their surprise, the fencing held. Charlie ended the story saying, "And that was the death knell for the open range."

"This is such a lovely place," I said. "I'm sure these walls have seen their share of romance."

"Yes, ma'am. Many a courtship has taken place here. When Eisenhower was stationed at Fort Sam Houston, he wooed Mamie here. After they married, they lived here until their quarters were ready. My first wife and I had our wedding reception here, though our marriage wasn't as long-lived as the Eisenhower's." Charlie reached over and took my hand. Sitting there with candles glowing on our table, gas lights flickering on the walls, and lace-curtained windows looking down on us from the rooms above, I imagined myself sitting on the patio one hundred years earlier. I closed my eyes and for a moment, heard spurs jangling and skirts swishing as cowboys and their ladies walked by.

Later that night, as we lay in bed, I said, "I know longhorns descended from cattle the Spaniards brought to Mexico, but how did they get to Texas?"

"The Spaniards brought the first cattle into Mexico in the 1500s. In the late seventeenth century, Spain expanded north into what was then called Tejas and took cattle with them. Some escaped and others were turned loose to graze. For the next two hundred years, the cattle fended for themselves. That's when they developed the traits that make them unique: longer horns for protection, a high tolerance for droughts, and a willingness to eat pretty much anything. They also developed an important trait missing in a lot of breeds. Want to guess what it is?"

"How could I possibly know?"

"Because it wouldn't surprise me if somewhere in that well-stocked mind of yours you have the answer."

I thought for several minutes and said, "I give up."

"Many heifers have a difficult time giving birth to their first calf. Not longhorns. That's because during the years they were wandering around, there were no people to help a cow if she was having trouble. She and her calf would just die, so that trait didn't get passed on. When Stephen Austin brought the first settlers into Texas, they integrated feral longhorns into their herds of European cattle and saw this benefit. That's the reason commercial cowmen today try to have some longhorn blood in their herds."

"I assume your grandfather had longhorns?"

"Of course. Longhorns were what most Texans had after the Civil War."

"Why?"

"Because while the men were fighting the war, their herds roamed free and propagated to the point Texas was overrun with them. After the war, whoever could round them up and put his brand on them owned them. Longhorns are one of the reasons Texas recovered from the war faster than some of the other Southern states. Grandfather did his part because for many years, longhorns comprised most of his herd. It's estimated he sent about 150,000 head up the trail to market in Kansas. What's amazing is that in only twenty years longhorns went from being overabundant to almost extinct."

I sat up in bed, "How could that happen?"

"Longhorn meat doesn't have a lot of fat. Other breeds—Angus, Herefords, shorthorns—were brought in and bred with the longhorns, which meant pure longhorn bloodlines were diluted. Another reason was longhorns got listed as a game animal because they were so wild and difficult to shoot. A few old-time cowmen kept herds of longhorns for sentimental reasons. Finally the government realized what was happening, stepped in, and established herds at the Wichita Mountains Wildlife Refuge in Oklahoma and the Fort Niobrara Wildlife Refuge in Nebraska. I knew Grandfather had run herds of longhorns, so in the late 1950s I started going to the annual sale at the Wichita refuge and bought a bull and some cows."

"Was that when you started the longhorn association?"

"No. I didn't start the association until 1964."

"What took you so long?"

"Frankly, it never crossed my mind until I was at one of the sales and heard a guy from Oregon say he was thinking about starting a longhorn association. As soon as he said that, I thought, "No way in hell am I going to let some non-Texan SOB start a longhorn association." I contacted a couple of other breeders, and we went to Houston to talk to the founders of the Brahman association to learn how to start a breed association. I came home and filed a charter with the Texas secretary of state for the

Texas Longhorn Breeders Association of America. Since I already had a small herd, the first bull registered was my herd sire, Sam Houston, and the first cows registered were mine.

"Once there was an association, I had to figure out a way to make people aware of it so they'd join and start buying and breeding longhorns. Actually, it was my friend Ace Reid who had a fantastic idea."

"Who is Ace Reid?"

"He's a good friend who also does a cowboy comic strip. Don't worry. You'll meet him."

"So what was his idea?"

"A trail drive from San Antonio to Dodge City, Kansas. We'd promote it as commemorating the centennial of the Chisholm Trail and honoring all the cowboys and cattle who went up it to Dodge City, Kansas, including Grandfather, who sent about three hundred thousand head up the trail."

"How could you have a trail drive in the twentieth century?"

"It wasn't easy," Charlie said. "You wouldn't believe the logistics involved for both the steers and the people."

"How many steers were there?"

"Almost 100, and about 150 people."

Charlie started rubbing his hand across the top of his head and grinning. "Unbeknownst to those participating in the drive, I arranged for there to be an Indian attack as we were crossing the Red River into Oklahoma. It was staged by the Quanah Sherriff's Posse, and I made a point of doing it at Doan's Crossing because that's where most of the Texas herds crossed. As the cowboys were driving the steers across the river, the members of the posse, in feathers and war paint, came galloping toward them letting out war cries and shooting blanks." Charlie started laughing. "The steers stampeded and the cowboys had to go after them." By this time Charlie was laughing so hard he was in tears. "It took more than four hours to round up those steers.

"Believe it or not, ten years later Texas Tech convinced me to have another drive to Lubbock for the opening of the Ranching Heritage Center. I didn't stage an Indian attack, but we almost lost a US senator. He was somewhat inebriated and as we were crossing a river he started listing to the side taking his saddle with him. One of the cowboys was alert enough to right him before he went in the water."

As he told me this, I could see the boyish delight on Charlie's face. The trail drives accomplished their goal because in 1977 over twenty-three thousand longhorns were registered with the association and there were nine hundred members throughout the United States, Canada, and

Australia. Because the longhorn was such a hardy breed, commercial cow-calf operations were realizing the benefits of having longhorn genetics in their herds. There was also the romantic aspect of owning an animal who was a living part of the history of the Old West.

A few weeks later I met Charlie in Lawton, Oklahoma, for the annual longhorn sale at the Wichita Mountains Wildlife Refuge. The Wichita bloodlines were considered the purest and were highly valued by breeders. I saw more longhorns than I knew existed as Charlie tutored me in how to tell a good longhorn from a bad one. I did not realize how important this information would be later. Stopping at each pen, Charlie gave me a critique of the animal's horns, conformation, and disposition. Of one cow with droopy horns, he said, "She looks like a dwarf Angus who got her head caught in the gate." He pointed out a cow with an oversized bag saying the deformity would cause difficulty nursing her calves. There was a beautifully colored black and white cow who was limping after being kicked by another cow the previous day. The injury would make her less valuable even though it might heal with no ill effects.

The colors of the cattle ranged from solid brown, black, or white to variations of spotted and speckled coats. The speckled coats were Charlie's favorites, and he explained this was a trait where bloodlines played a role. Even though a cow might be a solid color, if you bred her with a colorful bull, or vice versa, you increased the likelihood of colorful offspring. Charlie carefully explained the difference between the horns in terms of whether they grew straight out or curved upward. They all looked the same to me, but as we approached a pen I would try to guess the sex before Charlie told me.

"How can you tell the bulls from the cows?" I asked. Charlie peered at me over the top of his glasses and said, "I'm assuming you mean other than the obvious way?"

I started laughing. "Well, yes, there is that isn't there?"

"Not everybody understands that. A lady was making me a longhorn steer weather vane for the lodge. She did a great job except she put testicles on the steer! I tried explaining to her a steer has been castrated, so it doesn't have balls, but she was determined her steer was going to have balls, so I never got my weather vane. I wasn't going to have an anatomically incorrect steer on top of the lodge. But there are other differences." We walked over to a pen and Charlie said, "Look at his head and shoulders. Look at their shape." Then we walked to another pen. "Tell me the difference between him and this cow."

The cow's head was much slimmer—she lacked the thick muscular

Y.O. Samson, the herd sire for the Y.O. longhorn herd. From the collection of Charles Schreiner IV.

shoulders of the bull but there was also a difference in the horns. The bull's horns were thicker, not as long, and turned up, whereas the cow's were thinner, longer, and twisted. As we walked around the pens, Charlie would stop occasionally and ask me to critique a cow or bull. By the time we finished, I was comfortable with my ability to tell a steer from a cow or a bull and determine if it met Charlie's definition of a good longhorn.

Before the sale we attended a luncheon held in a tent outside the sale barn. The odor of manure and cow urine intermingled with the savory scents of smoke and barbecue. Throughout lunch flies swarmed over plates, and I seemed the only one bothered by the relentless dive-bombing of the insects. The sale was a blur of cattle being driven in and out of the sale ring, the ring men calling out bids, and the auctioneer singsonging the bids as he tried to get the highest price. Three ring men worked the crowd, taking bids and relaying them to the auctioneer. I tried to determine who was bidding but signals were so discreet only the ring men saw the slight nod of a head, raising of a finger, or tilt of the sale catalog. Charlie explained the ring men received a percentage of the auction's profits, which was their incentive to get the highest bids.

I was surprised at how little bulls sold for compared to cows. Charlie explained one bull was enough to provide breeding services for all the cows in a herd, which was why only the best bulls were kept as herd sires. If a bull did not have herd sire potential but was colorful, he would be castrated and kept as a steer. Steers would go on to produce beautiful horns, and once they died their heads were often mounted. Less fortunate bulls would be sent to market. Steers served a function because once castrated they were more docile. This meant they could be ridden or become a school's mascot, like UT's Bevo, or used in cattle drives, like those Charlie organized.

After the sale we drove to Dallas to spend the weekend. We stopped in Fort Worth for Charlie to order more of his custom-made checked shirts at M. L. Leddy's. Established in the 1920s, Leddy's originally made boots and saddles. Over time the store had expanded into Western clothing, both off the rack and custom-made. After Charlie placed his order, he told me to pick out some fabric so he could have shirts made for me. As the salesman was writing up the order Charlie reminded him to be sure the Y.O. brand was on the left pocket. I was wearing one of the shirts when I met one of Charlie's friends. He looked at my left pocket and said, "What's the other one named?" It took me a minute to get the joke.

Charlie wanted me to order a pair of custom boots. "I have plenty of boots," I said.

He harrumphed. "You have city boots. They aren't for walking over rocks and through cactus. Plus, a rattlesnake can bite right through them."

"You act like I'm going to be spending time at your ranch."

"That's what I'm hoping for," he smugly replied.

From Leddy's we drove to Dallas and stopped at Neiman Marcus for Charlie to purchase neckties. After finishing, he said, "Let's walk around and see what overpriced bauble we can find for you."

Taking the escalator to the second floor, Charlie steered me into the fur department. As we entered, he spied a full-length white fur on a mannequin. We walked over to it and a saleswoman magically appeared. Before I could protest she draped the coat across my shoulders.

"What kind of fur is this?" Charlie asked.

"Coyote," she replied.

"Oh no!" I declared, handing it back to her. "I would never wear a coyote coat."

"Why the hell not?" Charlie said indignantly.

"They're incredible animals." I said. "Intelligent, cunning, excellent hunters. They'll eat anything. Even fruits or vegetables."

"You're right about their eating habits. They regularly eat my lambs. I hate to tell you, but you cannot raise coyotes and lambs. I can't make any money off of coyotes but I can from lambs. Your opinion of Mr. Coyote would change if you ever saw one kill a poor defenseless little lamb."

Charlie began sneering and gritting his teeth. "Your cunning Mr. Coyote sneaks up on a poor little lamb and grabs its hind leg." Charlie snatched the air with his teeth to imitate this action. "Then he drags it down and tears open its stomach." He threw the imaginary lamb to the ground and tore at its stomach with his teeth. "Poor ole mama sheep can't do anything except bleat." Charlie bleated loudly. "The baby is struggling to get free but it's completely defenseless. But Mr. Coyote doesn't kill the lamb outright. He disembowels it and leaves it to die an agonizing death. And I'll tell you something else about your clever coyote's culinary habits. He wouldn't hesitate to eat your cat. There are coyotes living in a lot of cities, and cats and those yappy little dogs are one of their favorite meals. As far as I'm concerned this coat is the best use I've ever seen for a coyote."

Other shoppers had gathered around as Charlie enacted this tableau. As he finished, they burst into applause, which delighted him no end. He raised his hat and bowed.

"I am not wearing a coyote coat!" I declared. The following week a large package from Neiman Marcus arrived at my office. Inside was the coat with a note from Charlie reading, "If you don't want to wear it, you can let your cat sleep on it as revenge for the members of her species who were meals for your wonderful Mr. Coyote."

My cat slept on it regularly, and I wore it only when nagged by Charlie into doing so.

CHAPTER 7

"Oh, give me a home

where the buffalo roam,

where the deer and the antelope play."

BREWSTER M. HIGLEY

Home on the Range

I AWAKENED TO THE SOUND of Charlie's voice. At first I thought he was talking in his sleep, but as I came to consciousness, I realized he was talking to me and asking questions he expected me to answer. "What do you want for breakfast? How soon can you be dressed? I've decided it's time for you to see the ranch."

The previous night we attended the Charity Ball in San Antonio. Charlie's mother was one of the founders of the Charity Ball Association, whose primary goal was supporting healthcare for children. The ball, a black-tie event, was its major fundraiser. Charlie dutifully donned a tuxedo but balked at the idea of tuxedo shoes. "I'm not wearing any goddamn parlor slippers," he snorted, pulling on his black boots. The ball was held outdoors at La Villita, the three hundred-year-old neighborhood from which San Antonio grew. As soon as we walked in, a man slapped Charlie on the back and said, "Goddamn Charlie, you're dressed up enough to bury!" Turning to me he said, "And you must be Charlie's granddaughter."

Charlie glared and informed him I was his date, to which he responded, "It proves once more a woman's love is like the morning dew. It's just as likely to fall on a cow turd as a rose. You are one lucky old turd."

As the man walked away Charlie said, "Ignore him. He's just jealous because I'm with the prettiest woman here." Working our way through the crowd, we stopped every few feet for Charlie to introduce me to someone. Though I did not realize it at the time, most were from old and prominent

San Antonio and South Texas families whose forebearers, like Charlie's grandfather, played major roles in Texas history and economics.

Though we had been seeing each other for several months, I had not yet seen the Y.O. We were on the road by eight o'clock, and because it was Sunday morning, there was little traffic as we headed west on Interstate 10, hurtling along in Charlie's station wagon at eighty miles an hour. Charlie was rarely pulled over for speeding because his car was known to local law enforcement throughout the Hill Country. The station wagon was equipped with a car phone that worked only 50 percent of the time. Charlie often called me from this phone, and usually the call would disconnect as soon as I answered. Charlie Four complained about the expense of what he considered a useless piece of equipment, but it gave Three a false sense of accessibility to the world as he was out and about.

Traveling west from San Antonio, the land begins undulating as you enter the Texas Hill Country. For many Texans, this is the Elysian Fields of the state. It is not spectacular in its scenery, like the mountains of Colorado or California's Highway 1 running along the Pacific coast. But compared to the paved-over, freeway-glutted ambiance of the state's major cities, the gray murky waters of most Texas beaches, and the infinite flatness of the Panhandle, the Hill Country's gently rolling hills, spring-fed rivers, low-water river crossings, and small towns with German influenced architecture are the embodiment of understated beauty.

My first exposure to the Hill Country was when my family would travel to New Braunfels in the summer for my father to do work for the Christian Rural Overseas Program (CROP). The program solicited bulk produce from American farmers for those less fortunate in other countries. After his day's work was done, my father would take my brothers and me to Landa Park where he taught us to swim in its spring-fed pool. It was my first experience with cool clear water bubbling up through the limestone layers of the Edwards Aquifer. After swimming in those pristine waters, the ocean holds no allure for me.

My love affair with the Hill Country developed into a passionate crush when I moved to Austin to attend the University of Texas. Like so many before and after me, Austin captured my heart and soul. The author O. Henry, who lived in Austin for fourteen years, described Austin in one of his short stories as the "City of the Violet Crown." The first time I drove through its rolling hills at twilight I realized what an apt description it was. For a few minutes when the sun is setting, the hills do indeed have a violet hue.

The farther west one travels on Interstate 10, the more frequent and higher the hills become. As we drove, the highway climbed up and down, and on either side was hill after rolling hill covered by live oaks, Spanish oaks, cactus, and the omnipresent cedar trees (a misnomer because the tree is actually a juniper). This flora roots tenaciously in a few inches of impoverished soil beneath which are beds of solid limestone. Driving past the cuts blasted through the hills for the highway is a tutorial in Texas geology. The limestone was deposited during the Mesozoic Era when Texas was covered by shallow seas. In addition to providing a filtering system for rainwater and having numerous underground caves, it contains fossils ranging from dinosaur tracks to tiny sea creatures.

We had been driving a little over an hour when Charlie took the exit for the small town of Comfort. "There's something I want to show you," he said. We turned down a side street and parked in front of a twenty-foot-tall limestone monument with names engraved on its sides. A flagpole with a US flag flying at half-staff stood beside it. A Texas historical marker bore the heading "Treue der Union."

"Do you know about this?" Charlie asked.

"No. Why does it say True to the Union?" I asked, translating the German on the marker.

"It's a mass grave and has the same designation as a national cemetery, which is why the flag flies continuously at half-staff. There's one name in particular I want to show you." We walked to the other side of the monument and Charlie pointed to the last name in the first column, A. Schreiner. The heading on the list of names was "Gefallen am 10 August 1862 am Nueces" which translates to "Fell on 10 August 1862 on the Nueces." Turning to Charlie, I said, "I have no idea what this is about, but something tells me I'm about to learn. I also suspect A. Schreiner is a relative."

"Yes ma'am. Right on both counts. A. Schreiner is Aimee Schreiner, my grandfather's younger brother."

"I thought your grandfather fought for the Confederacy."

"He did but he was the only one of his siblings who supported the South. Like most German immigrants, Grandfather's brothers supported the Union. The men listed here knew it would probably get them killed so they decided to spend the war in Mexico. They were on their way there and camped on the Nueces River when a group of Confederate vigilantes massacred them. Their killers didn't even bury the bodies. Just left them to rot and be scavenged by animals. At the end of the war, their relatives recovered the bones and brought them here where they were interred in this common grave. The monument was dedicated in 1866, and it's the only German-language monument to the Union in the South."

We resumed our journey and an hour later Charlie took the Mountain Home exit onto State Highway 41. The road stretched before us with nothing to break its monotony except ranch gates on either side. Some were ostentatious with limestone pillars between which were iron gates with cutouts of cattle, whitetail deer, or other animals cavorting across them. Others were simple aluminum gates between cedar fence posts. The sign for the Y.O. was a combination of the two, simplistic in its use of cedar posts but large enough it couldn't be missed. The gate itself was aluminum with only signs attesting to membership in various livestock associations hanging from it. Though I was not originally enthusiastic about making this trip, once we passed through the front gate I found myself anticipating what lay ahead.

As we drove, Charlie pointed out animals, some of which I could see but others that eluded me entirely. I kept waiting for buildings to appear. After thirty minutes I saw the first one. On a hilltop was an imposing limestone structure with two chimneys towering above its roof. Before I could ask about it, I noticed a male ostrich behind a high fence pacing up and down with mouth agape and wings spread. Charlie turned onto a road leading into the enclosure. "This is our first stop," he announced. Charlie got out to open the gate and told me to drive the car through. When he returned he told me another rule of ranch etiquette. It is the passenger's responsibility to open and close gates, but since this was my first visit, he would not enforce it. A sign identified the area as Deer Park. Charlie came to a stop as the ostrich approached the car. "This is Junior," he said, rolling down his window as the bird began pecking on the side mirror. It seemed strange to be frightened by a bird, however, this was a six-foot-tall bird. Charlie told me even though the bird was flightless, he could kill a man or other predator with one kick from his leg, disemboweling the victim with his lethal toenail. The bird could also run more than thirty-five miles an hour for up to forty minutes, which gave it an advantage over predators.

"The term 'bird brain' doesn't exist for nothing," Charlie said. "His eye is bigger than his brain." The bird stuck his head through the window and as Charlie extended his roughened hand Junior began pecking at the diamonds in Charlie's ring.

"Is he tame?" I asked.

"Hardly. He kicked out the window of one of our trucks."

Behind Junior was the smaller less colorful female and behind her were several smaller birds Charlie told me were emu and rheas. The emu was from Australia and the rheas from South America. Behind the birds I saw a beautiful deer with a spotted coat and enormous antlers. "What kind of deer is that?" I asked.

"An axis. It's native to India just like the barasingha deer to its left. So is the blackbuck antelope over there." Charlie pointed to a black and white animal with spiraled horns. "The blackbuck is the second-fastest land animal. In India they once hunted them with cheetahs, which tells you who's faster."

"Do you hunt them in here?"

Charlie looked at me in exasperation. "Good God no! The ones we hunt are out in the pastures. These are for tourists to see."

"My grandfather was a fox hunter, but I've never been exposed to it. I have trouble seeing the sport in it when you're in a vehicle and have a gun."

Charlie looked over his glasses at me. "This ranch is divided into fifty pastures that range from three hundred to three thousand acres. You know what Hill Country land is like. It's hilly, rocky, and hasn't been cleared since God created it. There are more places for animals to hide in those pastures than there are game animals on this ranch, which is about ten thousand. The animals here have the same chance as any wild game anywhere in the world. Hunting is how we manage our game. In a year we take about 5 percent of our game animals, which is less than natural attrition. Do you still think we're taking advantage of these poor defenseless animals?"

"I still would never want to deliberately shoot one."

"Maybe this will make you feel better. We've been so successful breeding the blackbuck we've sent animals back to India and Pakistan to help them restore their herds."

As we drove around Deer Park, Charlie pointed out fallow deer from England, red deer from Europe, and sika deer from Japan.

"If your grandfather started this as a cattle ranch, when did the hunting start?" I asked.

"Mother leased part of the ranch for hunting to bring in money during the Depression. She was the first or one of the first ranchers to do this and we've never stopped doing it. In the 1960s the director of the San Antonio Zoo called to say he had some surplus animals and no place to put them. He wondered how well they would adapt to a new environment and asked if I would be interested in releasing them on the Y.O. I jumped at the opportunity. The first animals we released were blackbuck antelope and aoudad sheep. Next came the axis. They all thrived, so it

Y.O. flag. From the collection of Charles Schreiner IV.

wasn't long until we had a surplus. That's when the exotic hunting operation started."

We left the pasture and crossed a cattle guard onto a paved road. Charlie said, "This is our only paved road on the ranch. It cost us a fortune, but it's the most trafficked so we bit the bullet and did it."

Caliche roads veered off on either side with signs indicating they led to the Shearing Barn, the Live Oak, and the Airstrip.

"I remember you saying you had sheep and goats on the ranch, but I thought ranchers hated them. How did you end up having cattle, sheep, and goats?"

"You have more questions than a porcupine has quills," Charlie replied. "But, since you asked, Grandfather was responsible."

"I should have known. Which came first?"

"The cattle, but the sheep and goats were only a few years behind. Grandfather's brother-in-law, Caspar Real, was one of the first to bring sheep to this area in the 1860s, but they didn't really catch on until the 1870s. That's when Grandfather started running them and his timing was perfect because the Franco-Prussian War created a wool shortage and prices more than doubled. Grandfather used his bank to encourage other ranchers to run them. Whenever he loaned money to a rancher for livestock, the terms of the loan required that a portion be used to purchase sheep and goats. Then Grandfather set up a wool and mohair warehouse where he'd store and sell wool and mohair for a percentage of the sale price. Texas was the only state that had one until the late twentieth century. He also would pick up other ranchers' wool whenever they purchased supplies from his store. The wagons would carry supplies going out and wool and mohair coming back."

We pulled up to a large structure of stone and weathered cypress. A sign indicated it was "The Lodge." We walked past a flagpole on which flew the Y.O. flag. It bore a remarkable resemblance to the Texas flag except the Y.O. brand had replaced the star. Charlie Three created the flag and thought the state should consider his appropriating their design a compliment.

Looking down I saw the Y.O. brand embedded every few feet in the sidewalk. As we walked toward two massive Mexican doors, I saw one of the door handles was a large Y and the other an O. "Is there anything you don't put your brand on?" I asked as Charlie opened one of the doors. He smiled and I stepped into cool darkness scented with traces of oak fires, alcohol, and cigars. Charlie switched on the lights. I blinked several times, trying to take in all I was seeing.

CHAPTER 8

"Houses aren't refuge from history.
They are where history ends up."

BILL BRYSON

Shock and Awe

IT WAS AS IF I HAD STEPPED into a combination natural history museum and extravagant movie set. Mounted animals were everywhere. Over one hundred whitetail deer heads covered the walls. A grizzly bear reared on hind legs beside the fireplace. Five-foot-long elephant tusks stood on either side of the hearth. In the middle of the room were two whitetail deer with their horns locked together. Another full mount was a goat-like creature with a set of beautifully curved horns. Chandeliers made from old wagon wheels illuminated the room. Above the limestone fireplace hung the wooden blades and tail of an antique windmill. Written on its shaft was, "Chas. Schreiner, Kerrville, Texas."

On the wall opposite the fireplace was a ten-foot-long mirror and a bar in front of it complete with a brass footrail and spittoons. Two stained glass light fixtures hung at either end, each displaying the Y.O. brand. At one end of the bar stood a four-foot-tall carved wooden American Indian. Beside it was a spiral metal staircase leading up to a loft which overlooked the 5,500-square-foot lodge. Resting on the loft's railing were saddles. I was visually drowning in the multitude of images. As if my visual overload was not disconcerting enough, Charlie was overwhelming me with information about various objects.

"The bar came out of the Oklahoma Indian Territory which is why I decided it was appropriate to put Kaw-Liga on it. He survived the Casa

Grande fire and all my divorces. How many wooden Indians have managed that? When I found the bar, it was in pretty bad shape. I drug it home in pieces and Red, our ranch carpenter, put it back together."

Walking over to the goat-like figure, Charlie said, "This is Ivan, an ibex we got from the Albuquerque Zoo in the 1960s. He's a native of North Africa and became the herd sire for the Y.O. Ibex, a breed I developed. The federal government with its bureaucratic logic only allowed male ibexes to be imported. I figured if we bred him with a Spanish goat for several generations, we'd have an almost pure ibex. Ivan started that breeding program. He lived to be twenty and died happy." Charlie patted Ivan's rump approvingly. He pointed to the whitetail deer with their antlers intertwined. "One of the guides found these out in a pasture during the rut. They were fighting and their horns became locked. When he found them, one was dead and the other barely alive. Mother Nature can be damned cruel. Of course, to hear the bleeding-heart animal lovers tell it these deer died a death preferable to one who gets a fast death with a bullet through its heart." Charlie shook his head with disgust.

The rearing grizzly bear was killed by Charlie in Alaska. "By the way," he said, "did you know bears have a bone in their penis? I used to have this fellow's on my key chain, but it finally broke in half. I hope mine never does." He grinned and pointed to the elephant tusks. "I traded some guns for those." Directing my gaze upward, he pointed to one of the deer heads. "My father got that deer in 1905. It's thirty-six points, the largest deer ever taken on the Y.O., and it scored 240 points in Boone and Crockett."

I tried to determine which head he was pointing to because they all looked the same. I debated asking how he could tell one deer from another and what Boone and Crockett was but decided not to show my ignorance. I would learn Boone and Crockett is a standard scoring system developed by Theodore Roosevelt for North American big game.

Adjoining the Y.O. Lodge were a series of rooms which had been the house Myrtle built and gave to Charlie and Audrey, his first wife and the mother of his four sons. After their divorce, Charlie divided the house into rooms for overnight guests. On each door was a name, and the room was decorated accordingly. The Ranger Room contained photographs of various Texas Rangers and old chaps, hats, badges, and saddles. The Rio Grande had Mexican quirts, lariats, sombreros, and charro clothing items as well as pictures of Mexican vaqueros working cattle. In the Longhorn room were paintings of the bull Sam Houston and cow Carmella, the first longhorns Charlie registered when founding the Texas Longhorn Breeders

Association. Longhorn hides covered the floor, and a large steer head hung above the bed. Pausing before it, Charlie said, "For years I slept in this room with a picture of Audrey's mother hanging there. When I remodeled the room, I thought it only fitting to have an appropriate reminder of her." He chuckled with boyish delight at his mischievousness.

We left the Y.O. Lodge and walked over to a log cabin with a Wells Fargo stagecoach parked in front. On the way we passed a caisson that, Charlie explained, he'd found in the New Mexico desert when taking a back road to Colorado. Spying two wheels protruding above the sand, he stopped to see what it was and recognized the wheels were an army caisson. Charlie was being followed by one of the ranch hands pulling a trailer to haul back an antique soda fountain Charlie had bought. As they dug, Charlie realized an intact caisson was attached to the wheels. They dug it out, dismantled it, put it in the trailer, and it accompanied the soda fountain back to the ranch.

Around the Y.O. Lodge were log cabins, each from a different part of Texas. Texas historical markers explained one was previously a stagecoach stop and the other a schoolhouse. All had suffered years of neglect when Charlie purchased them. To move them to the ranch, each was disassembled, the logs marked for reassembling, and Red Alexander, the ranch carpenter, worked his magic restoring them. They had been decorated with antiques, cowhides, and various mounted heads by Audrey, Charlie's first wife.

We left the lodge and drove to a ten-acre area surrounded by a high fence. A sign outside the gate stated it was named Africana. As Charlie was opening the gate I saw zebras, elands, oryx, emu, and rheas. Driving slowly around the area, Charlie told me about the animals. The eland is native to eastern and southern Africa. When the Dutch named it, they used their word for moose or elk because that was what it reminded them of. The beisa oryx, with their distinctive black markings, are native to eastern Africa. Charlie said neither the eland nor oryx were hunted, nor were the zebras, though, Charlie said, he would gladly have shot one from time to time because they were "meaner than a snake" and "ornerier than a mule." Those at the Y.O. were Grant's, the smallest of the species.

"I've always wondered about the reason for the stripes," I said. "It seems it would make them stand out on the African plains."

"There're several theories. One is it gives them herd immunity and makes it more difficult for a predator to single out just one. Another is it protects them from flies because flies tend not to land on striped surfaces.

The home of Charles Schreiner III. Charlie designed the home on legal pads, and it was built primarily by Y.O. Ranch employees.

There's also a theory the striping helps regulate body temperature. The truth is no one knows for sure."

We returned to the main road and soon crossed over a cattle guard with ten-foot-tall limestone columns on either side. We begin ascending a steep incline and Charlie shifted the station wagon into low gear and pressed the accelerator. With wheels spitting out gravel, we lunged to the top, suddenly coming onto level ground. On the right I saw the oxcart Charlie purchased in Guadalajara. We circled around an island of trees and stopped in front of a house. Built of massive limestone blocks, it presented a rugged yet elegant façade perfectly matching the land on which it stood. Iron eagles perched atop the two chimneys and balconies jutted from upstairs doorways.

A pocked limestone walkway with wrought iron benches on either side led to an arched entryway. Weathered Mexican doors opened into an atrium that was enclosed on either side by foot-thick limestone walls, each of which contained a window in which resided a five-foot wooden wagon wheel. Saltillo tile steps led to a set of antique beveled glass doors that opened into a long hallway with a twelve-foot-high ceiling. From the exterior, the house appeared finished, but that impression changed when I stepped inside. Wires dangled from the ceiling, ladders were propped against the pecky cypress walls, and light fixtures sat in the middle of the floor, which was littered with sawdust, miscellaneous pieces of sheet rock, and other construction debris. I was struck by a sweet crisp odor Charlie told me was the cypress paneling.

"I've never heard of cypress paneling," I said.

"I did it out of respect for all the cypress trees we have beside the rivers and creeks in the Hill Country. A local mill made them." We walked down the hall, turned left, and descended two steps into the living and dining room. Charlie pointed to a corner. "The mill even squared off an entire tree for that corner." To the left was a limestone fireplace with doors on either side opening into a small garden area enclosed by a limestone wall. French doors ran the entirety of the wall facing us. Glass panels above the doors provided additional natural light. Outside the doors, a Saltillo tile patio ran the length of the house. The living room flowed into the dining room with French doors leading onto the back porch. In the middle of the dining room floor sat a Chinese Chippendale chandelier.

Walking up three steps, we entered the kitchen. Appliances were in place and cabinets covered every wall. An antique pie safe was recessed into one wall. Charlie told me it was his mother's and barely escaped the Casa Grande fire. An antique coal-burning stove stood as decoration at the end of an island containing a modern stove top.

Reentering the hallway, I noticed Saltillo tile flooring ran throughout the house. Several tiles had footprints from trespassing chickens, cats, or dogs walking across them before they dried. We turned into what Charlie called the garden room. The outer wall of the room was composed of metal-framed casement windows that ascended to the roofline. The adjoining wall was limestone, but at either end Charlie had incorporated the legs from several of the ranch's old wooden windmills as supports. Opposite this wall was a door leading onto the back porch. On either side of the door were ten-foot-tall live oak trees. Around each was a four-foot-tall limestone wall.

"They're real?" I asked, pointing to the trees.

"They were so healthy it seemed a shame to take them out," Charlie replied. "With the west wall being mostly windows and the roof plexiglass, they won't have a problem getting light."

"What about when they become larger?"

"We'll keep them trimmed, like bonsai."

In the center of the room was an iron spiral staircase leading upstairs. Charlie walked over to it. "When I found this, the room was almost finished, and the stairs lacked two inches being tall enough, but Red improvised to make it fit."

"Where does it lead?"

"To the upstairs sitting room. There's a regular staircase outside the gun room."

Charlie guided me back into the hallway. In only a few feet we were standing before a bank vault door with "Chas. Schreiner Bank" stenciled on it.

"It came from Grandfather's bank," Charlie said. He swung it open and flipped a light switch. We walked into a large room in the same state of construction as the rest of the house. The difference was the walls were of limestone, the ceiling was concrete, and there were no windows. "This is the room responsible for this whole project," Charlie said.

"From the looks of it, I think you succeeded in making it fireproof."

Most amazing to me was Charlie designing the entire house on yellow legal pads without consulting an architect. He told me he never could have done it without his accomplices, Red Alexander, the ranch carpenter, and Reyna Domotio, the ranch stonemason from Mexico. Except for the plumbing and electrical wiring, the house was built entirely by ranch laborers, many of whom were from Mexico and skilled craftsmen in rock work, tile laying, and carpentry. The running joke at the ranch and with Charlie's friends was the house would never be completed since Charlie had a reputation for starting projects and leaving them to a slow death as his enthusiasm moved to a new project.

Charlie guided me out of the gun room and upstairs. At the top of the stairs, leaning against the wall, were the twenty-foot-tall Mexican doors Charlie purchased the weekend we spent in Guadalajara. Turning right, we entered a massive bedroom. A large limestone fireplace stood along one wall with French doors on either side leading onto balconies. Behind the bedroom was the bath with closets anchoring either end. A Jacuzzi tub framed by antique windows overlooked the garden room below. Tiles in the shower and on the backsplash bore the Y.O. brand.

Across from the bedroom was a sitting room. The south and east walls were plate glass overlooking the main road and Deer Park. The southern end of the room extended like a balcony over a portion of the garden room. An antique Victorian iron fence served as a barricade. Looking out over the ranch was like a dream with equal parts illusion, reality, and ingenuity.

Charlie walked up and embraced me. "I have a request," I said. "What?"

"That you spend your first night in this house with me."

"Rest assured, you will have that honor," he said, nuzzling my neck. "I wouldn't want it to be anyone else. We'll make it a night to remember."

It certainly would be that!

Link for a tour of the Y.O. Ranch as it was when sold for the second time in 2022: https://www.texasranchsalesllc.com/listings/yo-ranch-headquarters-11200-acre -ranch-kerr-county/

Links for interview with Charles Schreiner III in his gun room at the Y.O. Ranch: Charlie III in the Vault—Part I of III—YouTube: https://www.youtube.com /watch?v=SOSTPMYtFAI

Charlie III in the Vault—Part II of III—YouTube: https://www.youtube.com /watch?v=Iu-3PzkCGCE

Charlie III in the Vault—Part III of III—YouTube: https://www.youtube.com /watch?v=8HqGWbgE1Qw&t=0s</List>

CHAPTER 9

*"No one ever made a difference
by being like everyone else."*

P. T. BARNUM

A Gathering of Texas Ranchers

WORKING OUR WAY THROUGH Dallas Fort Worth International Airport to our connecting flight reminded me of going through a receiving line because Charlie was stopping every few minutes to greet someone. After introducing me, Charlie would explain how he knew the person. They attended school together, or served together on a board, or their grandfathers had known each other or been in business together. Several were related by blood or marriage. Many of their surnames were prominent in Texas history, and others were prominent in the business world. No matter where we traveled, Charlie always crossed paths with people he knew. But nothing compared to the evening I accompanied him to a directors meeting for the Texas and Southwestern Cattle Raisers Association (TSCRA). The association was founded in 1877 by forty Texas cattlemen to combat cattle rustling in Texas, but soon its membership grew to include all of the Southwest.

One of the directors, Kerry McCan, was hosting dinner on Friday evening at his ranch outside of Victoria, Texas. Driving there, Charlie spotted a sign saying a historical marker was a mile away. I was amazed at Charlie's knowledge of Texas history and how minuscule mine seemed in comparison. Seeing the sign, Charlie asked, "What do you think happened?" This was his favorite activity whenever there was a historical marker. My usual response was, "How would I know?" Charlie would prod, saying, "Take a guess." Seldom could I formulate one but Charlie, using what he knew about the history of the area, would guess and most of the time was right.

"I haven't the faintest idea," I replied.

"Then I'll take a guess. Three Mexicans were killed in a wreck."

I looked at him skeptically. "I sincerely doubt that warrants a historical marker."

Charlie stopped at the marker, which stated three Mexican nationals were killed when their wagon overturned during an American Indian attack. Charlie beamed with pride. "See—wagon, car, it doesn't matter. It's still three dead Mexicans."

The dinner was held on the lawn surrounding the ranch house and barns. After parking the car, we walked a short distance and had to cross a cattle guard to reach the party. Like other women attending, I wore high heels. I marveled as they traipsed deftly across the iron rails. I balanced precariously on my toes while holding onto Charlie with a death grip. Try as I might, I never acquired this skill.

Kerry was a descendant of James Alfred McFaddin, who in 1877 established one of the largest cattle ranches in Southeast Texas. Kerry looked the part of a Texas rancher in his Western shirt, Stetson hat, and custom boots. His appearance belied that he graduated from Yale, served in the Marines, played polo, authored books, and traveled the world on hunting trips. I found him charming and easy to talk with. Kerry good-naturedly told me to resist all temptation to marry Charlie, no matter how much he begged. Charlie asked Kerry if he'd recently designed any unusual jewelry for his wife. Both broke into laughter. Kerry told me the year the screwworm fly was eradicated he gave his wife a custom-made diamond and ruby pin of the insect. He considered it a fitting gift given the decimating effect the screwworm inflicted on the state's cattle and deer. Charlie said Mrs. McCan was not nearly as enthusiastic about the gift as her husband.

As we walked away, I asked, "What was so bad about the screwworm?"

"Everything! Ranchers lost millions of dollars because of those little buggers. They feed on any warm-blooded mammal and lay their eggs in a cut or wound. Once an animal is infested, there's no cure. Its biggest toll was on deer and cattle. Finally in the 1950s, two scientists figured out if sterile males were introduced into the wild, females would still mate with them but there wouldn't be offspring. Once the program started, screwworms soon disappeared in Texas. But, that created another problem. It brought the whitetail deer back in such numbers now they're a pest, as anyone who drives in the Hill Country knows. There's more deer killed by cars now than by hunters. During the rut, deer have only one thing on their minds, and it leads to their bolting in front of cars. There's a body repair shop in Kerrville that advertises on a billboard, "Not IF but WHEN you hit that deer, remember us."

I would learn the wisdom of Charlie's words firsthand. I have hit two deer and don't know anyone living in the Hill Country who has not hit at least one. One of my friends has hit eight!

Charlie stopped to greet the governor of Texas, Dolph Briscoe, and his wife, Janey. The Briscoes owned a ranch in Southwest Texas. Unlike many large ranches, which shrink in acreage as they pass through the generations, the governor's ranch had grown from the 190,000 acres he inherited when his father died in 1954 to 300,000 acres. By 1980, the Briscoes would be the largest individual landowners in Texas with approximately 640,000 acres. I met the governor during the legislative session, and, to my surprise, he remembered me and introduced me to his wife, Janey.

Charlie asked the Briscoes how they were faring with the drought Texas was experiencing. Because the Briscoe ranch was in Southwest Texas, one of the most arid parts of the state, Charlie's inquiry was not made casually.

"Oh, Charlie," Janey Briscoe replied, laying her hand on his arm. "I'm afraid we'll be burning cactus in another month if we don't get some rain." Burning thorns off prickly pear cactus provides food for the cattle when there is no grass and is common practice during a drought.

Other members of Texas ranching royalty in attendance were from the King Ranch, Four Sixes, Armstrong, Waggoner, and Gage ranches. The men and women comprising this group had known Charlie most of his life. In many cases, their grandfathers and uncles were friends. In others, they served on boards or attended the University of Texas together.

Gage Holland, whose ranch was in the Big Bend area of West Texas, became one of my favorites. He was a bear of a man who walked with a rolling gait and had a growly voice. Gage advised me that should I decide to move to the Y.O., do not move all my belongings. "It will make it easier to escape," he said with a wink. Gage's ranch was established by his grandfather, Alfred Gage, in 1883. By the time he died in 1928, he owned approximately five hundred thousand acres in West Texas. Gage's ranch now covered around two hundred thousand acres.

Though one would never suspect it, Gage was an accomplished landscape and still-life painter and had several awards proving it. Gage asked Charlie if he was still raising "those ornamental cattle," referring to

Charlie's longhorns. Charlie shot back, "Yes, and I bet you're still carrying on a love affair with those teary-eyed white-faced Herefords."

Charlie and Gage discussed their mutually shared problem of cowboys wearing inappropriate attire, specifically baseball caps rather than cowboy hats. Gage told us about a cowboy he recently hired who wore not only a baseball cap but sneakers. Gage said the young man was one of the best cowboys he ever had and an exceptional roper. When Gage could stand it no longer he asked the young man if he would be willing to wear a cowboy hat and boots if Gage paid for them. The cowboy shuffled his sneaker-clad feet a few times, cocked his head, looked at Gage and said, "Well, sir, Mr. Holland, if it's all the same to you, I'd rather not dress up like no truck driver."

Charlie laughed and said, "I've told my employees we're running a ranch, not a camp for baseball players, and I better never see them in a baseball cap."

Several board members were from the King Ranch, which at one time was over a million acres. Founded in 1853 by steamboat captain Richard King, it occupies a large swath of South Texas and was the inspiration for Edna Ferber's novel *Giant* and the movie of the same name. Charlie introduced me to Tio Kleberg, whose auburn hair and impressive handlebar mustache made him instantly identifiable. At the time, he was head of ranching operations. Also present were two of his cousins, B. K. Johnson and B. K.'s half-brother Bobby Shelton. Their mother was the granddaughter of Capt. Richard King. Each of their fathers died shortly after they were born.

After their mother died in a car accident, they were reared by their aunt and uncle, Helen and Robert (Bob) Kleberg. Bob Kleberg ran the ranch for fifty years and was responsible for developing the Santa Gertrudis cattle breed, King Ranch bluestem grass, and thoroughbred racehorses. Because of their close relationship with their uncle, after he died B. K. and Bobby thought they would play major roles in managing the ranch. When that did not happen, each decided to sell their shares back to the ranch. Charlie told me rumor was the ranch had to borrow money for the payouts. Consequently, a rule was passed that family members could not sell their shares. With his money, Bobby Shelton purchased several ranches in the Kerrville area, which became his home base. In a strange twist of fate, B. K. would marry Charlie's fifth wife after she and Charlie divorced.

Jim Clement became my favorite member of this ranching dynasty. He was a tall, distinguished man who looked somewhat out of place among all the cowboys. When Charlie introduced us, Jim immediately asked me where I was from and how Charlie and I met. When I told him of my political involvement, he asked more questions. I would always look forward to seeing Jim and discussing a wide range of subjects with him. I never knew what his official role was until writing this memoir. He was the president and CEO of King Ranch when we met. I also learned he graduated from Princeton with a degree in politics, which explained why we always discussed politics.

Like Charlie, most of those attending wore their ranch's brand in one form or another. The men had them embroidered on their shirt pockets or cuffs. Many also wore their brand on a belt buckle or hat band, and some branded their boots. The women also wore brands, often in diamonds, on necklaces, bracelets, and earrings. Driving back to our hotel, Charlie casually mentioned that around ten million acres of Texas were represented at the party.

There was one thing about the gathering I found curious. "Are there any women directors?"

"Heavens, no!" Charlie exclaimed. "A woman? As a director? That doesn't make sense."

"Why? It's obvious those women know as much about ranching as their husbands. What about all the women who inherited the ranch, but their husbands are running it? This is the twentieth century for God's sake! When are you good ole boys going to wake up to the fact things have changed?"

"God willing, not in my lifetime," Three snorted. "And, by the way, there's something I've been meaning to ask you. No matter who I introduce you to, you never have a problem talking with them. The governor, bank presidents, my sons, a cowboy, it doesn't matter. You find something to talk about. Most of my wives lacked that skill. What's your secret?"

I laughed. "That, Mr. Schreiner, was first learned as a preacher's daughter, honed as a flight attendant, and perfected working in politics."

"When were you a flight attendant?"

"I dropped out of college my sophomore year, after having my heart broken. My job required talking to strangers, some charming and some jerks. I was fairly shy when I started the job but quickly overcame it. If I wanted to survive, I had to! When I became a flight attendant, my mother was certain I would marry a pilot and never finish college, but I failed to live up to her expectations. Why are you asking? You aren't reticent about striking up a conversation with strangers."

"I'll tell you a secret. I'm actually shy. When I was a boy I stuttered really bad whenever I was nervous. I finally managed to conquer it, and one of the ways I did was forcing myself to talk to strangers. I still get nervous doing it. It's like jumping into cold water. I have to brace myself. Same thing is true when I have to speak before a group."

After Charlie told me that, I noticed the telltale signs when he met someone. There would be a slight stutter, and he would clean his glasses to avoid eye contact, just as I remembered him doing the day we met in Jim Nugent's office.

I was also introducing Charlie to my world. He escorted me to political events, and even though he was out of his element with my liberal friends, he was so genial, knowledgeable, and witty he charmed everyone. When they teased him about his political views and the risk of my changing them, he replied we were proof that politics makes strange but happy bedfellows. When we attended a fundraiser for Mickey Leland, one of the first African Americans since Reconstruction to be elected to the Texas House of Representatives, Charlie and Mickey had an in-depth conversation about the cost of insurance for employees.

As he met my friends, Charlie commented several times on how fortunate I was to have so many genuine friends because he had few. I replied I found that hard to believe given how many people he knew. He said most were better described as acquaintances, not what he called "three o'clock in the morning friends," the ones you could call any hour of the day or night and count on them coming to your aid. He said many people became friends with him to gain something—a loan from Schreiner Bank, an invitation to visit the ranch, or a free hunt.

That I remained friends with the former men in my life astounded Charlie. "How in the hell do you do that?" he asked.

"If someone is good enough to sleep with, they're good enough to remain friends with, or at least be civil to when you see one another."

Charlie shook his head. "I wish I could say the same. My first wife would just as soon see me dead. She's told me her secret desire is to see me as a shoulder mount over her fireplace."

I put my arms around him. "No matter what happens, Charlie, I can't imagine ever hating you."

CHAPTER 10

"Every creature stalks some other,

catches it, and is caught."

MIGNON MCLAUGHLIN

Looking Forward into the Past

"I THINK THE MOST IMPORTANT THING to know about Charlie is he's a hunter," Jim Nugent said. I looked at him quizzically but said nothing. I knew not to interrupt when he wanted to tell me something. "For him the thrill is in the pursuit, not the kill. Once he's got his trophy, it becomes part of his collection and he moves on to his next conquest. You might keep that in mind."

"I don't understand."

"You're a smart woman. You'll figure it out."

Nugent had flown to Austin that morning for a meeting with the governor, and because I was going to the ranch for the weekend, I flew back to Kerrville with him. Changing the subject, Nugent said, "Has Charlie told you his Uncle Louis donated the land for the Kerrville airport?"

"No, but that explains why it's Louis Schreiner Field. I noticed that when we flew into it from Van Horn."

Charlie was waiting when we landed. He said he needed to run some errands and offered to take me to the hotel where we would be spending the night rather than making a late-night drive to the ranch. I said I'd accompany him, adding, "I came to Kerrville twice during the legislative session but both were quick trips so I saw nothing of the town."

"What in God's name brought you to Kerrville?"

"The first time was to be on a local radio talk show about the Equal

Rights Amendment, which led to my second trip to speak to a women's group about the ERA."

Charlie grinned and said, "It's a shame our paths didn't cross then."

Our first stop was Charles Schreiner Bank where Charlie introduced me to everyone from the president to the tellers. Interspersed with the introductions, Charlie told me the bank's history. "For several years it was part of Grandfather's general store. He didn't have a safe, so every night he put the money under a loose floorboard and rolled a barrel over it. His customers also entrusted him with their money, which he kept in the same place. Once a month Grandfather would deposit the money in a San Antonio bank. The money was carried there by Grandfather's most trusted employee, Simon Ayala, a one-legged cowboy. Ayala carried the money in a nose bag attached to his saddle by a grass rope. Because of Ayala's humble appearance, no one ever suspected a small fortune rather than food for himself and his horse was contained in the nose bag. The bank finally moved into a separate building in 1914.

Charlie went on to say that until 1959, when it became a state bank, Schreiner Bank was an unincorporated bank, relying on the financial standing of the Schreiner family. Charlie told me there had always been a gentleman's agreement between his grandfather and Col. Tom Frost, who founded Frost Bank in San Antonio, that neither would expand into the other's territory.

"What's it like to own a bank?"

"I don't own it. I'm just one of the board members. When Grandfather divided his holdings among his children, Uncle Louie got the bank. Grandfather had groomed him for it by having him work at the bank starting when he was a teenager. He worked there until he died at ninety-nine."

We walked across the street to the two-story Schreiner's Department Store, which started life on Christmas Eve, 1869, as Chas. Schreiner General Merchandise. Charlie told me the first sale was for two dollars' worth of coffee. The company had come a long way since its humble beginnings, now selling everything from cosmetics to fine china and crystal, to hunting and fishing equipment.

Next door was the former home of Captain Schreiner, a hulking mass of limestone blocks with deep porches upstairs and down. It was built where the captain's original cypress shack store was. In front of it was a Texas historical marker, and a plaque for the National Register of Historic Places was mounted by the front door. Captain Schreiner commissioned well-known San Antonio architect Alfred Giles to design the house in 1879. Giles designed many houses and courthouses throughout South

Texas, most of which are in the National Register of Historic Places. The house had been vacant several years but one of Charlie's cousins was raising money to make it a museum.

Charlie asked if I would like to see where he would be buried. Although some might think this strange, I did not. It is a common southern phenomenon not only to know from an early age where your bones or ashes will come to rest but to visit that place occasionally. Within a few minutes we were turning into Glen Rest Cemetery. Immediately I saw a large grey granite monument with only the name Schreiner on it. Clustered around it were the graves of Captain Schreiner, his wife, and many of their children and their spouses. Charlie led me to the graves of his father and mother.

"I'm surprised you don't want to be buried at the ranch," I said.

"I'd rather be here with all the other Schreiners."

"Is anyone buried at the ranch?"

Charlie grinned. "If they are, we don't know about it."

We pulled out of the cemetery and within several yards turned into Schreiner College. "And where does this fit into your family?" I asked.

"Grandfather donated the land and first building in 1917. Uncle Louis donated a couple of dorms and Uncle Gus was on the board and left all his money to it. It started life as Schreiner Military Institute, a male-only high school and junior college. I went here for a short time. In the early 1970s, it became coed and the military training was discontinued."

We drove back through town, crossed the Guadalupe River, and turned into a driveway with limestone pillars on either side of a wrought iron gate. We drove up a hill and stopped in front of a majestic columned two-story mansion.

"This was Uncle Louie's home," Charlie said. "I wanted you to see the view from here."

"I assume this is the same Uncle Louie who ran Schreiner Bank and for whom the airport is named?"

"None other. In addition to inheriting the bank, Uncle Louie also got three thousand acres. He decided this was the best spot for a house and built it in 1920. I wish you could see inside. It's beautiful. Marble floors, fountains, six bedrooms. It's fallen on hard times since Uncle Louis died. I keep hoping someone will buy it and restore it."

Charlie would get his wish a few years later when businessman Lloyd Brinkman bought the home for his company headquarters and returned it to its former glory. As we walked around the property, Charlie pointed out various Kerrville landmarks. Uncle Louie's three thousand acres were now consumed by businesses, a mall, and a subdivision. I could imagine how impressive it would have been to visit the house in the roaring twenties when it stood sentry over those virgin acres. I could almost hear a band playing ragtime as women in flapper dresses arrived.

That evening we dined at Riverhill Country Club. Before dinner Charlie took me on a tour of the clubhouse, which was originally the home of Gustave Fritz Schreiner, Captain Schreiner's second child and son. Compared to the other Schreiner homes, Uncle Gus's was modest, though there was a ballroom occupying the third floor.

"Uncle Gus managed the cattle operations for his father and was a conservationist long before it was a trend," Charlie said. "He played a major role in preserving the whitetail deer when the screwworm was taking such a toll. He also was on the board of Schreiner College until he died."

Lying in bed that night, I thought about all the places Charlie showed me that day. I had to give Charlie credit. He did a good job of portraying himself as a simple sheep and goat rancher. I wondered how big a burden Charlie found it to be heir to such a legacy and why he was giving me this tour. Impressive as his family's history was, I was not overwhelmed or intimidated by the opulence of the homes they lived in, the enormity of how much land they owned, or the influence and power his grandfather wielded in the worlds of banking, commerce, and ranching. There were equally distinguished branches on my family tree.

My ancestors did not play the prominent role in Texas history the Schreiner's did, but my roots in the United States and Texas went deeper than the Schreiners. My father's and mother's ancestors came to America in the mid-1700s and fought in the Revolutionary War and the War of 1812. My father's family descended from three brothers—Shadrach, Meshach, and Abednego Inman—who landed in Virginia, moved to North Carolina, then Tennessee, and became scouts for Daniel Boone. Abednego was the progenitor, or, as Charlie would say, herd sire, from which my father's ancestors came. In the 1800s, they moved from Tennessee to Georgia and then to Texas in the early 1900s. Inman Street in Houston is named for my paternal grandfather, who worked at the Houston Cotton Exchange.

My mother's paternal ancestors originally settled in Alabama and moved to Texas in 1865. My mother's maternal ancestors arrived in Texas in Stephen Austin's second colony of settlers in the early 1830s. The Spanish land grant they received in Montgomery County is still in the family. A cousin, T. A. Binford, was sheriff of Harris County, where Houston is located, for twenty years (1917–1937). His reputation as a tough lawman led to him being mentioned in a version of the classic prison song:

"If you ever go to Houston.
You better walk right;
You better not stagger,
You better not fight;
Sheriff Binford will arrest you,
He'll carry you down,
If the jury finds you guilty,
You're penitentiary bound."

Another maternal cousin, Price Daniel Sr., was a US senator and governor of Texas from 1957 to 1963. From 1973 to 1975, his son, Price Daniel Jr., was speaker of the Texas House, where members ignominiously nicknamed him "Half-Price" for his indecisiveness. His final notoriety was being killed by his second wife, who prior to their marriage was a waitress at the Dairy Queen in Liberty, Texas.

We drove to the ranch the next morning, taking the back road through Ingram and Hunt rather than Interstate 10. Charlie said, "I think this is the prettiest road in Texas. It takes longer to come this way, but it's worth it." The farther we drove the more I agreed. The headwaters of the Guadalupe River provide the source for numerous creeks that wind their way through cypress trees and limestone cliffs. Occasionally there was a gray heron or white egret standing still as a statue in the river waiting to spear a fish or frog. When we arrived at the ranch's front gate, I remembered my duty as passenger and got out to open and close the gate. We drove in silence until we reached the paved portion of the road. Rather than going to his house, Charlie turned left at the shearing barn sign. After a short distance, he turned right onto a steep road that gradually plateaued on the top of a hill. A windmill was the sole occupant, its sucker rod squeaking as it rose and fell. A slight breeze stirred the branches of the live oak trees around us. A few Spanish oaks were beginning to change color, or what passed for color in a Texas fall. We came to a stop in front of a sign proclaiming we were at Gobblers Knob.

"This is my favorite place on the ranch," Charlie declared. "I wanted to build my house here, but there wasn't enough room."

We got out of the car and I followed Charlie as he made his way up a small rise. He threw open his arms exclaiming with boyish delight, "As far as I can see in any direction is mine!"

Slowly I turned in a circle trying to imagine what it would be like to be able to make such a statement and to know from childhood it was your legacy. For the first time I understood the vastness of the ranch and why Charlie loved it as he did.

Charlie took me in his arms. "Do you know what I've always wanted to do here?"

"Have a picnic?" I coyly asked.

"I've done that."

"Hmmmm," I said. Placing my arms around his neck, I kissed him. "The only problem is this ground doesn't look very comfortable."

"I can solve that problem," Charlie said. He went to his station wagon, pulled out several furniture pads, kicked the largest rocks out of the way, and spread the pads on the ground.

"You think of everything, don't you? Did you plan this?"

"I figured if there was any woman who would indulge my secret fantasy it was you."

I smiled, put my arm around his neck, and said, "Let's give you another reason for this to be your favorite place on the ranch."

It wasn't the most comfortable place to make love, but there was a certain symbolism to it, especially with the windmill's sucker rod squeaking an accompaniment.

When we were dressed, Charlie said, "I've got something for you." He pulled a small box from the pocket of his jeans and handed it to me. Opening it, I saw it contained a smaller version of his Y.O. ring. Three removed the ring from the box and placed it on my finger. "I've said this before, but I'm going to say it again. I think you're the smartest, prettiest, most spirited woman I've ever met. Do you know how hard it is to get all those coons up one tree? I wish I'd met you five years ago. It would have saved me a lot of grief and money. I'm old fashioned and believe in marrying someone if you love them. If you won't consider marriage, will you come to the ranch to live? Just to see what it's like. All I'm asking is you think about it and wear this ring while you do."

I was flabbergasted. And surprised. And not sure how to respond.

Learn about the history of Capt. Charles Armand Schreiner and his Kerrville home in an online video, https://youtu.be/yRZUkSWMwsM
Link on founding of Schreiner Institute: https://youtu.be/oMMikvuzoNg

━━━━━━━━━━━━

CHAPTER 11

"I've married a few people I shouldn't have,

but haven't we all?"

MAMIE VAN DOREN

━━━━━━━━━━━━

The Wives of Charlie Three

CHARLIE OFTEN TOLD ME he would have preferred living in the late 1800s when ranching and cowboys were at their zenith. He believed something was lost from those times when a handshake sealed a deal, a man's word was his bond, and "women were women and didn't want to be men." Notwithstanding being reared by a strong-willed and independent mother, Charlie believed a woman's place was in the home and did not understand why any woman would prefer having a career. Charlie was certain he could quash my ambition, tame my willful ways, and convince me to be his obedient wife happily basking in his shadow. He even put it in writing when he gave me the book he wrote, *A Pictorial History of the Texas Rangers*. He inscribed it to "a very gentle lady all dressed in harsh 'womens' [sic] lib clothes . . . a real tigress to the legislature; but really only a sweet docile pussycat." Reading those words, I wondered whether he really believed them or wrote them in jest. In time I would discover the answer.

I was as delusional about Charlie as he about me. The twinkle in his eye, impish grin, and vigorous wooing made him hard to resist. My expectations for a relationship were based on my previous marriage of twelve years. R. C., my ex-husband, and I were equal partners sharing decision-making, managing finances, and encouraging each other in our ambitions. This was the relationship I naively assumed Charlie and I

69

would have. What neither Charlie nor I realized were the characteristics attracting us to each other posed the biggest threats to our relationship.

Charlie was as an old school Texas man who believed in removing his hat when greeting a member of the opposite sex, rising when a woman entered a room, walking on the street side when escorting a lady, opening doors, saying "ma'am," and never uttering in mixed company certain four-letter words now in common usage by both sexes. He liked women who were smart but didn't flaunt it, self-reliant but knew when not to be, ambitious but not aggressive, sexy but not cheap, and who could hold their own when drinking and telling stories. The woman Charlie most admired was his mother, Myrtle, for being successful in the male-dominated ranching business after the death of his father. Charlie often told me I reminded him of her, and I considered it a high compliment.

Like Charlie, I am also a contradiction. I am not offended by men being polite or expecting me to be a lady to their gentleman. Just as I was charmed when Charlie stood and removed his hat when we were introduced, I was also charmed by his employees and friends who took off their hats when talking with me and called me, "ma'am" and "Miss Norma." I was, however, taken aback and amused the first time one of them called me, "little lady." I thought it was a term used only in Western movies. I soon learned it wasn't. Accepting being treated like a lady did not mean I sacrificed my intelligence or beliefs about equality for women.

Charlie was forthright in giving me details of his previous marriages and his interpretation of why each failed. He admitted he was not a perfect husband but believed his previous wives were not blameless. Each had an aversion to living on the ranch full-time. As I would discover, Charlie probably contributed to this aversion.

Charlie met his first wife, Audrey, while both were attending the University of Texas. They married in 1950 in San Antonio, and his mother sent them on a three-month honeymoon to South America. This was not so the newlyweds could have time to get to know one another but so Charlie could study Brahman cattle and consider integrating this bloodline into the Y.O. herd. When they returned to the ranch, Myrtle presented them with a house she had built and furnished. When Charlie told me about the honeymoon and house, I wondered if Audrey felt appreciation or resentment at her mother-in-law's intrusion into their lives.

But if I thought Myrtle was presumptuous, Charlie one-upped her when his sons were born. Audrey agreed the first son would be named after his father and great-grandfather. The following three sons were named for

Left to right: Audrey Schreiner, Louis Albert Schreiner, Walter Richard Schreiner Jr., Texas Governor John B. Connally, Charles Schreiner IV, Gustav Louis Schreiner, and Charles Schreiner III, circa 1960s.

Charlie's father, Walter, and uncles, Gus and Louis. When Charlie told me this, I asked what Audrey thought about it. He proudly replied, "She didn't have any say. I named them while she was still under the anesthesia."

As fault lines developed in the marriage, Audrey and their sons begin spending more time in San Antonio at her mother's home. Attempting to salvage the marriage, Charlie bought a house in Alamo Heights, an incorporated city within San Antonio. The plan was for Audrey and the boys to spend the school year there and come to the ranch weekends and summers.

As he was telling me about their divorce, he asked, "Do you know how to shoot a gun?" I replied, "No."

"I taught Audrey how to shoot and did too good a job. She was an expert marksman, and there were several times she got so mad at me I thought she might kill me. During those times I'd deliberately not stay at or drive by the house."

In the late 1960s Charlie became involved with Patricia Lopez, the secretary for the Texas Longhorn Breeders Association. Charlie filed for divorce in 1970. Audrey countersued, accusing Charlie of desertion, cruelty, and adultery with Patricia. Their case went to trial in 1973. As part of her settlement, Audrey asked for thirty-three thousand acres of the Y.O. When the divorce was granted, this demand was denied.

Within hours of receiving the news, Charlie and Patricia were on a plane to Las Vegas and immediately married. The next day Charlie's attorney called saying Audrey filed an appeal because she did not receive the requested portion of the Y.O. The divorce would not be final until the Texas Court of Civil Appeals ruled. Charlie flew back to Texas and left Patricia to get a quickie divorce in Las Vegas. Charlie held his breath, fearing Audrey would find out about the marriage and charge him with bigamy. She did not, and a month later the appellate court ruled Audrey was not entitled to any of the Y.O. because it was Charlie's separate property that he inherited at the age of six when his father died. Charlie and Patricia remarried, but Charlie told me Patricia felt uncomfortable on the ranch because she thought ranch employees and Charlie's friends blamed her for his divorce. Charlie also told me that even though he knew Patricia had been in relationships with women, he was sure marriage would change her. He was wrong, and the marriage was short-lived.

Shortly after divorcing Patricia, Charlie married a woman he termed his "menopausal wife." One of the ranch employees told me twenty-year-old Sully Vandenberg came to the ranch as Walter's guest and left as Charlie's fiancé. The wedding was an extravagant formal event, held at the lodge with the bride and groom departing via helicopter for their honeymoon. When Charlie told me about it, he said, "I made a total ass of myself." Sully kept an apartment in New Orleans, often going there to visit and, Charlie suspected, to see other men. She talked of wanting a child, and Charlie was afraid she would become pregnant. With this in mind, he secretly combined his annual mule deer hunting trip to New Mexico with obtaining a vasectomy. Sully found the receipt in his wallet and was livid at his duplicity. Shortly thereafter, Charlie filed for divorce.

It never occurred to me to ask Charlie for specific dates as to when each marriage and divorce occurred. Had I done so, I would have learned his most recent two marriages and divorces had occurred in the last four years. Another vital piece of information I didn't know was Charlie filed for divorce from each wife. He was the poster boy for marrying in haste and repenting at leisure—but while repenting he was on the prowl for his next trophy.

CHAPTER 12

▬▬▬▬▬▬▬▬

"Enjoy the flavor of life. Take big bites."

ROBERT A. HEINLEIN

▬▬▬▬▬▬▬▬

Strange New World

I WAS FOLLOWING CHARLIE'S STATION WAGON into a blinding sunset and could hardly see the road much less Charlie's vehicle going its usual eighty miles an hour. We stopped in Kerrville to have dinner and by the time we started to the ranch it was almost ten o'clock at night. Charlie resumed his warp speed climbing up and down hills on a winding back road. Trying to keep his taillights in view was all I could concentrate on. Suddenly my peripheral vision caught an object hurtling toward my car on the passenger side. I turned my head as a twelve-point buck crashed into the car. I began shaking uncontrollably and slowly came to a stop. Charlie's car had disappeared into the pitch darkness.

Should I get out and look for the deer? What could I do if I found it? I sat in my car shaking and hoping Charlie would come back. Minutes passed with no sign of Charlie. I steered my car back onto the road and after a few miles I saw taillights stopped ahead. I flashed my lights, and as I stopped and rolled down my window, Charlie approached and said, "What the hell happened to you? I was starting to get worried."

"I hit a deer! We need to go back and check on it."

"Trust me, the deer is dead. Even if he isn't, there's nothing we can do."

"You could shoot it and put it out of its misery."

"No, I couldn't. It's against the law. Only a game warden can shoot one injured by the side of the road."

This was my first lesson, but by no means last, in leaving wild animals to their plight, cruel though it may be.

My mother, in addition to believing in the power of prayer, was a great believer in dreams, premonitions, and signs. It was not unusual for her to call me and start the conversation saying, "Are you all right? I had a dream about you last night." Because she passed this superstition on to her children, I was now wondering if the blinding sunset and hitting the deer were warnings telling me not to drive blindly into the future. When I quit my job and moved to the ranch, I made it clear to Charlie this was not a commitment but an opportunity to see whether the reality of living on a ranch in any way resembled the romantic vision I conjured as a child. Charlie assured me I could leave at any time.

Until his new house was completed, Charlie was living in a trailer located between the Y.O. Lodge and the Chuckwagon. He apologized for bringing me to such cramped quarters and promised completing the upstairs of his house would be a priority. Charlie was up at five each morning and, after the scare of a mild heart attack two years before, exercised by walking to the Chuckwagon. The Chuckwagon was the dining facility for many ranch employees and all visitors to the ranch. It also housed the ranch offices and was where ranch visitors checked in and out. At eight thirty, he would arrive back at the trailer, and I would accompany him as we drove around the ranch stopping to check on his various projects; it was also an opportunity for me to begin learning my way around the ranch and how to identify the many animal species.

From volunteering at the Houston Zoo, I was familiar with many of the exotic animals on the ranch; however, differentiating between the species of deer was difficult. I thought I would never master it until I devised my own touchstones for telling them apart. The axis deer were my favorite with their beautiful spotted coats and antlers ascending straight up as if trying to pierce a cloud. Their hides were used for upholstery throughout the Hill Country and made into purses and vests. Like the axis, the antlers of the barasingha grew straight up but were not as spectacular, and its coat was a lackluster brown. Another Asian deer was the sika. It was distinguished by a white rump that looked like a bullseye. At one time this deer roamed throughout Asia and Russia but is now found primarily in Japan where its abundant numbers make it a pest, much as the whitetail deer is in Texas. When I visited northern Japan, I saw sika deer roaming freely through the streets and yards of towns just as the native whitetail does in parts of Texas.

The fallow deer came in a variety of solid colors, but some were spotted, making it difficult for me to distinguish them from the axis. When I told Charlie this, he said, "All you have to do is look at their antlers. They're palmated." He held up his hand pointing at his palm. "Like a moose, with a wide central portion or palm. And whatever you do, don't go calling antlers 'horns'. Deer have antlers. Antelopes, cows, sheep, and buffalo have horns."

"There's a difference?"

Charlie rolled his eyes. "Yes ma'am there certainly is. Antlers are extensions of the animal's skull. They grow out during the rut and fall off when it's over. As deer age their antlers usually grow larger each year. Horns are permanent. The interior is bone and the exterior is keratin, like our fingernails. Horns are never shed and continue growing throughout the animal's life. If a horn gets broken, it doesn't grow back."

One morning as we drove around Deer Park, I saw a blackbuck antelope with his neck stretched out, his head high in the air, and his upper lip curled back exposing his teeth. "What's he doing?" I asked.

"He's flehming. It's the German word for exposing the upper teeth. It means he's breathing through his mouth, not his nose. Lots of animals do it, even your pussy cat. There's tissue in their mouth that picks up certain scents the nose doesn't, especially if a female is in heat."

One of the more frustrating skills for me was how to tell whitetail bucks apart by the shape of their antlers, a talent Charlie and all the hunting guides excelled at. One night as we sat in the lodge entertaining guests, I realized I was sitting in the perfect classroom to master this. I began spending time there studying each mount and the shape of their antlers. Suddenly, differentiating between them was easy.

Like most people from the city, I had urban eyes and could look directly at a deer standing in foliage and not see it. As we drove around the ranch, Charlie would say, "There's an axis at one o'clock." I would stare where Charlie was pointing and see nothing until Charlie taught me to examine each individual object. Soon the animal would emerge, and I would wonder how I could have missed it. Years later when I traveled to Africa and India to see wildlife, the guides expressed surprise at my animal sighting abilities. My answer was, "I was taught by an expert."

Several times when we were in pastures Charlie would ask me what kind of grass was growing there. The first time he did this, I looked at him quizzically and said, "What difference does it make? Grass is grass."

"No ma'am, it is not."

From then on, wherever we were Charlie made a point of telling me the names of various grasses and their good and bad characteristics—side oats grama, buffalo grass, and bluestem varieties including King Ranch bluestem, developed by that ranch to survive the harsh soil and weather of South Texas. Charlie knew his grasses, but I never mastered them.

In a pasture housing a large elk, Charlie taught me how to "read signs." Reading signs is closely examining every detail of your surroundings to determine which animals have been there and what they were doing. Deer are browsers that prefer tender buds and succulent young leaves. Looking at the ends of stems and branches reveals whether deer browsed the ends. Urine and feces tell how recently an animal was there and its species. Studying the ground can reveal tracks, and disturbed soil and grass indicate there was a fight or an animal bedded down.

Charlie pointed to the trunk of a tree where some of the bark was missing. "Remember I told you deer drop their antlers after the rut? When they grow back in the fall they're covered in velvet. These marks are where a deer was rubbing velvet from his antlers."

I interrupted. "I know about velvet."

"How?"

"From reading, of course. In Rudyard Kipling's *The Second Jungle Book* a barasingha deer is befriended by a man who helps the deer rub the velvet from its antlers. The deer repays the favor by warning the man the mountain he lives on is collapsing."

"You never cease to amaze me with all the information you have filed away in that brain of yours. Let's see if you have an answer for this. What's the reason for velvet?"

"It supplies oxygen and nutrients while the antlers are growing. I learned that while volunteering at the zoo. When they stop growing, the velvet begins coming off and the deer assist by rubbing their antlers against trees or whatever else they can find."

When driving around the pastures, we used Charlie's ranch vehicle, a Ford Bronco customized with a quarter-inch steel bottom. Charlie drove it with reckless abandon across rock-strewn pastures, through impenetrable cedar stands, over boulders, up hillsides, and down into gullies. I held on for dear life as we bounced from one rock to another. The Bronco was coated with dust inside and out. If it had ever been washed, the event was a long-forgotten memory. The interior contained various tools, unmated gloves, pieces of wire, empty soft drink and beer cans, plastic glasses and cups, rope, chains, notebooks, and man's best friend, duct tape. When I mentioned to one of the hunting guides the abandon with which Charlie drove the Bronco, he laughed and told me one time Charlie was guiding several of the state's elected officials. As he bounced off a particularly large boulder, the state comptroller's rifle went off, blasting a hole in the top of the Bronco.

My first ride in this vehicle was when Charlie took me to see his longhorns. The only ride I experienced comparable to it was years later riding across the Mongolian steppes in a Russian army jeep. As we drove around the pasture, there wasn't a longhorn to be seen.

"I guess we're out of luck," I said.

"Be patient," Charlie said, stepping from the car. He went around to the back, got a large sack, and began bellowing while shaking the sack. In less than a minute longhorns came loping down a hill. Charlie continued bellowing while shaking out the sack's contents. I watched entranced as the massive beasts consumed their reward with clashing horns and saliva dripping from their mouths. It was easy to imagine what a cattle drive would have been like with hundreds or thousands of these animals being trailed to market in a cloud of dust, their horns clashing and cowboys yipping and twirling lariats to keep them moving.

Charlie returned to the car. "What was in the bag?" I asked.

"Range cubes. They're cow candy."

"And that horrific sound you were making?"

"That's how you call cattle."

"I want to learn how to do it."

Charlie looked at me over the top of his glasses. "I'll try but you won't be able to do it."

"Why not?" I replied indignantly.

"Because your voice has to come from your balls, and you don't have any."

"We'll see about that," I thought.

We drove to another pasture and I got out of the car and began bawling, doing the best imitation of Charlie I could, sans balls. It was not long before longhorns came crashing through the cactus and underbrush.

"I've got to admit, you're pretty good for a girl," Charlie said grudgingly.

Unbeknownst to both of us, that skill would save my life almost forty years later. I was on a ship sailing across the Drake Passage to Antarctica. The ship was moving at fifty knots trying to outrun a weather system. I went onto my balcony and left the sliding glass door open. Suddenly the ship listed, and the door slammed shut and locked. Knowing the staterooms on either side were unoccupied, I realized demurely calling for help would not get me rescued. "I've got to use my cattle calling voice," I thought and began bawling, "Help!" After a terrifying thirty minutes I was rescued.

When I arrived at the ranch, I was an urban-reared animal lover. To live in a rural environment requires understanding and accepting the brutality of nature. One day as we drove into Kerrville there was a fawn frantically running up and down one side of a high fence as its mother and twin followed on the other. I innocently asked Charlie to stop the car and help. "There's nothing I can do. They're wild animals and will run away from me. Most likely the fawn found a hole in the fence and went through it. Either it will or won't find it again."

Another day we were driving through a pasture on the ranch and came upon a deer caught in a fence. This is a common occurrence when deer jump a fence because their back foot will catch between the two top strands of the fence's wire. In struggling to free itself, the deer pulls its leg muscles and, even if freed, the animal is badly lamed and becomes easy prey. This deer was still alive and struggling. Charlie quickly put it out of its misery. The day would come when I would have to perform this act, and it was among the most difficult tasks I've ever carried out.

One day as I was approaching a cattle guard while driving into the ranch, I saw something protruding between the metal grids. Suddenly it disappeared and then reappeared. I stopped several feet from the cattle guard and saw two lamb heads pop up and then disappear. Getting out of my car, I saw the mother standing in a grove of trees calling to them. I had on a dress and heels but got down on my knees and extracted both lambs from the cattle guard. They hightailed it over to their mother and the three of them trotted away without even a departing glance of gratitude.

Dogs were tolerated on the ranch only if they did not chase deer and cattle, a behavior as instinctive for dogs as catching birds is for cats. Occasionally a group of dogs would find its way onto the ranch. It is the rule of all farmers and ranchers that when this happens, the dogs are shot on sight. When I lived in Bandera, I adopted a dog who was shot for this reason and consequently lost a front leg. I'm sure feral cats were abundant, but only one ever came up to Charlie's house, where he received free room and board.

The animal situation that I found most disturbing was four jaguars kept in cages behind the house of Charlie's son Walter. The cages were only about four-by-eight feet with concrete floors and chain-link fence enclosing them. The jaguars were captured in Mexico in the early 1970s by Capt. Bob Snow. Like so many associated with the Y.O., Snow was a larger-than-life character. As a young man he worked on the King Ranch and then for the Texas Rangers along the Texas-Mexico border. From there he became a game warden with Texas Parks and Wildlife. After retiring, he came to the Y.O. and worked as a hunting guide and trapper, making frequent trips to Mexico to hunt and trap mountain lions and jaguars. Why the jaguars were left at the Y.O. is unknown, but my heart bled each time I drove by their cages and saw those spectacular creatures in such cramped and unnatural conditions.

In addition to coyotes, golden eagles were also predators of lambs, and Charlie despised them. At the time, the US government protected the eagles because they were endangered. Every spring during lambing

Letter sent by Charlie Three to the US Fish and Wildlife Service.

Y-O RANCH / MOUNTAIN HOME, TEXAS 78058

October 16, 1978

Office of Endangered Species
Fish and Wildlife Service
U.S. Department of the Interior
Washington DC

Gentlemen:

In September of 1978, I wrote you, urging you to come and get your protected Golden Eagles and Bald Eagles before they kill our baby lambs again in December of 1978.

We suffered economic losses of lambs due to Eagles, in 1976 of approximately $42,000 and in 1977 of $56,000. We anticipate that the Eagles will return in November to kill and claw to death more of our baby lambs. You must provide us protection against your protected Golden Eagles and Bald Eagles.

Come and get your eagles; we must protect our own private property.

We have not received a satisfactory answer to our September letter. There are only a few more weeks until the Eagles will come and kill our baby lambs -- again.

Sincerely,

Chas. Schreiner III

CS/dd

season, the eagles would migrate north from their winter nesting grounds to the south. As far as Charlie was concerned, their favorite route was over the Y.O. where they could take advantage of the lamb buffet he provided for them. For several years, Charlie called the Department of the Interior to express his ire. With tongue in cheek, I suggested he might get better results if he put his complaint in writing, which he did. Whether it was responded to, I do not know.

Bordering the Y.O. on the northeast was the Moody Ranch. It was built in the 1920s by William L. Moody III, whose family was as distinguished and integral a part of Texas history as the Schreiners. The first William Moody established himself trading cotton in Galveston during the 1850s, and his son expanded the business into banking and insurance. The Y.O. leased the Moody Ranch for hunting; because it had a lodge with nineteen bedrooms and its own cook, it increased the number of hunters the ranch could accommodate. The Moody family also owned the Menger Hotel in San Antonio. We often saw Mary Moody Northen, the eighty-six-year-old grande dame of the family, when staying there. Charlie always made a point of greeting her, and she would always ask about the Moody, how much rain there had been, and how the wildlife was faring.

One fall afternoon Charlie and I drove across the Y.O. to visit the Moody. It took us over an hour since we traveled on the Y.O.'s rutted caliche roads. As we drove Charlie pointed out various animals, and as the sun lowered itself into the hills, the grass took on a golden tint as the crisp coolness of the evening set in.

We pulled up to a beautiful 1920s style Spanish hacienda. Charlie told me it was designed by Carl Weyl, who was an art director for the movies and designed numerous buildings in Los Angeles. The Moody's cook came out to greet us and show us to our room. Dinner was served at a large table in a formal dining room. As we were the only guests, after dinner we explored every room. Numerous antiques were casually placed throughout the lodge, including carved jade and ivory pieces and old books, many of which bore book plates of members of the Moody family. Like everything I did with Charlie, I felt immersed in Texas history, part of a sweeping narrative with people and places I'd read about in books.

Of all the places Charlie showed me during my first days on the ranch, the most beautiful was Bear Creek Ranch, eight hundred acres of pristine Hill Country he purchased in the 1960s and put in a trust for his sons. To get there, we turned off the state highway into a pasture and drove cross-country until we came to Bear Creek, which emptied into the North Fork of the

Guadalupe River. Huge cypress trees loomed over us as we drove slowly through the shallow water. Charlie added to the setting's ambiance, telling me we were driving through wagon ruts left by early settlers. Whether this was true or his providing a dramatic effect I never knew, but I was so enraptured I believed him. Suddenly the trees disgorged a flock of white egrets screeching at our intrusion. A doe and her fawn flashed across the creek, and a fox froze on the creek bank as we passed. I wished time would stop and Charlie and I would be frozen here for eternity, like the fossils embedded in the limestone cliffs surrounding us.

CHAPTER 13

"In order to be irreplaceable,

one must always be different."

COCO CHANEL

A Colorful Cast of Characters

IMAGINE YOU ARE VISITING the Y.O. Ranch for the first time. You've driven an interminable forty-five minutes, because you're driving a low-slung European sports car that could be swallowed whole by one of the road's many craters. Finally, you cross a cattle guard onto a paved road. You see a sign saying "Chuckwagon" with an arrow pointing ahead. You follow it until the road ends in a large, paved parking lot where there's a flagpole flying the Y.O. flag.

The parking lot is filled with various makes and models of all-terrain vehicles, trucks, and jeeps. It's obvious many of these vehicles have been subjected to hard labor. Their paint is scratched and gouged, their bodies dented and smashed. Windshields have nicks and cracks, many so severe you wonder how the driver manages to see out. Useless side mirrors dangle from doors. Hoods and bumpers are lashed in place with bailing wire. Duct tape holds a rear light in place or mends a shattered window. One of the trucks is skillfully painted with zebra stripes. Several vehicles have a dead animal lashed to their hoods.

Walking up to the Chuckwagon, you notice a twelve-foot mound of shed deer antlers and wonder how long they have been accumulating. Looking down you see the sidewalk has the Y.O. brand every few feet. As soon as you open the Chuckwagon door, your senses are overwhelmed by the aromas of food and an oak fire burning in the fireplace.

Norman "Button" Forehand, the official Y.O. bartender and greeter of guests.

"Welcome to the Y.O. Ranch," booms a disembodied baritone. "We've been expecting you folks and you got here just in time for dinner, or what you probably call lunch." The voice greeting you is coming from a short squatty man who personifies the way you imagined someone working on a ranch would look. He extends his hand over the counter. "I'm Button." You're immediately impressed by Button's perfectly groomed salt and pepper handlebar mustache and beard. In his mouth is a chewed unlit cigar that bobs up and down as he speaks. He comes from behind the counter, and you see his attire is as impeccable as his facial hair. He wears a white cowboy hat and a white Western shirt starched to perfection. Over it he wears a plaid vest, the pocket of which holds several cigars. His jeans are tucked into knee-high cowboy boots.

If Button had a title, I never knew it. Button was a combination greeter of ranch guests, receptionist, breakfast cook, matchmaker of guides with hunters, stagecoach driver, bartender, and occasionally a guide for hunters and tours. His given name was Norman, but I never heard it used and I doubt if many people knew it. He earned his nickname growing up on a ranch in Arizona. As soon as he could, Button would ride with the cowboys, and their tradition was to nickname the youngest cowboy "Button." Whether by accident or intent, the name stuck. Button had

Bertie (Miss Bertie) Varner, the Y.O. cook extraordinaire, 1978.

been at the Y.O. since 1963 and seen the ranch evolve into what it was as its centennial approached.

Button takes you by the arm and steers you to a counter where you see a large pot of pinto beans, a green salad, fried chicken, mashed potatoes, brown gravy, green beans, and freshly made cornbread. Wondering how you can possibly consume a portion of each, you then spy a large pan of peach cobbler.

"We don't stand on formality here. Just get a plate and help yourself." The voice is that of a short, plump woman with salt and pepper hair and a welcoming smile.

"This here is Miss Bertie. She's the best damn cook in the state of Texas," says Button as Bertie blushes. The veracity of this statement would be acknowledged in 1987 when Bertie was one of the cooks featured on the Public Broadcasting Service series *Great Chefs of the Southwest*.

You take a small sampling of each dish, including the peach cobbler, and sit down at a ten-foot-long table covered with red-and-white-checked oilcloth. As you're dining, you take in your surroundings. You notice the andirons supporting the firewood are a "Y" and an "O." The walls are covered with photographs of hunters posing with their Y.O. trophies, shoulder mounts of various animals found on the Y.O., and paintings of ranch employees. Restroom doors have the head of a buck painted on one and a doe on the other. A woman walks up to them and looks perplexed. A tall barrel-chested man appears and explains she should use the door with a doe's head. Smiling broadly, he walks over and extends his hand. "Welcome to the Y.O. I'm Butch Ramsey, the game biologist."

Another man appears who only reaches to Butch's shoulders. He grins and says, "I'm Tommy Thompson, one of the hunting guides." Pointing at Butch he says, "You can also call him Cannibal because he's mean as a wild hog."

"I am *not* a cannibal," Butch states, looking you in the eye. "I was involved in a little altercation in a bar in Junction and bit off the ear of my adversary. But I spit the ear out so he could get it sewed back on. If I was mean, I'd have swallowed it."

Butch and Tommy break into laughter. Tommy says, "At least I don't go around kissing other men when they do me a favor." Tommy points at Butch and says, "He lost a very expensive knife he borrowed from one of the other guides. We'd been out in the pasture for hours looking for it and I looked down and if it'd been a snake it would've bitten me. I called Butch over and showed it to him and the SOB picked me up and kissed me! On the mouth! What if a hunter and guide saw us? Or Charlie Three?" Butch puts his arm around Tommy, kisses him on the head, and they make their way to the buffet.

Whenever my friends visited the ranch, I requested Butch and Tommy give them tours because they were so entertaining. My friends agreed, and Butch and Tommy reciprocated and told me I had the "best friends of all of Three's wives."

As Butch and Tommy walk away, an older distinguished man approaches with his tray of food. "Mind if I join you?" he asks, setting down his tray. He removes his white cowboy hat, extends his hand and says, "I'm Warren Klein but everybody calls me Uncle Warren. You can do the same. I'm the ranch's nearest neighbor. Matter of fact, you drove across my land to get to the front gate."

"How long have you known the Schreiners?" you ask.

"I was born three miles from here and have known all the Schreiners starting with the captain. I remember when Mr. Walter, Charlie Three's father, brought Miss Myrtle back as his bride. Mr. Walter was a fine man. A man of his word. It was a sad, sad day when he died." Uncle Warren shakes his head. "I figured Miss Myrtle would sell the ranch to one of Walter's brothers since she knew nothing about ranching, but she took over and didn't have to take her hat off to no man. She sent Charlie Three off to

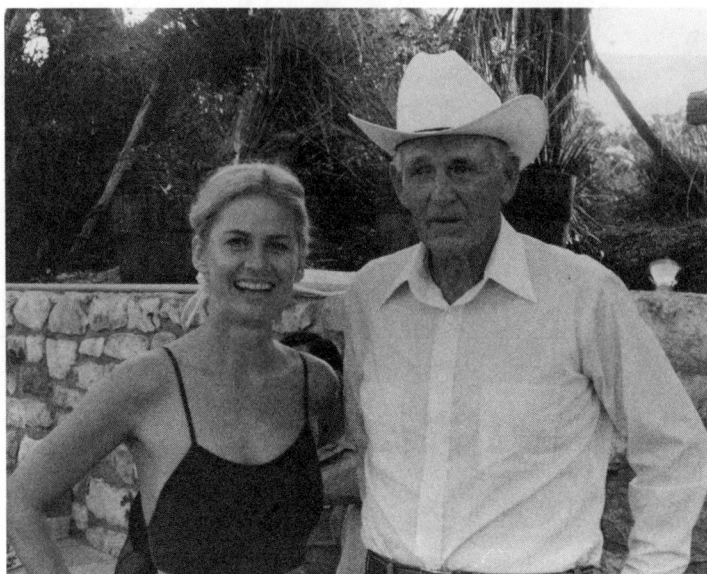

The author with Warren (Uncle Warren) Klein, the Y.O.'s nearest neighbor, 1982.

school in San Antonio so she could devote all her time to the ranch. She told me she hated doing it but was determined to save the ranch for him. Charlie ran away and hitchhiked to the ranch a couple of times, but he wasn't any sooner in the front gate than Miss Myrtle was sending him back."

Uncle Warren takes a bite of fried chicken and waves at another man. "Chester, come over here and join us." As Chester sits down, Uncle Warren says, "Chester's done just about everything there is to do on the Y.O. Worked on windmills, built fences, helped with the livestock, and managed the Live Oak section. He's also the Y.O.'s official rattlesnake killer and the proud husband of Miss Bertie, who's responsible for this delicious lunch we're having." Chester lifts his hat and extends his hand.

Intrigued by the introduction, you ask, "How did you become the rattlesnake killer?"

"I know where they den up for the winter," Chester replies succinctly.

When it becomes obvious Chester is not going to elaborate, Uncle Warren adds, "Knowing where they den up makes them easy to find in the spring when they come out and take naps on the rocks outside their den."

"I use rat shot," Chester adds. "That way it doesn't mess up the skin so you can make a belt or hatband out of it." As Chester says this, a young man enters the Chuckwagon. Chester nods in his direction and says, "Donnie's got one of them on."

You look over and see a handsome dark-haired young man who could have stepped out of a Western movie. He's wearing a rattlesnake skin belt. Uncle Warren calls him over and introduces you to Don McMinn, saying, "Donnie's official title is Maintenance Supervisor but like everybody here he does whatever needs doing."

About that time, you notice a middle-aged man wearing a shirt that matches the tablecloth standing at the adjacent table and speaking Spanish to a guest. You understand enough of the conversation to know the guest has asked what he does at the ranch. The man looks down at his scuffed boots and says, "Whatever needs to be done. Right now I'm supervising the building of a house."

Uncle Warren and Chester look at one another and shake their heads. Uncle Warren turns to you and says, "That's Charlie Three. He loves acting like he's just one of the hired hands."

For visitors to the ranch, its employees exceeded expectations in being colorful and unique characters. Many of the Y.O. crew have appeared in commercials filmed at the ranch and on television programs, both national and local, featuring the ranch.

Years after leaving the Y.O., I was living in Hawaii. One of the men I worked with was a native Hawaiian and surprised me when he said his favorite author was Larry McMurtry, a fellow Texan. I asked him why. "His characters," he replied. "They're so colorful. I've always wondered how he makes them up."

Immediately the Y.O. came to mind. "Trust me," I said, "he doesn't make them up."

Soon after I moved to the ranch, hunting season for the native whitetail deer and turkey began and with it my initiation into the man's world that dominated life on the ranch. At every meal, the Chuckwagon was crowded with male hunters. Conversing with them reminded me of lobbying the Texas legislature. All I had to do was sit, murmur an occasional response, and listen as they extolled every detail of their day's hunt. Leaving the table, they would say, "It certainly was nice talking with you, ma'am." I always thought, "But you did all the talking."

Unlike many game ranches where the hunter pays a fee regardless of whether he shoots an animal, the Y.O. did not charge a hunter for an animal not taken. It was the job of the hunting guides to ensure a hunter got his animal. Before hunting season, the guides drove around the ranch learning the patterns of the various animals and sharing the information with each other. I never heard of a hunter failing to get the animal he came for, and often a few others as well.

Charlie told me the hunting operation and visitors to the ranch played a major role in the ranch's cash flow. For this reason, Charlie and his sons made a point of adding a personal touch by mingling with hunters and guests during meals at the Chuckwagon. Whether intentionally or by osmosis, Charlie's sons were as proficient at gracious humbleness as their father. After dinner, hunters would gather at the Y.O. Lodge for drinks, and several of the guides would sing while accompanying themselves on guitar, fiddle, and mandolin. Seldom was a song requested they did not know. If Charlie Three was on the ranch, he would stop at the lodge after dinner.

Hunters at the Y.O. covered a wide spectrum, including astronauts, movie stars, state and local politicians, international political and business leaders, writers, journalists, people from almost every state and profession, as well as visitors from foreign countries. Most were men but occasionally there was a couple or lone woman. There were also unexpected visitors, like the two men who showed up at Charlie's house one evening after landing on the ranch's airstrip. I heard a knock on the front door, which was unusual because most people walked in and yelled to announce their presence. When I opened the door, they explained they were on their way to West Texas when night descended. The pilot said he was not comfortable flying at night so they would sleep in their plane, but he wanted us to know they were there. I invited them in, made drinks for them, and called Charlie Four since Three was off the ranch. Charlie Four arrived a few minutes later, took the guests to one of the cabins to spend the night, and told them to go to the Chuckwagon for breakfast the next morning.

Of the many outdoors writers who regularly visited, my favorite was Byron Dalrymple from Kerrville. From the moment Charlie introduced us, Byron and I were friends. Byron attributed it to the fact we were both Leos sharing August birthdays only a few days apart. Originally from Minnesota, Byron's career included playing the saxophone in jazz bands, writing music for the movies, and authoring numerous articles and books on wildlife, hunting, and fishing. Byron told me he began his literary career writing pulp fiction, a job that paid a penny a word. When he was told what he would be paid, he thought it would be the easiest job he ever had, given how many words are in the dictionary. He soon discovered getting the right words in the right order could be a maddening exercise.

Paul Calle was one of the many artists who visited the Y.O. The Franklin Mint Gallery commissioned him to do a series of paintings depicting life on a modern ranch and the Y.O. was chosen as the ranch. Calle was best known for the numerous postage stamps he designed, especially the one depicting the first moon landing. When Calle was introduced to George Hey, who had been at the Y.O. twenty-five years, he immediately asked George to pose for him, saying George exemplified what a ranch hand should look like. After the artist left, George was in the Chuckwagon telling of Calle's request to paint him. "I think," George said, "he was telling me I was a dried-up crusty looking old bastard."

George performed many jobs on the ranch and had become "the wind-mill man" with the responsibility of maintaining the ranch's forty-plus windmills. There was no running water on the ranch and windmills were the ranch's life blood, bringing water from underground aquifers to the surface for humans and animals alike. George's responsibilities included repairing leaking pipes and broken pumps and checking water levels at the tanks where animals drank. George told me several of the ranch wind-mills were fifty years old and a few were pushing seventy-five, including a wooden one still pumping in the Gilmer pasture.

George's seniority on the ranch was exceptional. Most of the work-ers and cowboys were itinerant in nature, working for short periods of time before moving on. The majority were from Mexico. Some were in the country legally while others walked across the border illegally fol-lowing trails handed down through generations. Their routes followed back roads and crossed private property, especially the large ranches in West and South Texas. Many of those whose land they crossed left food and water along the trails. When returning to Mexico, they walked along major roads hoping to be picked up by immigration officials, thus insuring them a ride back to Mexico. Many had been working at the Y.O. for years. Once a year they returned to Mexico to spend time with their families and then trekked back to the ranch. They risked the perils of such a jour-ney so they could provide their families with a higher standard of living. On paydays they handed over their checks to Dian Dixon, Charlie Four's assistant, who made purchases for them of money orders or clothing that she mailed to their families.

Charlie Three referred to his illegal workers as "exchange students," meaning it in the most respectful way. Three and Four held these men in high regard and told me the ranch could not function without them. They were the cogs that made the Y.O. wheels turn. They were provided with room and board and paid according to their skills. An unskilled worker was paid minimum wage and those with specialized skills, such as cow-boys or stonemasons, earned more. The unskilled workers assisted in the kitchen, cleaned ranch buildings, and did manual labor, usually outdoors and strenuous, such as moving rocks and jousting with the hard caliche ground with picks and shovels to repair and replace fences. I wondered what led them here and did they ever receive letters or phone calls from their families? What did they think of this country so geographically close to their own but light years removed in technology and standards of living? The words of Porfirio Diaz often crossed my mind. "Poor Mexico. So far from God, so close to the United States."

I asked Three if he ever considered hiring US citizens. He grimaced and said, "Very few are willing to do the hard work required on a ranch, much less live without female companionship. These men are willing to do it because they can't make a decent living in Mexico."

"What do they do for entertainment?"

"Play games—baseball, soccer, cards, checkers. They have a radio and television in their dining area, but, as you know, reception is erratic." Indeed, it was. This was before satellites, cable, or streaming. Whether the ranch received the San Antonio radio and television stations was up to the whims of the airwave gods.

"Do they ever get to be with women?"

"That would be a recipe for disaster given the machismo nature of Mexican men."

"Not even occasionally? It would seem some type of arrangement could be made."

"Absolutely not! We make that clear when they're hired."

I found out otherwise one Saturday night when I walked into the Chuckwagon for supper and was immediately pulled into the office area by Mary Helen, Four's wife, who frantically whispered, "There are four prostitutes at the front gate waiting to be let in. What should we do?"

"I thought that wasn't allowed," I said.

"It isn't but Roberto [a ranch employee who lived in Kerrville] arranged it and was going to escort them in and out of the ranch without anyone knowing. His car broke down and now it's up to us to decide what to do since your Charlie and my Charlie are off the ranch."

Mary Helen and I batted the quandary back and forth several minutes, neither of us anxious to make the decision.

"I feel sorry for the women" Mary Helen said. "They've come all the way out here and if we send them back to Kerrville they'll have wasted their time when they could have been working."

"I agree, but you know how Three feels about it. What if a fight breaks out and one of them is injured? We'd never be able to explain. Let's call

Donnie and ask him to escort them and make it very clear to their customers if there is any type of fight, even if it is only verbal, those involved will be fired on the spot." Donnie came to our rescue, and the event was never discussed again. Three and Four were none the wiser.

One day Charlie and I went out to a pasture where the cowboys were working cattle. It was lunchtime and the cook was preparing their meal over an open fire. As Charlie talked with the cowboys, I walked over to watch the cook. He was making tortillas and explained beans and tortillas were the Mexican cowboys' main food when walking to and from Mexico. I expressed surprise that tortillas could be made over a campfire. As I watched, he took a small amount of flour, added lard and water, and began working it. Forming it into a ball, he laid the dough on a flat rock, took a round stone from his pocket and rolled the dough into a circle. He placed the dough on a griddle straddling the fire, flipped the tortilla several times with his fingers, removed it from the griddle and handed it to me. It was delicious, and to this day, I seldom have a tortilla without being transported back to that pasture with cattle bawling, horses kicking up dust, and cowboys' lariats spiraling above cattle.

Lupe Ortega had been Three's housekeeper for several years. Charlie told me most Mexican men considered domestic work an insult to their manhood, but Lupe was the exception. Because he worked for the *patron* of the Y.O., Lupe was held in high regard by the other Mexican workers. Lupe arrived at the trailer each morning with a cooler of ice and laundry from the previous day. He would change the sheets, wash the dishes, and clean the trailer. Once Three and I moved into the house, Lupe's duties greatly increased as he took over responsibility for not only the house but the yard. Lupe and I communicated with hand signals, his smattering of English, and my smattering of Spanish. Though we tried to teach each other our respective languages, neither of us was very successful. Lupe, like I, could understand the other language better than communicate in it.

Whenever I hear the Robert Earl Keen song "Mariano," Lupe and the other Mexican workers at the ranch come to mind. My eyes mist and tears often fall at the lines, "He says that he comes from a place not far from Guanajuato. That's two days on a bus from here, a lifetime from this room."

In 1985, the *Great Chefs* TV show featured Y.O. Ranch cook Bertie Varner: https://greatchefs.com/chef/bertie-varner-y-o-ranch-chuck-wagon/

CHAPTER 14

Bernstein: "There's a lot of statues in Europe you haven't bought yet."

Charles Foster Kane: "You can't blame me. They've been making

statues for some two thousand years, and

I've only been collecting for five."

FROM *Citizen Kane,* BY HERMAN MANKIEWICZ
AND ORSON WELLES

Citizen Charlie

A MONTH AFTER I MOVED to the ranch, the upstairs of Charlie's house was ready for us to move in. Charlie informed me it was my job to decorate it. This was the first I'd heard that this would be my job. I assumed Charlie and I would do it together. As I was to learn, you assumed nothing with Charles Schreiner III.

Charlie's last wife had purchased several pieces of furniture and reupholstered others that Charlie had inherited from family members. These were in four large storage barns together with an array of items Charlie had collected and inherited through the years. I was in no way prepared for what I saw when Charlie opened the first barn door and flipped the light switch. Before me was a topsy-turvy jumble of chairs and tables, lamps, animal shoulder mounts, chandeliers, animal hides, and numerous boxes stacked haphazardly throughout the barn. I was too stunned to do anything but stare as Charlie pointed out items he wanted at the house. We moved to another barn that resembled the first in its mass of objects and lack of organization. Once more Charlie indicated items of special significance. Then came another storage barn, and another, each resembling the first in the density of objects and haphazard arrangement of them. Whereas previously I felt like a character in *Giant,* this time I felt as though I had stepped into *Citizen Kane* after Charles Foster Kane died and all his possessions had been assembled to be disposed of. I wondered if Charlie's "Rosebud" was somewhere in this jumble.

Charlie handed me a set of keys and told me a work crew would meet me at the first barn the next morning. I consider myself organized, but this was the ultimate test. Throughout the night I awakened thinking of how to pursue the task. The next morning I had the workers empty the first barn, and then I started organizing the items. The pieces Charlie had pointed out were moved to the house. I labeled the contents of the boxes, some of which went to the house and others back into the barns. Charlie came by occasionally to see my latest discoveries and tell stories on their provenance. Each day, I never knew what treasures awaited me. One day it was boxes of photographs. The next day antique holsters, wooly chaps, concho belts, quirts, spurs, or a buffalo hide coat. There were more than one hundred antique tin advertising signs interspersed with bronzes and paintings by contemporary Western artists. Antique carousel horses rested on zebra, eland, and longhorn hides amid countless antlers and horns.

Several boxes contained twelve place settings of monogrammed Sevres china. Charlie was thrilled at the discovery, saying they were his Aunt Mimi's, one of Captain Schreiner's daughters. Not one piece was broken or chipped, a miracle considering the pieces had no protective wrapping and were stacked precariously in boxes. There was Charlie's collection of bird eggs from his boyhood, each meticulously labeled. Eighteenth-century Limoges vases formerly belonged to Uncle Louis as did a limited-edition, leather-bound autographed copy of *Big Game Hunting in the Rockies and on the Great Plains* by Theodore Roosevelt. Mexican pottery from the 1950s nestled in the same box with Steuben plates and glasses. Chinese vases, foo dogs, lacquer ware, and cinnabar were souvenirs of Myrtle's trips to Japan and China. As each of these items appeared, Charlie expressed delight and said he would love to see them displayed in the house. I began to fear most of the barns' contents were going to the house.

Furniture included an elegant Louis XV chair frame, an eighteenth-century French hutch, a coromandel screen, a set of Victorian wicker furniture, a seven-foot-tall paper umbrella painted with red flowers, and trunks of all sizes and types, some of Chinese and Japanese origin and others bearing the Wells Fargo stamp.

One of the boxes was filled with pine cones. When I asked Charlie about it, he shook his head and said, "I remember her colleting those."

"Who?"

"Audrey. She collected them when we were living in Two Dot, Montana. She'd never seen a pine forest and was fascinated by pine cones. She decorated them and used them for Christmas ornaments."

"When was that?"

"During the seven-year drought in the 1950s. We stuck it out here for four years but finally moved all the cattle to Two Dot in 1954."

"How long did you stay?"

"Almost four years. Once it started raining in Texas, we hauled ass back. I'll take a Texas summer over a Montana winter any day."

"Do you want to keep these?"

"Hell, no. I didn't know they were still around. Throw them away."

But I didn't. There was something touching about Audrey gathering them in a place so far from home. I still have them and have added others to the collection through the years, even bringing several home from Jigokudani Snow Monkey Park in northern Japan.

My dilemma of sorting through the barns was replaced by a new one: how to make these diverse pieces fit together without the house looking like an antique mall. My good friend Kay Howard was an interior designer with an appreciation and ability for melding eclectic pieces into sophisticated and unique decors. Best of all, she had a special appreciation for Texas and Western antiques. Kay lived in Austin where, in addition to having an interior design business, she taught at the University of Texas. Explaining the task before us, I asked her to come to the ranch for a weekend. She was thrilled at the opportunity.

After showing her the house, I took Kay to the storage barns, which now had a semblance of order to them. As I pointed out items, Kay immediately suggested one or more locations where they could be placed. She also allayed my fears about making several of the modern items purchased by Charlie's last wife blend with Victorian furniture and Western art. Speckled longhorn hides could mute the chartreuse rug in the bedroom. Red lacquer Chinese chests and rosewood Chinese stools subdued the chartreuse and white couch. Kay assured me strategically placed Western paintings and bronzes could be integrated with the Asian pieces. Following her guidance, I set about making the upstairs comfortable and reflective of Charlie's diverse collections.

As I was placing Aunt Mimi's Victorian furniture in the upstairs sitting room, Charlie arrived with a mounted longhorn steer head strapped to the top of his station wagon. The steer was one of Charlie's favorites, and after it died, Charlie had the head mounted at the taxidermy shop owned by the Y.O.

"Where can we hang this?" Charlie asked.

"It's perfect for the upstairs sitting room. We can put a spotlight on it to make it the focal point as guests pull up to the house at night." I always got a thrill at the sight of it when I crested the hill at night.

All was in readiness for us to spend our first night at the house. The downstairs remained a construction zone, but the upstairs was a preview of what the house would look like once completed. Charlie was effusive in thanking me for integrating so many diverse pieces into a cohesive whole. After supper at the Chuckwagon, we returned to the house ready for a romantic evening. Lupe had iced champagne and prepared a fire. Charlie lit the fire and I opened the champagne. Within minutes the room was filled with smoke and tears were streaming down our faces. Charlie hastily put out the fire. I turned on the ceiling fan and opened the balcony doors as romantic notions fled with the smoke. Lying in bed, Charlie contemplated why the chimney hadn't drawn properly and decided it wasn't high enough. The next morning Reyna, the ranch's stonemason, was on the roof raising the chimney several feet. That solved the problem.

Several nights after we moved in, I was awakened by a horrific bellowing reminiscent of what a banshee or demon spirit might make. I lay there tensing with fear and trying to imagine what it could be. I was about to awaken Charlie when he patted me and said, "Hear that old bull bellowing at the moon?" I breathed a sigh of relief and eventually went back to sleep.

With the upstairs decorated, I decided it was time to start learning my way around the ranch. One day I took Charlie's Bronco and headed toward the Live Oak section. I saw some longhorns in the distance and drove across the pasture for a better look. It was almost lunchtime and I started back in what I thought was the right direction. It wasn't, and I was lost with no idea how to get back to the main road. From out of nowhere Chester, Bertie's husband, appeared in his battered pickup.

"Are you okay?" he asked pulling up beside me.

"I hate to admit it, Chester, but I'm lost."

"I was afraid that might happen. That's why I followed you. If that ever happens again, just look for the nearest windmill and climb it to get your bearings."

"Thank you. I'll remember that." I silently prayed I would never have to do that since I suffer from acrophobia. If I have to choose between being lost and climbing a windmill, I'll gladly opt for the former.

One afternoon as I was working at the house, Charlie called. "Guess who just showed up at the Chuckwagon?" He did not wait for me to answer. "Rusty!" he exclaimed.

Like several ranch employees, Rusty was an itinerant presence on

The author with Rusty Cox at the Y.O. Trail Drive Party, 1979. Photo by Ron Dorsey.

the ranch, showing up between other events in his life and staying until another opportunity, usually a woman, presented itself. His arrival now was no doubt due to hunting season and the prospect of guiding and performing at the Y.O. Lodge. Charlie and I often discussed what a shock it would be to Rusty when he returned to the Y.O. and found me there. Charlie was relishing the opportunity to best Rusty in the wooing department.

Rusty's buffalo coat was the catalyst for Rusty and Charlie meeting. Charlie was driving down a back road in Texas and passed a beat-up pickup stopped by the Highway Patrol. As Charlie drove by, he saw the truck's driver, who was standing beside the road with the officer, was wearing a buffalo coat. Charlie, who also owned a buffalo coat, thought, "I've got to meet this guy." He promptly did a U-turn and drove back, stopping behind the patrol car. Charlie managed to talk the officer out of giving Rusty a ticket and Rusty ended up working, occasionally, but never very hard, on the Y.O.

I waited upstairs as Rusty and Charlie entered the house. Charlie called me on the intercom and asked me to come downstairs. When I walked into the living room, Rusty was sitting on the couch with his back to me.

"Here she is," Charlie said. "I was just telling Rusty what an amazing lady you are."

Rusty rose and turned around. He shook his head several times in amazement. He then clutched his chest, repeating, "It can't be!" and fell in a dramatic swoon onto the couch.

Unmoved by Rusty's theatrics, I said, "You always said you were going to show me the Y.O. but I got tired of waiting."

"So, you went all the way to the top. Good job, Norma Sue!"

Charlie was preening like a peacock as this played out.

As we talked, Rusty told us he had been in Hollywood for the last six months acting and doing stunt work in movies. Most of it involved horses since Rusty was a good rider and loved being in Western movies. Charlie invited Rusty to stay around for hunting season and Rusty gladly obliged.

The sons of Charlie Three, left to right, front row: Louie, Charlie Three, Gus. Back row: Walter and Charlie Four. From the collection of Charles Schreiner IV.

Gradually I settled into a routine. When I was not accompanying Charlie on one of his jaunts around the state, I was sorting through the seemingly endless array of items from the storage barns. The number of boxes of photographs was incredible and compiled a pictorial history of the Schreiner family and the Y.O. Some were in formal studio settings, but most were informal and multigenerational, ranging from Captain Schreiner and his children to Charlie and his sons, all with multiple copies.

Photographs of Charlie as a boy and young man revealed a slim man with an abundance of dark hair and a lean patrician face. His four sons were equally handsome but each in a different way. When I mentioned to Charlie how attractive they were, he replied, "No reason they wouldn't be. Good sire and good dam." It seemed odd there wasn't a single photo of Charlie with his sons when they were babies. Charlie proudly told me he never changed a diaper and had little to do with his children until they were able to walk and talk.

The photographs of Charlie's grandfather and father were startling in their likeness to each other and to Charlie. Both had mustaches and I wondered if Charlie grew a moustache to emphasize this resemblance. I was most intrigued by the pictures of Charlie's mother, Myrtle. One of the most striking was from the 1920s. Myrtle was in a beaded flapper-style dress with opera length pearls, one hand akimbo, the other resting lightly on the pearls. Her hair was short and wavy, and though she was not smiling she looked self-confident and happy. I wanted to know more about her. What were her roots? How did she meet Walter? What did she think coming to the Y.O. when it lacked running water and electricity and was even more isolated than now? What were her feelings after Walter died and she was thrust into running the ranch? Would I ever know or had she taken her past with her to the grave?

CHAPTER 15

"Dare to live the life you have dreamed for yourself.

Go forward and make your dreams come true."

RALPH WALDO EMERSON

Taking a Chance

SETTLING INTO LIFE ON THE Y.O., I found myself torn between return-ing to the excitement and tension of a political consulting career and my growing love for Charlie and the ranch. His marriage proposal hung in the air, dangling before me like the fruit tree before Tantalus. One night as I was reading, I came across the epigraph for this chapter. I had my answer. Not marrying Charlie would leave me forever wondering what might have been. In my romantic, idealistic mind, I saw myself as Charlie's perfect mate. His other marriages failed in large part because his previous wives didn't want to live on the ranch full-time. For me it was the answer to my childhood fantasies. Charlie was fascinating. He wooed me with a vigor no other man had shown. Living among animals most people saw only in zoos, giving tours of the ranch, and entertaining guests in Charlie's impressive new home utilized to the fullest my talents and interests. I was certain I was the wife Charlie was searching for.

When I accepted Charlie's proposal, he said, "I never doubted you would." We set the date for January 6, 1978, because Charlie always wanted to marry on his birthday. For me, its significance was in it being Epiphany. In addition to its religious significance, epiphany means an illu-minating discovery, realization, or disclosure. Little did I know that reali-zation would be one I never could have guessed.

Charlie told me he was not as well off as people imagined. "Sure, we could sell the ranch and retire handsomely, but what kind of life would that be? I was brought up to run this ranch, and I plan to do it until the day I die."

Charlie told me his attorney insisted there be a prenuptial agreement. I would be the first wife to sign one and had no objection to doing so until I read the document. Reading it, I felt like a high-priced courtesan. Every month Charlie would deposit a specific amount in an account only I had access to. This amount would negate all claims for a settlement should we divorce. Charlie and I had already discussed this, so it came as no surprise; however, the next section did. It stated there would be no community property. Community property is property acquired during a marriage and owned equally by both spouses. Charlie's list of separate property consisted of five items: the ranch, his house, his livestock, his Western art collection, and his gun and knife collection. As I read the document, I had the impression it was written anticipating our divorce.

The morning after Charlie gave me the prenup I called Nugent at his Kerrville office. He could tell I was fighting back tears and said, "Get your duds on and get down here." An hour later I walked into his office and handed him the prenup. He read it several times, picked up the phone, and called Charlie. When Charlie answered, Nugent said, "I've got a young lady here who has some concerns about that document you gave her last night. I'm going to take her to lunch. We'll meet you in my office in an hour and a half."

When we returned from lunch, Charlie was pacing outside Nugent's office. Once in his office, Nugent dispensed with pleasantries and said, "Norma thinks this marriage contract makes her nothing more than a concubine." Charlie started to interrupt, but Nugent held up his hand. "She's of the opinion if there's no community property, there's no reason to be married. And, I see her point. There's nothing to draw you together and give you a common interest. What would you say to giving Norma some longhorn cows? Say ten? She could pick them, but you could help her. She'd keep them at the ranch and use the ranch bulls for breeding at no cost. It would be a common interest."

"Fine by me," Charlie said, turning to me for my reaction.

The proposal caught me off guard, but I liked it. It seemed a practical solution, and the idea of starting my own longhorn herd was exciting. I happily agreed.

"Then I'll draft it and send it to Charlie's attorney," Nugent said, reaching across his desk to shake our hands.

Charlie and I agreed the ceremony would be small with only family and a few friends attending. He let me decide where to say our vows and I picked the living room at the house. Doing so would, I hoped, send the message I would be as permanent a fixture on the ranch as the house. On a primal level, I was marking my territory. Not only would I be the first woman to live in the house with Charlie, but I would also be the first and, I hoped, only wife to marry there. It was also a way of emphasizing the house was a joint project we were working on together, even if it was his separate property. I asked Charlie if he would object to my father marrying us. He was pleased at the prospect. Charlie wanted to have a reception at the Y.O. Lodge "for a few friends" after the ceremony. He told me to make a list of those I wanted to invite and give it to Dian, Four's assistant.

The next month was frantic as I rushed to finish decorating the kitchen, living, and dining rooms. Amid all this, Charlie decided I needed to accompany him to Austin because there was something he wanted to show me. I balked, saying there was too much to be done. Finally, I agreed if we would only be gone two days. When we arrived in Austin, Charlie drove to an antique store and introduced me to the owner, saying, "I want her to see your eagle." We walked into a room where a massive carved wooden eagle, its wings splayed on either side took up an entire wall. It reminded me of the eagle on the German coat of arms, except this eagle

The eagle that was the author's wedding gift from Charlie Three.

had its head turned to the left with a cluster of grapes hanging from its beak. Each feather was individually carved, and on close examination I saw a whitish residue making me wonder if it was once gilded. The shop owner knew nothing of its provenance except it was European in origin. There were no markings to indicate where it came from or who made it.

As I examined it, Charlie asked, "What do you think?"

"I love it! Don't you wish it could talk and tell us its past?"

Charlie beamed and said, "I'm buying it for you as a wedding gift. It guarantees I'll never divorce you because I don't want to lose both of you. The only problem is, where do we put the damn thing?"

"At the top of the stairs," I exclaimed. And that is where it hung until the day it and my other possessions left the ranch in a horse trailer. As I moved around the country, the eagle determined my choice of housing. Walking into a potential home, the first thing I looked for was a wall to accommodate the eagle's height and wingspan. In 2019 I had the eagle appraised and learned it was from the eighteenth or nineteenth century, possibly of German origin, and carved from linden wood. The whitish residue on its feathers was traces of gesso indicating it may have been gilded. The appraiser surmised, because of its imposing size, it may have been part of an armorial device.

The day after we returned home, I came in from my daily jog on the runway and found Charlie sitting in the living room with Tony Harden and his girlfriend, Rhonda Real, one of Charlie's cousins who became Tony's wife. Tony was a good friend of Walter's, often staying at Walter's house. He was the epitome of the hail-fellow-well-met, offering to help with whatever task was at hand. He was often requested as a hunting guide and ran many errands for Three, who knew he could send Tony on the most unrealistic task and Tony would accomplish it. Charlie often referred to Tony as his fifth son, and I think Tony viewed Three as a father figure. Evidence of this is that Three taught Tony how to construct buildings in what Charlie Four dubbed "Three's Style," which was using native materials, such as limestone and cypress, together with architectural antiques and Mexican tiles to create what Four dubbed "grandiose Hill Country ranch style."

"Tony's brought us a wedding gift," Three exclaimed.

Tony rose to greet me, smiling his impish smile.

The wedding gift was the kind of gift only Tony would think of and only Three would fully appreciate. We walked out to the patio beside the living and dining rooms where sat a four-foot-diameter tree trunk with roots still attached, curling and twisting in a Medusa like pattern. Both Tony and Three thought it would be a perfect planter, which is what it became.

I received another unusual wedding gift from one of Charlie's friends. It was panties in various colors with the Y.O. brand embroidered on the left hip. What I did not realize was if I wore them under a light-colored pair of jeans, the brand showed through. This was brought to my attention one day when someone remarked, "So he branded you too."

Charlie told me my wedding band, which he was having his jeweler design for me, would not be ready in time for the wedding. I replied I really didn't care if I had a ring. Charlie adamantly declared that he did care and on the day before our wedding, we drove to Kerrville to purchase my ring. When we parked in front of the dime store, Charlie said, "There's no sense paying a lot of money for something I'm going to replace." Charlie greeted the lady running the store by name and told her what we were looking for. A quizzical look came onto her face, but she led us to the rings. Charlie took my left hand and started placing rings on my finger. Only one fit. By default, it became my ring. It was a wide faux gold band with a brushed finish and cost ten dollars.

After we returned home, I made a final inspection of the rooms where those attending the ceremony would gather. In the entry hall stood Captain Schreiner's nine-foot-long oak sideboard with Myrtle's electrified cobalt blue oil lamps anchoring each end. At the end of the hall was a hat stand with a finial of an eagle spreading its wings. A variety of cowboy hats, including one of Charlie's sweat-stained Stetsons, adorned it. Standing on the floor behind it were two shotguns, and in front were a pair of petite cowhide boots alleged to have been Annie Oakley's. A longhorn head hung over a small table with a guest registry bearing the Y.O. brand.

The living room was elegant but welcoming. An antique marble soda fountain occupied one wall where it had traded its original function to serve as a bar. Moving it into the house had required the service of every able-bodied man on the ranch. Around it I hung antique advertising signs for various beers and soft drinks. Descending on the bar was a life-size carved wooden eagle with talons poised to seize a libation and fly away.

The yellow couches and armchairs I once thought would be out of place blended well with Myrtle's Imari lamps and a large Aubusson rug, chosen by Three, in hues of blue, rust, and creme. Foo dogs sat on either side of the limestone fireplace guarding the hearth with its Y.O. andirons. Above the fireplace hung an oil painting by Western artist Joe Beeler of cowboys

The living room of Charlie Three's house. Photograph by Ron Dorsey.

herding longhorns across a river. On the mantle I placed one of my favorite pieces, Beeler's bronze *Widow Maker*. The horse stands in a pose of defiant exhaustion, ears back and feet firmly planted on the ground. Reins dangle from its halter. Between its front hooves is the rider's hat. The rear of the saddle is partially suspended in the air, having not yet come to rest after ousting its rider. In one stirrup is an upside-down boot indicating the rider was pitched so vigorously he came out of it. To me, the empty boot was a nod to the military tradition dating back to Genghis Khan of a riderless horse with boots reversed in the stirrups for a fallen leader.

In the dining room, the antique Chinese Chippendale brass chandelier had risen from the floor to hang over a malachite dining table, one of the pieces chosen by Charlie's previous wife. In the plate racks of an antique French hutch once belonging to Charlie's mother, I intermingled a variety of plates ranging from flow-blue to colorful Mexican pottery to Sevres china. Beside the hutch, antique doors with stained-glass panels led to the kitchen where Myrtle's pie safe anchored the opposite wall. Charlie's collection of antique tins sat atop the cabinets. On the counter below, I placed Charlie's boyhood bird egg collection. Beside it was the pitcher Charlie told me he used as a child to pour milk onto cereal. It was white with a tuxedo cat handle.

On the afternoon of January 6, 1978, my father married us. Charlie's sons and a few close friends were the only attendees. Charlie's close friend Jimmy De Lesdernier stood up with Charlie and Jim Nugent with me. It was a beautiful day, and my father suggested we have the ceremony on the patio overlooking Deer Park. Before the ceremony began, Charlie

The soda fountain bar in the living room of Charlie Three's house. Photograph by Ron Dorsey.

introduced my father to the assembled group saying he was glad to be getting a father-in-law that was older than he was. This was his tongue-in-cheek reference to his last marriage. My father began the service reflecting on the beauty, peace, and harmony of the natural setting and praying these values would be found in our marriage.

We planned to stay at the house until six o'clock when the reception at the Y.O. Lodge started, but that changed when Charlie learned the lodge was rapidly filling with guests. When we entered, a crowd of several hundred broke into applause. Turning to Charlie, I said, "Is this what a few of your friends looks like?" He sheepishly ducked his head. I searched the crowd for my friends, but they were lost in a sea of strangers. One of the more memorable guests was Charlie's longtime friend Ace Reid. Ace created the cartoon *Cowpokes*, which was syndicated in newspapers throughout the West and Southwest. Ace took my hand, kissed it, and said, "Miss Norma, you are a lovely lady and I'm sure you're as sweet as sugar. I hope you won't take this personally, but I've learned not to get too attached to Charlie's wives since they don't stick around very long." He winked at me. "It makes it less painful for both of us."

I wasn't sure how to respond. Charlie took Ace by the arm and led him away. When he came back, he said, "My apologies. Ace has had a few too many." Later I learned that one of Charlie's friends who was unable to attend sent him a special delivery letter saying he was sorry he couldn't be there but would be at Charlie's next wedding. These incidents stung me and made me realize it would not be easy convincing people I would be Charlie's last wife.

CHAPTER 16

"When two people are under the influence of the most violent, most insane, most delusive, and most transient of passions, they are required to swear that they will remain in that excited, abnormal, and exhausting condition continuously until death do them part."

GEORGE BERNARD SHAW

Off to a Frigid Start

I WAS WALKING ACROSS THE BEDROOM when I realized I had experienced this exact moment in a dream. Throughout my life I've had such déjà vu instances, but this one was different because I remembered exactly when it occurred—Christmas night of 1974. My then husband, R. C., and I had a tradition of inviting friends over on Christmas night. Rusty Cox, occasional employee of the Y.O., attended if he was in town, playing his guitar and singing songs interspersed with stories about the Y.O. That night I dreamed I was standing exactly where I now found myself and was there because I was married to the owner of the Y.O. Ranch. Every detail of the room was precisely as it was in reality, even to the chartreuse rug and ostrich egg lamp sitting on my desk.

The morning after the dream, I told R. C. about it, and he grinned and asked, "What was your new husband's name?"

"I don't know," I replied. We laughed about how ridiculous the dream was and the improbability of its occurring, but now I was standing in that dream. It was my first dream about Charlie and would be followed by more than I can count.

Charlie always attended a gun show in Las Vegas at the end of January. I assumed I would accompany him. A week before the show, I asked Charlie how long we would be gone. He looked over his glasses and said, more firmly than I thought necessary, "You're not going."

I was stunned. "Why not?"

"Because you aren't interested in guns and you'd be bored."

I could tell by his tone any further discussion was out of the question. I let the subject drop, but only temporarily. Later in the evening, I brought it up again and received the same answer but this time with a hint of anger. I refused to take no for an answer. "I agree I'm not interested in guns, but I can entertain myself doing other things while you're at the gun show. Then we can be together in the evenings."

"Missy," he said. "You aren't going, and I don't want to hear any more about it."

"We'll see about that," I thought. I went into the bedroom and closed the doors. There was no lock on the massive Mexican doors, but I had devised one for nights I spent alone in the house. The brass handles were of the pull variety, a foot long with several inches between the pull and the door. I found a three-foot-long board I could slide between the handles that prohibited the doors being opened. I inserted it and went to bed. As I was lying there reading, I heard Charlie's footsteps on the stairs.

Charlie pulled on the handles and when they did not respond yelled, "Norma! What's wrong with these doors?"

"I locked them."

"The hell you did. These doors don't lock."

"They do now. There's a board between the handles. You can spend the night in one of the cabins. In the morning we can revisit my going to Vegas with you."

I heard his footsteps descending the stairs. "That was easier than I expected," I thought as I resumed reading. Minutes later I heard a rasping sound. Looking over at the doors, I saw the blade of a saw coming through the crack. I watched as it made slow but steady progress cutting the board in half. Having achieved his goal, Charlie stood in the doorway, saw in hand, a triumphant look on his face.

"I'll teach you to lock me out of *my* bedroom." We both begin laughing. Charlie came over, took me in his arms, and we made up. But I did not go to Las Vegas with him. A year later I would discover why he was so adamant in his refusal.

I did not want to stay at the ranch while Charlie was away, so I asked my mother to join me in San Antonio. My mother, who refused to fly, rode the bus to San Antonio. Her seat mate was a young man from France named Guy LeBlond who was spending several months traveling around the United States via bus in order to see as much of our country as possible.

Charlie Three and French cowboy Guy LeBlond, February 1978.

He found the size of Texas daunting and asked my mother what she recommended he see. As they talked, my mother had an idea. I am my mother's daughter, and as soon as she introduced me to Guy, I had the same idea.

When I returned to the Y.O., Guy accompanied me. He spent several days at the ranch during which time he stayed in one of the log cabins, accompanied one of the guides on a hunt, learned to shoot a rifle, and rode a horse. For the latter, Charlie outfitted him in wooly chaps, a cowhide vest, bandana, and vintage Stetson. Photographs were taken so when he returned home, he would have proof of his Texas adventure. Once he returned to France, we exchanged a few letters but then lost touch. Writing this and looking at the photographs, I wonder where life took him and hope he delights in telling his grandchildren stories about playing cowboy in Texas on the Y.O. Ranch.

On February 5, Charlie and I left for our LCRA-sponsored honeymoon. The LCRA (Lower Colorado River Authority) was established in 1934 as electricity was coming to rural Texas. In addition to having responsibility for producing and delivering electric power throughout Central Texas, the authority manages the lower Colorado River (thus its name) and its park system. Jim Nugent was responsible for the governor appointing Charlie as a director. The LCRA was having a bond sale in New York, and Charlie, ever one to take advantage of a free trip, decided it would be our honeymoon. As the plane descended into the city, densely swirling snowflakes made it seem we were encased in a snow globe. Taxiing to the gate, the captain announced we had the dubious distinction of being the last flight allowed to land that evening. Incoming flights for the next twenty-four hours were canceled.

Unbeknownst to us, we had just landed in what would become a blizzard of historic proportions. As we were in the air, a nor'easter formed and was now dropping record-breaking snows on New England, New Jersey, and New York City. On the way to our hotel, the cab driver told us high winds and snowfall of up to twenty inches were predicted. As Texans who seldom saw even a sprinkling of snow, Charlie and I were entranced at the prospect of spending our honeymoon in a snow-covered New York City. We checked into our room, opened the curtains, and watched in wonder as the snow fell, and fell, and fell. It did not stop snowing until Tuesday evening, February 7. The storm brought all transportation, including the city's ubiquitous yellow taxis, to a halt and, in another rare event, the public schools were closed for the next three days. The selling of the LCRA bonds was postponed until later in the week.

Even after the snow stopped falling, moving around the city was difficult and dangerous until roads and sidewalks were cleared. I discovered just how difficult when my leather boots offered both insufficient warmth and lack of traction on snow and ice. I made a trip to Bloomingdale's to procure less precarious and warmer footwear. When Charlie gave the saleswoman his credit card, she looked at it and said, "Mr. Schreiner. It is so nice to meet you. I visited your ranch last year on a tour." Charlie went into his humble sheep and goat rancher act as I marveled at the odds of the encounter.

On the recommendation of our hotel's concierge, we had dinner one evening at one of New York's classic French restaurants, Le Boeuf a la Mode. There were paintings on the walls of scenes from Paris and the French countryside. Many heads turned when we entered the restaurant. Throughout our visit to the city, Charlie had no qualms about revealing his country of origin, wearing his cowboy boots and felt Stetson. I was slightly intimidated when the waiter, with his authentic French accent, handed us the menus, saying he would return shortly. Obviously, Charlie was not intimidated, because when the waiter returned Charlie pointed to the lamb chops and said, "My good man, I have a question. How can you in good conscience charge that much for two little lamb chops?"

The waiter was unflappable. "Sir, it is the market price. You would find it comparable in any fine dining establishment in the city."

Charlie took off his glasses and begin wiping them with his napkin. "I raise sheep for a living and what we get per pound when we sell them makes this price a travesty. Do you have any idea how hard it is to raise sheep in the part of the country I come from?"

"Oh no," I thought. "Please don't go into your routine of the baby lamb being mauled by the coyote."

To his credit, the waiter kept his composure and sense of humor. "Sir, perhaps it would behoove you to sell your lambs directly to us."

Charlie replied, "Well, I want to have these high-priced lamb chops so I can go home and tell about paying the cost of twenty lambs for two of its ribs."

When we returned to the ranch, I told Charlie I wanted to start choosing my longhorn cows. There was nothing Charlie loved better than visiting his longhorns, and he was delighted to begin this project. We started visiting the pastures where the longhorns were, and as Charlie told me about the various cows, I took notes on their bloodlines, horn size, conformation, and age. As I reviewed my notes each evening, I realized how difficult it was going to be to decide which cows I wanted.

Often as Charlie and I stood in the pastures, I would hear voices, not distinctly but a faraway susurration. The first time it occurred, I turned in the direction from which they were coming, expecting to see their source, but no one was there.

"Did you hear voices?" I asked Charlie.

He gave me his skeptical look. "There's no one within five miles of us."

"I guess it was just the wind," I said.

It became a recurring event, whether I was alone or with Charlie, and always took me by surprise. Perhaps it was just the wind in the live oak trees but to me it was the souls of previous occupants of this land. I wondered whether they were welcoming me or trying to warn me.

CHAPTER 17

"It is not enough for a rider to know how to ride,

she must also know how to fall."

MEXICAN PROVERB

A Horse Wreck

IT WAS A BEAUTIFUL MARCH MORNING, crisply cool, with the sun taking most of the chill out of the air. Wildflowers of gold, pink, blue, and red added rare beauty to the usually dull palate of the pastures. It was a perfect day for riding horses, which is what Charlie and I were going to do. We had ridden several times since I moved to the ranch, and I had chosen a sorrel gelding with a white blaze on his face as my horse of choice. I named him Desperado, much to Charlie's chagrin. "There isn't a desperate bone in that horse's body," Charlie snorted when I told him the name.

What Charlie didn't know was I did not name him for his disposition, which was indeed anything but desperate, but for the song by the Eagles. Many lines in the song spoke to me and seemed prescient, especially, "These things that are pleasing you can hurt you somehow." During the past two years, there had been major changes in my life: moving to Austin, my first lobbying job, my divorce from R. C., and my moving to the ranch and marrying Charlie. Often I felt as if my life was on fast-forward with no time for adapting to one change before the next occurred. I was reluctant to confide in my friends, fearing they would think me ungrateful for my exciting new life. When I tried to discuss it with Charlie the only solace he offered was to pat my hand and say, "Everything will be fine," and then change the subject.

One of Charlie's gifts to me was a presentation saddle probably awarded to a cowboy for a rodeo event. It was ornately trimmed in silver, but the

The author on the not desperate Desperado, 1978.

stiffness of the leather implied it had never been ridden. Charlie decided this was the day for me to ride it and had Lupe take it to the corral. When we drove up, I saw that it was on a white mare.

"Where's Desperado?" I asked as we got out of the car.

"One of the cowboys probably took him by mistake," Charlie replied.

I looked at the mare and felt uneasy. "I don't want to ride her."

"Don't be ridiculous," Charlie said. "You're a good rider. It's a beautiful morning and we're going for a ride." He began mounting Dunny, his horse.

Though I love horses, I envy those who are as casual with them as I am with any type of cat, dog, or bird. I can approach any cat, put it at ease, and pet it, regardless of its size or disposition. When hiking through the forests on the Hawaiian island of Molokai, a yellow cat walked out of the dense foliage, flopped down in front of me, and waited to be petted. When I visited the Kenya Safari Club Animal Orphanage on my first trip to Africa, I petted a cheetah who gave a rousing purr of appreciation.

Horse people have the same effect on horses. The trainer Diane Hanrahan is one such person. I met Diane forty years later when she helped me hone my riding skills for a horseback trek across the Mongolian steppes. The horse I was training on, Joey, had a mind of his own, a tendency to pull, and knew he could bully me and get by with it. I was filled with anxiety whenever I mounted him. He took full advantage of it. But the minute Diane walked up to him, he came to attention, saluted smartly, and seemed to say, "Yes, ma'am. What would you like me to do?"

Because it is a prey animal, a horse comes by its perceptiveness and flightiness naturally. Added to this is its poor peripheral vision, which leads to bolting when something appears there. Even with my riding experience, I remain wary of horses, knowing the bodily harm they can inflict. My intuition told me I had no business getting on this horse, and the horse knew it. But Charlie had thrown down the gauntlet, so I mounted the mare. Swinging my right leg over the saddle I noticed my foot did not slip easily into the stirrup. The leather was stiff, and the stirrup turned outward rather than toward the horse. I struggled to get my foot into the stirrup.

We left the corral at a walk and stopped at Walter's house for Charlie to check on something. We dismounted and walked around to the back where numerous horns and skulls hung on Walter's back fence. Among them was the frame from a television sans screen. I smiled remembering the story behind it. One night Rusty was at Walter's watching television. Rusty took umbrage at something on the screen and shot the television. This was Walter's tribute to Rusty's marksmanship.

Returning to our horses, I noticed the mare shied as I approached her. I stroked her neck, speaking to her softly hoping to calm her. As I mounted, the wayward right stirrup once more eluded my foot. I bent over to adjust it, and the mare sprang forward almost throwing me off. I grabbed the saddle horn as my right leg floundered outside the stirrup. I tried to rein her in but she did not respond. I needed to let go of the saddle horn so I could use the force of both arms. As I did so, I could tell I was off-balance and not sure where to focus my energies.

Should I try to get my right foot in the stirrup or put all my concentration on reining her in? My left foot was now trying to come out of its stirrup. I was pulling her head so forcefully to the side we were almost eyeball to eyeball. Any rider who has been on a bolting horse knows the futility of trying to stop the animal until it is ready to stop. Michael Korda in his book, *Horse People*, describes this happening to him in New York's Central Park. When I read his account, years after the mare bolted with me, I was back in that saddle, trying to hang on for dear life and scared shitless.

I could hear Charlie yelling, "Rein her in, damn it. Rein her in."

I turned my head and yelled, "I'm trying to." Then my problem was solved. The mare galloped under a live oak tree and a low-hanging branch knocked me off. I hit the ground on my hips and started rolling. I saw limestone rocks as I hurtled by them, and prickly pear cactus that I somehow missed being impaled on. The theorem a body in motion tends to stay in motion came to mind as my body tumbled uncontrollably.

Once I came to rest, I was surprised I had not lost consciousness. Excruciating pain shot through my left wrist and arm, so intense I let out an anguished cry. Where in the hell was Charlie? It seemed an eternity before I heard hoofbeats and he came galloping up and dismounted. By then I was sitting up, rocking back and forth, moaning as I cradled my left arm. Charlie took my face in his hands and said, "Look at me and listen to me. I'm going to get the car. I'll be back as soon as I can. Do you understand?" I nodded and kept rocking back and forth. He hurried over to Dunny, seeming to spring into the saddle, and galloped away. I tried to stand and discovered I could not because of the severe pain in my left ankle. I hobbled over to a large rock and sat down. I fought to keep from throwing up and managed not to.

Finally, Charlie's station wagon came racing across the pasture. He stopped within a few feet of me and simultaneously he and Lupe jumped out. Three opened the rear of the station wagon where there was a mattress, pillows, and blankets. Lupe got on one side of me and Three on the other as I hopped to the car and slowly climbed in. As Charlie was placing blankets around me I heard him muttering, "Goddamn green broke mare. I'm going to shoot that goddamned horse." He continued muttering it as we bumped across the pasture and onto the main road.

"Please slow down," I groaned. Every bump sent spasms of pain through my body. I buried my face in the pillow, cradling my arm as best I could, hoping once we were on the highway there would be some relief. The pain was increasing to the point I was drifting in and out of consciousness. I was dreading reaching Kerrville and having to stop for traffic lights but Charlie had thought of that. At some point in our journey we were met by a member of local law enforcement who escorted us to the hospital with sirens screaming. At the hospital's emergency entrance, I looked out and saw a flock of white coats surrounding a gurney. Charlie screeched to a stop and suddenly many arms were reaching inside to help me out.

"No!" I declared fearing someone would touch my arm. "I'll get out by myself." Which is what I did ever so slowly. Charlie told me the first part of me to appear was my boot. One of the nurses turned to him and said, "I better find something to cut off those boots. It's been a while since we had to do that for a patient."

Someone said, "I'm going to give you something to relieve the pain."

"Wait!" I said. "Where's Charlie?"

Charlie appeared, took my unbroken hand, and said, "They're going to take good care of you."

I grabbed his shirt and pulled his ear to my mouth. "Don't you dare kill that horse."

When I awoke, Charlie was hovering over me. "Hi, cowgirl. You should have heeded the advice given to Julius Caesar."

"What?" I replied groggily.

"Today's the ides of March," he said chuckling. He added, "I didn't shoot the goddamned horse."

<hr>

CHAPTER 18

"The hardest-learned lesson:

that people have only their kind of love to give, not our kind."

MIGNON MCLAUGHLIN

<hr>

A New Side of Charlie

WHEN I AWOKE THE NEXT MORNING, there was a nurse by my bed squeezing the fingers of my left hand, which was in a cast and suspended from a pole by my bed.

"What are you doing?" I asked in a voice bearing no resemblance to mine.

"Making sure you're still getting blood flow to your hand."

"Am I okay?"

"For the moment," she replied. "With a break as bad as yours, we have to make sure there isn't swelling to inhibit blood flow.

"Why is it suspended?"

"We need to keep it immobile the first few days." She asked if I was in pain. I wasn't. She told me if I had pain to ring for a nurse to increase the morphine. I noticed it took all my willpower to keep my eyes open.

As the nurse left, Dian Dixon, Four's assistant, walked in. She was on her way to the ranch. "We've been so worried. All Three told us was you had surgery to set your arm but were okay. But when he spent last night in town we knew it was serious." She looked at my suspended arm. "What do you need from the house?"

I told her where to find my gown, robe, hairdryer, and makeup. Then I said, "I know this sounds silly, but when you go to the house see if you can find Ms. and tell her what happened and I'll be gone a few days."

The author and Lupe Ortega, 2010.

To her credit, Dian did not bat an eye at my request to explain my absence to a cat. "I'll be happy to," she said.

The next morning when Dian brought the requested items she told me she explained what happened to Ms. "Do you know, I think she understood me."

I smiled. "She did and we both thank you."

I was in the hospital four days. In addition to breaking my wrist, I also fractured my left ankle and tore ligaments in that leg. Several ribs were bruised as well. When the doctor visited, he said I was, "damn lucky you didn't break your neck." He also told me the break in my wrist was "very serious," and there was a good chance I would have impaired mobility once it healed. The pins extending from my hand and arm were to hold the broken wrist in place, he explained, and would be removed in six to eight weeks.

On the third day my arm no longer needed to be suspended. That was when I realized how constraining the cast was. My arm was bent at a right angle with the cast extending from the middle of my hand to several inches above my elbow. I was grateful it was my left arm, but even so I could not hold a knife to cut meat, pull up a zipper, fasten a necklace, or blow-dry my hair. The process of showering and dressing was a several hours ordeal leaving me drenched in sweat and exhausted. Doing my hair and applying makeup were also challenging, but I succeeded in time to receive my first visitors, Lupe and Charlie. With Charlie acting as

translator, Lupe asked what he needed to do to prepare for my return to the ranch. I told him I was going to need a lot of pillows for my arm. He grinned broadly and nodded he understood.

Rusty came by with his paints and brushes and painted a derringer on the underside of my cast. Butch Ramsey ambled in, carrying flowers, telling me he was representing the ranch employees who looked forward to my return. Jimmy De Lesdernier, who stood up with Charlie when we married, was another visitor. "Jimmy Dee," as he was called, was an inspector for the Texas and Southwestern Cattle Raisers Association (TSCRA). In this capacity, he investigated agricultural fraud and the thefts of horses and cattle, and he found the owners of stray livestock. He was a commissioned law enforcement officer through the Texas Department of Public Safety. The Texas writer J. Frank Dobie compared the TSCRA inspectors with Scotland Yard, the Royal Canadian Mounted Police, and the Texas Rangers. Jimmy looked every inch the part with his black Stetson, starched and monogrammed white shirt, boots, and ever-present unlit cigar clamped between his teeth. Walking into my room he took off his hat and said, "I swear, Miss Norma, you do look like that ole horse got the better of you. I thought you were smarter than to have a battle of wills with a 1,200-pound animal."

"So did I, Jimmy, but she had a mind of her own and I wasn't changing it."

"I can't believe Three let you ride her. He's got a rule that he never rides a mare because they're just like women. They'll buck you into the next county without thinking twice. Speaking of that, I brought you something."

He handed me a package wrapped in brown paper with twine ribbon. As I struggled to open it, Jimmy took out his knife and cut away the wrapping. He handed me two framed cartoons. "When I told Ace Reid about your little horse wreck, we decided you should have these." One of the cartoons was of a cowboy lying in a hospital bed swathed from head to foot in casts and bandages. One arm was suspended from a pole as mine had been. Standing by the bed was his friend saying, "Reckon I oughta told you that ole hoss might pitch." Across the top Ace inscribed, "Get Well Soon Norma!" The other cartoon showed a cowboy holding on for dear life as his horse, with a Y.O. brand, plunges off a cliff. The cowboy is yelling, "WHOA, DAMIT—W-H-O-A!" I laughed, the first time I had done so since my accident, and I was immediately reminded of my bruised ribs. "These are perfect, Jimmy! Thank you so much! And thank Ace for me."

The cartoons still hang in my home and always make me smile, both at the cartoons and at the kindness of Jimmy and Ace in thinking of me. Jimmy sat down and began telling me stories about miscreants, rustlers, and other blackguards he had encountered on his job. I loved Jimmy's stories because he sprinkled them with sayings that were pure Texas. He told me about a cattle rustler he caught and summed up the story saying, "I told that ole boy there are lots of people in this world who need killing, but nothing ever needed stealing, especially a cow or horse. He was damn lucky he didn't live one hundred years ago when I would have strung him up from the nearest tree." That story served as a springboard to the next about a former lawman who preferred "killing the suspect to having to fill out the paperwork to put him in jail." Then he told of a judge who ruled a shooting death a suicide. "He certainly was one dedicated suicide," Jimmy said. "He shot himself in the back six times." My latest dose of morphine was kicking in, and I was fighting to stay awake. Jimmy noticed and stood up. "I've got to get back to work. You take care of yourself, Miss Norma, and don't go getting on any more of those wild-eyed Y.O. mares."

I was released the next day with an ample supply of Percodan and instructions to take it anytime I was in pain. I slept most of the drive to the ranch, awakening when Charlie stopped at the front gate. Charlie drove directly to the Chuckwagon, saying, "Bertie gave me strict orders to stop there first so she could see for herself you're okay."

When I limped inside I was met with applause from the assembled ranch employees. Bertie had cooked my favorite meal, chicken-fried steak, cream gravy, and mashed potatoes. Though I had little appetite, I tried to consume as much as I could. I could not cut the meat and asked Charlie to do it for me. He looked at me as if I had asked him to pet a rattlesnake. "I can't hold the knife," I said, showing him the restrictions caused by my forty-five-degree angle cast. Rolling his eyes, he cut my meat.

As soon as we got to the house I went upstairs and was soon in bed. Lupe had taken my request for pillows to heart. There were six on my side of the bed. As I was arranging them, I noticed there was a new addition to my bedside table. The bronze *Widowmaker* was sitting there. Propped beside it was a sheet from one of Charlie's notepads declaring he was giving it to me. The pain in my wrist was building and I took two Percodan. Once I was in bed, Ms. appeared. She bedded down beside me, and we slept the rest of the afternoon. When I awoke, I saw a note on my bedside table. "3 P.M. You and fat cat fast asleep, From neither of you a peep. CSIII." It was one of the few personal notes Charlie ever wrote to me.

The next morning, I forced myself out of bed, took a shower, and dressed. When Charlie arrived to take me to lunch, I asked him to fasten my necklace and zip my jeans. He gave me the same look as when I asked him to cut my meat but complied. When we returned to the house after lunch, Charlie said, "In the future when you need help getting dressed call the Chuckwagon. Dian or Bertie or somebody will help you. I can't be spending my time dressing you."

I was too tired to argue. "Okay," I said. I was too proud to call for help and instead found ways to work around the problems involved in dressing. My appetite was greatly diminished, and soon I lost enough weight I could zip my jeans with one hand and a pair of pliers. I would button blouses and then slip them over my head. With practice, I gained more proficiency and stamina and soon was able to shower and dress in one hour rather than three.

One morning as I lay in bed, Ms. jumped onto the bed making a guttural sound that meant she had something in her mouth. I opened my eyes and saw her sitting beside me with a squirming rat clenched in her jaws. Moving faster than I thought possible, I sprung up on the bed, flattening myself against the wall. She dropped the rodent, which begin scurrying across the covers. Lupe appeared in the doorway brandishing a branding iron. Ms. retired to the floor to watch the mayhem as Lupe's arm descended with a decisive whack. We burst into laughter as Ms. made off with the carcass.

One day at lunch, Doc Thomas, the Y.O.'s veterinarian, sat beside me. He was curious about my arm, which bones were broken, the pins running through it, and how I was adapting to "flying with one wing." After I finished telling him, Doc said, "If you were a horse, we'd have put you down." I smiled wanly, thinking, "It might be preferable to hobbling around in these casts." Then Doc said, "When we have an animal with a break that can heal we give it bonemeal to help it heal faster. Why don't you start taking some? Hell, it couldn't hurt and might help." The next morning Dian brought me bonemeal tablets, which I took faithfully until my cast was removed.

Charlie began spending less time at the house. Before the accident, his habit was to return midmorning to check on me. Now, I did not hear from him until lunch when he called to see if I needed a ride to the Chuckwagon. Once I gained the confidence to drive with one hand, these calls stopped. He would return to the house after lunch for a nap and then leave again, returning at five when he mixed his daily iced tea-size glass of Scotch with a splash of water. He started inviting ranch employees or guests who were at the ranch to join him at the house for drinks before dinner. After dinner, he would drop me off at the house and go to the Y.O. Lodge to mingle with guests. I would be asleep by the time he returned home.

Becoming more frustrated and resentful at Charlie's ignoring me, I exacerbated the situation by refusing to come downstairs to entertain guests and seldom going to the Chuckwagon for meals. He responded with anger that the woman he married had changed into a haranguing harpy. I was worn down by the constant pain in my arm and frustrated by the limitations my casts placed on my activities. As I was learning, nothing made Charlie more uncomfortable than discussing motivations for his actions or feelings. The more I asked, the more remote he became. During this time, one of Charlie's friends, Bob Berry, came to the ranch to visit. I liked Bob and decided to seek his advice. I told him of Charlie's behavioral changes and asked if he had any suggestions for me.

"Charlie was reared by cowboys and in military schools," Bob said. "I don't have to tell you neither of those groups believe in showing feelings. Think of all the cowboys in the movies. They're stoic and the only emotions they show are happiness and anger. That's the role model Charlie grew up with. I was the one who called Charlie to tell him his mother was dead. You know how much he loved and respected her, but even then he didn't break down or even get a catch in his voice. Charlie has mastered the art of keeping his emotions to himself and I doubt he's going to change. I don't think he ever allows himself to dwell on his feelings or spends time in self-examination. I've always thought it was the reason he stays on the move like he does. That way he doesn't have time to think. I can't tell you what to do. I think you're Charlie's best wife. I hope you can make it work."

I was wondering if I could.

CHAPTER 19

"Cowboys ain't easy to love and they're harder to hold. . . .

If you don't understand them and they don't die young,

they'll probably just ride away."

ED AND PATSY BRUCE

Cowboys Aren't Easy to Love

"WHY AREN'T YOU DRESSED?" Charlie asked.

"Because I'm not going. My arm hurts. I'd rather stay home and read."

It was six weeks since my horse wreck. The pain in my arm was constant, and I was living on Percodan and little else. The kickoff party for the annual Y.O. Trail Drive weekend was that night and Charlie was expecting me to attend.

The Y.O. Trail Drive was Charlie's tribute to the trail drives of one hundred years before and the men and animals who endured them. It was one of his favorite events because it allowed him to play cowboy in the grandest way. A costume party on Friday night started the festivities. Male guests came as lawmen, outlaws, or cowboys, with many wearing firearms loaded with live ammunition. Women were mostly dance-hall girls or schoolmarms with an occasional Annie Oakley or Calamity Jane thrown in.

Charlie left the house in a huff, stomping down the stairs with more vigor than usual. When I told him several weeks before I would not attend, it was payback for his abandoning me since my horse wreck. But in the week leading up to the event, my heart softened and I decided to surprise him by going. When cleaning out the storage barns, I discovered several charro suits. The charro is a Mexican horseman or cowboy who dresses in an elaborately embroidered and decorated outfit of tight-fitting pants, embroidered jacket, and sombrero. After trying on several of the suits, I

123

Charlie Three and the author at the Y.O. Trail Drive party, 1978.

decided on a brown one. A friend arrived to assist me in dressing and we drove to the Y.O. Lodge.

It was several minutes before Charlie saw me but when he did, he broke into a wide grin and hugged me for the first time since my accident. The rest of the night he escorted me around the party, delighting in showing me off. One of his friends looked at my cast and said, "Well, Charlie, I know you don't like to take no for an answer, but did you have to break her arm to get her to marry you?"

When we returned home, I asked Charlie to help me undress. He chided me for being so helpless, saying how uncomfortable it made him to help me. Finally he blurted, "I've never been comfortable around handicapped people."

"I'm not handicapped," I declared. "This isn't permanent. I just need your help until my cast comes off."

"To me you're handicapped, and being around you and having to help you makes me uncomfortable."

I was shocked at his stupidity. I knew from experience nothing I could say would change his mind so, being a mature adult, I returned to being sullen and withdrawn.

Several weeks later, we hosted the directors of the Lower Colorado River Authority for a weekend at the ranch. Before dinner on Friday night there was a cocktail party at the Y.O. Lodge. Charlie and I drove down in silence, which was now our established method of communicating. Entering the Lodge, Charlie walked away from me to mingle with the other directors. Their wives gathered around me asking about my injuries and how well I was coping. As we were talking, an intense wave of nausea swept through me and I broke out in a cold sweat. Later the doctor told me this was a result of the high dosage of Percodan I was taking and how little I was eating. The circular staircase leading to the loft was behind me and I began stepping back to sit on one of its steps. As I did, I lost control of my body. My last thought was to protect my arm, and I pulled it against me as I collapsed. I was told my head hit the floor with a loud thud. I carried visible proof of this for several days with a large bump and bruise on my forehead.

Regaining consciousness, I found myself surrounded by a circle of concerned faces. As I was being helped to my feet, I heard Charlie say, "She's fine. Y'all head on down to the Chuckwagon. We'll be there in a minute." After everyone left the lodge, Charlie grabbed my right arm and said, "That was one hell of a stunt, Missy. You'll do anything to get sympathy won't you? Well, it's not going to work. You just pull yourself together pronto because you aren't going to get out of dining with our guests." I was too weak to reply, however, a rage I had never before experienced consumed me.

After dinner everyone returned to the Y.O. Lodge, but fainting gave me a reason to beg off. Once I was in the house, tears of anger and sorrow started flowing and would not stop. Why would Charlie think my fainting was an act? Where was the Charlie who wooed me with charm and humor? I walked out onto one of the bedroom balconies, took off my ten-dollar wedding ring, and hurled it into the night. Charlie had never bothered to replace it and pride kept me from nagging him about it. It was several days before Charlie noticed it was missing.

"Why aren't you wearing your wedding ring?"

"I threw it away after the way you treated me when I fainted. Why would you think I faked that?"

"Why would you stoop to pulling such a stunt? If you're going to be throwing away my wedding rings, I won't give you any others." He left the ranch and was away several days.

In May the cast was removed from my arm, the pins came out, and I was finally rid of the constant pain of the previous two months. Several days after returning to the ranch, I had my first attack of dizziness, cold sweats, and tremors. I went to bed and waited for it to pass. Fortunately, the next day the symptoms were less pronounced and within a few days they were gone. It was years before I realized what I experienced was withdrawal from the Percodan. Soon my old persona returned, and just as quickly, Charlie reverted from the evil Mr. Hyde to the charming Dr. Jekyll I fell in love with. In the best marital tradition, we swept our hurt and resentment under the rug, where it would lie dormant and festering.

Much to the orthopedic surgeon's amazement, I regained 100 percent mobility in my wrist. I told the doctor I gave some credit to my excessive exercising of my wrist once the cast came off, but others claimed credit as well. My mother and father attributed it to their unrelenting prayers to the Almighty. Doc Thomas, the Y.O.'s veterinarian, attributed it to the bonemeal he recommended. "But," I said, "I give your skill as a surgeon most of the credit and brought you a small token of appreciation."

The surgeon had treated many famous athletes, dancers, and Texas luminaries. There were autographed photographs of these patients throughout his office. He mentioned during my recovery he never treated anyone who sustained injuries from a horse. It seemed fitting to give him a photograph of me on Desperado. I inscribed it, "To the man who put me back in the saddle again." The surgeon did warn me that as I aged the injuries would plague me. He was right, and on a daily basis I am reminded of my horse wreck.

A few weeks later, Charlie and I attended the dedication of the Robert J. Kleberg Animal and Food Science Building at Texas A&M University in College Station. Kleberg was the grandson of the ranch founder, Capt. Richard King. He ran the ranch for fifty years and was responsible for starting the Santa Gertrudis cattle breed, developing King Ranch bluestem grass, and breeding thoroughbred racehorses, one of whom, Assault, won the Triple Crown in 1946.

The building featured a "branded stairway" with 254 oak panels for each Texas county. For the grand opening, the officers and directors of the Texas and Southwestern Cattle Raisers Association were invited to be the first to place their brands in the appropriate panel. Then they signed their names, brand, and ranch's name in a leather brand book, and left their branding irons for display in the building. The first name for Kerr County was Chas. Schreiner III.

Because I did not participate in the branding, I was able to enjoy the chaos as the A&M staff and students scurried around trying to heat 150 branding irons and then cool them down. I was privy to one conversation where the order was given to turn off the smoke alarms in the building and another where, because there were not enough buckets of water to cool the branding irons, the toilets were requisitioned for this purpose.

After the ceremony, there were stories told about branding mishaps and mayhem. My favorite was about Charles Goodnight, for whom the Goodnight-Loving Trail was named and who was the model for Capt. Woodrow Call in Larry McMurtry's Pulitzer Prize-winning novel, *Lonesome Dove*. Goodnight's ranch was in the Panhandle of Texas near Palo Duro Canyon. During a roundup and branding, Goodnight and some of his cowboys came upon a camel, probably a stray from the Army's failed experiment with them. The cowboy asked Goodnight what to do with the beast. Goodnight replied, "He's eating my grass so he can wear my brand." It was a good story but given the recalcitrant nature of camels I doubt the brand was successfully applied.

Now that I had the use of all my limbs, my goal was to have the gun room and garden room completed by the time Charlie had his gun show at the end of June. With its concrete floor and ceiling beams, limestone walls, and antique vault door from the original Schreiner Bank, Charlie's gun room achieved his objective of being fireproof. Cabinets from a London apothecary shop lined three of the walls and contained Charlie's gun and knife collection. Rusty helped Charlie label and arrange the guns, most of which were previously owned by Texas Rangers or notorious outlaws. Beside the fireplace were two framed displays of different types of horseshoes. Charlie gave one of them to me on condition I "lend" it to the gun room. On either side of the hearth was a small cannon with vintage holsters draped on them. Cowhide sofas framed an Oriental rug with a hunting scene that had been purchased by Charlie. A Gatling gun pointing at the door occupied center stage. Charlie was particularly proud of it because few collectors had the means to purchase one. Foolishly, he taught his fifth wife how to dismantle the gun, which allowed her to achieve the ultimate revenge when Charlie decided to divorce her. She dismantled the gun and threw the barrel into the Guadalupe River. Charlie Four told me it cost Three "a small fortune" to replace it.

The gun room was barely completed in time for Charlie's annual gun show, an all-male weekend attended by a select group of Charlie's gun collector friends. I made a point of staying out of the way because the good times consisted of consuming lots of alcohol, firing guns into the air, and

The 1900 University of Texas football team, which was captained by Walter Schreiner, Charlie Three's father. Walter is in the center in a striped jersey and holding the football. Date unknown.

telling tall tales. The highlight of the weekend was each of the attendees getting to fire the Gatling gun.

The garden room was finished a few weeks later and contained the greatest mishmash of styles, running the gamut from wicker furniture, Myrtle's Oriental pieces, Wells Fargo trunks, antique carousel horses, and zebra and cowhide rugs. The room overlooked the backyard, where Charlie planned to put a swimming pool. When living in Austin I was a daily swimmer at Barton Springs, a natural spring-fed pool of clear, six-ty-eight-degree water. Until the pool could be built, I was swimming in the horse tank by the corral. Its water was as refreshing as Barton Springs since it also came from underground aquafers, but the sides and bottom of the tank were covered with slimy algae. It was also not unusual for a horse to stop for a drink while I was swimming. Often my hand would touch a horse's nostril as I reached the side.

In the downstairs hallway, I hung Schreiner family photographs. One of my favorites was of Charlie's father, Walter, surrounded by his teammates of the 1900 undefeated University of Texas football team. Walter, the team's captain, sat in the center holding a football. He was the first Schreiner to attend the University of Texas, establishing a tradition that would be continued by his son and grandsons. In 1899 he was selected for the All-Southern Team, comparable to All-American today, and is the only athlete in UT history to win five letters in varsity football. He was nicknamed "Crip" because of the numerous broken bones he incurred during his playing career.

I hung each photograph, often requiring me to climb to the highest step on a six-foot ladder and balance precariously as I drove nails and hoisted pictures onto the wall. My hunch that others would find them as interesting as I did was confirmed by visitors to the house who lingered in the hallway.

It occurred to me I should include my family photos as well. Even though I queried Charlie about his family, he never asked about mine, not even after I hung their photographs. I did not yet realize this is a common male trait. Men are delighted to tell you every detail of their lives but never inquire about yours. When I became a widow, only one of my several suitors inquired about me.

Because Charlie's house was the first sign of habitation visitors saw from the main road, they assumed it was the headquarters. There was no lock on the front door, and on a daily basis I would discover a ranch visitor wandering through the house. I would politely explain it was a private residence and give directions to the Chuckwagon. Charlie often sent guests up for a house tour without letting me know. One day as I left the shower with a towel wrapped around me, two couples confronted me. I do not know who was more surprised, them or me. They apologized profusely saying, "Charlie told us to come on up. You must be Norma." I answered in the affirmative and told them if they would give me a few minutes to dress, I would be glad to show them around.

When I expressed my displeasure at this constant flow of visitors, Charlie said, "You should be happy people want to see your house." I rebutted it wasn't my house but his house, and I didn't mind showing people around but would like some warning. After many discussions, Charlie grudgingly agreed to put a "Private Residence" sign in front of the drive leading to the house.

In the evenings, Charlie and I drove out to see the longhorns so I could finish selecting my ten cows. Studying my notes, I agonized over which ten to pick. There were so many good cows, and I wanted to impress Charlie with my selections. After much agonizing, my list was complete and I presented it to Charlie one night after dinner. As he read, he began running a hand across his head, a sign indicating there was a problem. "Are my choices so bad?" I asked.

Charlie shook his head. "Anything but. You just topped my herd. There's no way I can give you these ten cows. My sons would kill me."

"The terms of our prenup said ten cows of *my* choosing. Those are the ones I chose. You have to give them to me. I may have topped your herd, but I'll be damned if I'm going to cull it for you. Besides, I thought you were a man of your word."

The next day I called Nugent. He found the situation humorous. "Charlie doesn't own a bad cow so come off your high horse and compromise. You do remember how to do that, don't you? As I recall you were pretty good at it as a lobbyist."

The compromise was Charlie would give me five of the original cows I chose but he would determine which ones. I would choose five more with his approval. He said it had not been easy getting his sons to agree. It never occurred to me Charlie did not have sole decision-making power about the ranch. I tried to console myself but remained resentful and wondered what other terms of our prenup would be summarily changed as circumstances warranted. It shed a new light on many aspects of my living there, especially if something were to happen to Charlie.

CHAPTER 20

"Life's single lesson: that there is more accident to it

than a man can ever admit to in a lifetime and stay sane."

THOMAS PYNCHON

Where the Giraffes and the Antelopes Play

"WHAT DO YOU THINK ABOUT getting some giraffes for the ranch?" Charlie asked as we were having supper at the Chuckwagon.

"No ranch is complete without some," I quipped. I didn't give it another thought. I was too busy planning for twenty-five of my friends to spend the weekend at the ranch to celebrate my birthday. As I prepared, I thought about the previous year when I spent my birthday in Guadalajara with Charlie. Had someone told me where that encounter would lead, I would not have believed them. My guest list included friends from high school, college, and politics. Surprisingly, the diverse group melded together and the weekend provided stories that would be told for years to come. One of my favorites was when Rusty's former girlfriend mooned him from the back of the tour bus as we were going out to see animals.

Soon after, Charlie and I left for Oklahoma City to visit the Oklahoma City Zoo, which had a pair of giraffes for sale. Because Charlie avoided the interstate highway, we went through Mineral Wells, Texas. Charlie pulled up in front of a fourteen-story brick building looming above the town. "This is the once famous Baker Hotel," Charlie said. "It closed a couple of years ago but in its prime it was quite the place. It opened in 1929, and people came from around the world to partake of the waters. Lots of movie stars stayed here and several presidents. There's an Olympic-size pool in the basement that was filled with mineral water and a grand ball-room on the top floor. I came here a couple of times with Myrtle."

"I'd love to see inside."

"I bet I can grant your wish." Charlie made a phone call and fifteen minutes later we were touring the hotel from the basement to the ball-room. Even in its bedraggled state the former grande dame was impressive, and I could imagine what a perfect respite it once offered the rich and famous. As we drove away Charlie said, "I wish somebody would restore it, but it will take very deep pockets." It took forty years, but in 2019 a group of investors purchased the Baker and began restoring the building to its former grandeur.

We continued on our meandering route and finally arrived at the Oklahoma City Zoo. Charlie, of course, knew the zoo's director, who gave us a behind-the-scenes tour. When we stopped at the lowland gorilla exhibit, one of the male gorillas ambled up to the bars of his enclosure and extended his hand. The director took some grapes from his pocket and placed one in its palm. He handed several to me, and each time I placed them in the gorilla's outstretched hand the animal looked into my eyes. I have looked into the eyes of many animals, some wild and some domesticated, but never have I experienced the connection I did with this creature with whom humans share 98 percent of our DNA. Years later I would have the same feeling in the Bwindi Impenetrable Forest in Uganda when a female mountain gorilla, with her baby clinging to her back, brushed against my arm as she walked by.

We went to the zoo director's office to discuss what special provisions the ranch would need to accommodate the giraffes. The major prerequisite, which the Y.O. was lacking, was a giraffe house with proper heating, including a heated floor. Giraffes are very susceptible to cold temperatures and not adept at acclimating to them. For them, like many Texans, cold is anything below fifty degrees Fahrenheit. Once a giraffe is chilled, it is difficult for the animal to regain its normal body temperature without assistance from an external heat source. The zoo director told us giraffes had died of hypothermia in captivity because their entire bodies were not kept warm. Even though Hill Country winters are mild, there are many days and nights with temperatures below fifty, and it is not unusual to have sustained days of temperatures in the teens, twenties, or thirties. There can also be brutal ice storms. During one such event, the ranch lost many of its blackbuck antelope because, being native to India, they lacked the instinct to paw through the ice to get to the grass.

One of the Y.O.'s new residents with the Giraffe Hilton in background.

Charlie was certain he could build a giraffe house in three months so there was no reason not to ship the giraffes to the Y.O. as soon as possible. Charlie and the zoo director shook hands and Charlie said he would be back in touch with a shipping date. On the drive back to the ranch, Charlie started planning the giraffe house as I took notes. The giraffes would be in the Africana pasture with the zebras and oryx. Their house would be built of twenty-foot-tall telephone poles with insulation between the poles and the interior wood walls. Copper tubing in the concrete floor would provide heat for their lower bodies, and electric heaters on the ceiling would keep their upper bodies warm. Even the giraffe house could not escape Charlie's penchant for using antiques. Two antique hay mangers Charlie had been wondering how to use would be perfect for feeding them. As the structure went up, ranch employees dubbed it the "Giraffe Hilton."

Within weeks of our returning from Oklahoma, the giraffes were on their way to the ranch. Just as they required special housing, they required special shipping arrangements. The journey from Oklahoma City would be nonstop in an open trailer. The drive would take ten to twelve hours, depending on traffic and allowing for stops for meals and gas. A major consideration was that the open trailer with its eighteen-foot-tall cargo could not go under overpasses. Thus, each time there was an overpass, the truck would have to exit and go around it.

The giraffes arrived at the ranch on a moonlit night. A call from the

A Y.O. cowboy welcomes the ranch's newest residents.

front gate alerted Charlie when they arrived. The word was spread and everyone assembled in the Africana pasture. The bed of a pickup truck contained ice and several cases of bubbly. Plastic cups with the Y.O. brand were filled in anticipation of the arrival. As the truck and trailer slowly made its way into the pasture, a cheer went up. The truck drove to the middle of the pasture and stopped. The two giraffes tentatively looked around as the trailer doors opened and the ramp extended; without hesitating, the animals made a stately entrance into their new kingdom. There was cheering and clapping as glasses were raised. We stood watching as the giraffes inspected their new home. It obviously met with their approval because they would live long lives there, producing numerous offspring who still reside at the ranch.

There were other additions to the ranch that summer. The ranch had been contacted by a German tour company wanting to bring large groups to the Y.O. for a cowboy experience. To accommodate the numbers of guests anticipated, an additional entertainment area was needed. Three was more than happy to design and supervise the building of a multi-function pavilion behind the Y.O. Lodge to serve as an additional area for cocktails, dining, and dancing. In anticipation of this new tourist enterprise, eight red mules joined the ranch menagerie. It would be their job to pull wagons of tourists around the ranch. In the interim they stayed in shape by jogging with me. One of the best places to run was on the ranch's caliche airstrip because it was relatively smooth and I did not have to worry about traffic. One day as I was jogging along, I heard hoofbeats behind me. I looked over my shoulder and saw the mules trotting behind and gaining on me. I stopped. They stopped. I begin walking. So did they. I started running again and they followed suit. I repeated the stop, walk, run sequence several times, and they mimicked my actions. From then on they became my jogging buddies, forming a phalanx around me as we ran up and down the airstrip.

A new longhorn breeder, who would be a major influence in marketing the breed, visited the ranch that summer. Charlie Four and Walter showed him the longhorns, after which Three and I drove down to the corral and were introduced to Red McCombs. I had no idea who he was but soon discovered Red was a major figure in the San Antonio business world; in the coming years, his business acumen would make him a billionaire. His business career started with a Ford dealership, and in 1973 he was one of those responsible for bringing the San Antonio Spurs to San Antonio. He went on to own the Denver Nuggets basketball team and the Minnesota Vikings football team. In the summer of 1978, Red decided to get in the longhorn business, which is why he was at the Y.O. Red would bring his superior sales and marketing skills to the longhorn business, and within a year longhorn prices were soaring. Whenever I sold one of my longhorns, Red was usually the top bidder. "You succeeded where I failed," he told me. "You got some of Charlie's best cows. How did you do it?" I told him the story of topping Charlie's herd and can still see him laughing with delight.

The summer ended with Charlie and I hosting a fundraiser for our matchmaker, Jim Nugent. Having the fundraiser at the ranch, with a tour of the house included, provided an incentive for people to attend. The guest list included the state's elected officials and numerous business-people. One of those attending was Chase Untermeyer, who represented the eighty-third district in the Texas House. Chase had been a freshman representative in the 1977 legislative session when I was a freshman lobbyist for the Equal Rights Amendment. Proving politics makes strange bedfellows, Chase, a Republican representing the affluent River Oaks district of Houston, became friends with Mickey Leland, the Black representative for Houston's predominantly Black Fifth Ward. During the session, Chase and Mickey hosted a party that I attended. The invitation read, "The Fifth Ward Gets Down With River Oaks." Both Chase and Mickey entertained—Mickey recited one of his epic poems, and Chase sang a repertoire of Cole Porter songs. I was impressed that Chase knew not just the lyrics but the introductions to every song. After the fundraiser, Chase sent his bread and butter note in the form of a poem which read in part:

DON'T FENCE ME IN

(Newly discovered lyrics by Cole Porter; not to be confused
with Leonard Bernstein's "Y.O., Y.O., Y.O., Did I Ever Leave Ohio?")

Oh, give me land, lotsa land
Where the oryx all run free,
Don't fence me in.
Let me drive, stay alive
In the wilds of Kerr County,
Don't fence me in.
Let me wake with the dawn
Be a rise 'n' shiner;
Eat a cowboy breakfast
With an interior designer;
And debate the E.R.A.
With Mrs. Norma Schreiner.
Don't fence me in.

Chase would become Vice President George H. W. Bush's executive assistant and then assistant secretary of the Navy. When the vice president was elected president, Chase was his director of presidential personnel and later appointed director of Voice of America. President George W. Bush appointed Chase to be ambassador to Qatar.

Of all these ranch events, the most significant was one that led to my almost being shot by the ranch's nearest neighbor, Uncle Warren Klein.

CHAPTER 21

"Love is a mighty pretty thing but like all other delicious things,

it is cloying when the first transports of passion begin to subside,

which it assuredly will do. . . . There is no truth more certain

than that all of our enjoyments fall short of our expectations."

GEORGE WASHINGTON IN A LETTER TO HIS
STEP-GRANDDAUGHTER

The Bloom is off the Rose

CHARLIE AND I WERE IN LAWTON, Oklahoma, for the annual long-horn sale at the Wichita Wildlife Refuge when we were awakened by a phone call at two in the morning. Charlie answered the phone and Charlie Four greeted him with, "Hello, grandpa!" Mary Helen had just given birth to Tiffany Nell Schreiner, Charlie's first grandchild, who was born on what would have been the eighty-second birthday of her great-grand-mother Myrtle.

As soon as Charlie hung up the phone I said, "You owe me one hundred dollars."

When Charlie Four and Mary Helen announced the pregnancy, Charlie immediately started referring to the baby as "he." "Are you so certain it will be a boy?" I asked.

"My first grandchild wouldn't dare be anything but a boy!"

I was not about to let such arrogance go unchallenged. "I'll bet you one hundred dollars it's a girl." Charlie immediately accepted.

"Pay up," I said.

"Now? I'll pay you in the morning."

"Nothing doing. Now," I said, holding out my hand.

Grudgingly, Charlie got out of bed and wrote a check. After I cashed the check, I framed it and gave it to Mary Helen, who later gave it to Tiffany.

In addition to winning me one hundred dollars, Tiffany's arrival allowed me to leave the longhorn sale and return to the ranch. When I first attended longhorn sales with Charlie I found them interesting, but a year later the novelty was gone. Since reading a book would have been too obvious a sign of boredom, I started doing various forms of needlework as a distraction. One of those pieces was an alphabet sampler, with each letter represented by an animal, which I gave to Four and Mary Helen as a baby gift. Presciently, the baby for whom I made it now provided the perfect excuse for extricating myself from the sale.

I arrived at the Kerrville hospital that evening, visited with Mary Helen, and drove to the ranch. It was almost midnight when I arrived at the front gate. There were two locks on the gate. One was a combination lock that for security often had the combination changed. Only a few people had a key for the other lock, and I wasn't one of them. When I entered the combination, the lock refused to open. I tried again and failed again. No one was at the Game Warden's Cabin because it wasn't hunting season. There was a phone at the front gate, but it only rang at the Chuckwagon and Y.O. Lodge. I tried both but no one answered. This was 1978 and cell phones were a thing in the distant future. My options were to sleep in my car until morning or make the hour drive back to Kerrville and get a hotel room. Neither appealed to me.

Then it occurred to me. Uncle Warren would have a key to the gate lock. I drove to his house and knocked loudly on the front door. No response. I went to the back door and knocked. No response. I went back to the front door and pounded to no avail. I tried to open the doors but they were locked. I concluded Uncle Warren wasn't there, but his phone would be, and I could call Charlie Four. Getting to the phone would require breaking one of the windows. I found a large rock, picked out a front window, and was about to hurl the rock when the front door opened. Uncle Warren stood there holding a shotgun. He was as surprised to see me as I was to see him. He said his wife awakened him saying she thought she heard someone knocking on the door. I explained my predicament, and he graciously unlocked the front gate for me. When I told Charlie Three about the incident, he saw that I received a key to the gate lock. I still have the key. It is one of those items we collect as we go through life that I simply cannot bear to part with.

Several weeks later one of Charlie's gun collector friends, H. G., came to visit. H. G. and I met at the first gun show I attended with Charlie. H. G. was Charlie's mentor, tutoring him in how to collect guns that would increase in value. Charlie specialized in collecting Colt single-action army

My key to the lock on the Y.O. front gate.

The drawing Charlie Three did for the author when explaining the parts of a gun.

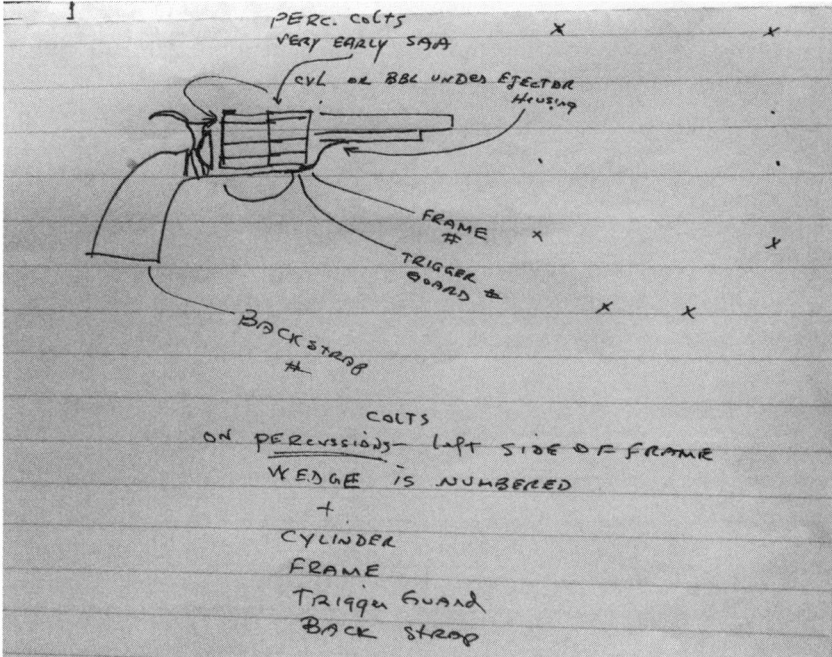

and navy revolvers, Bowie knives, and an occasional rifle. He had a predisposition for guns owned by Texas Rangers because of his grandfather's having been a Ranger. As we walked around the gun show, Charlie told me the Colt single action, invented in the 1830s by Samuel Colt, was "the gun that won the West" because it gave the white man an advantage over the horseback Native American's skill with a bow and arrow. Charlie had written a book about the Texas Rangers, and as we walked around the gun show he told me about Jack Hays, whom he especially admired and who was instrumental in making the single action successful.

We stopped at a booth and Charlie picked up a gun that was on display. He told me the most important characteristic to check in antique guns was matching serial numbers on the cylinder, frame, trigger guard, and back strap. Though this gun met those criteria, its value was lessened because the natural patina of the original finish, a crucial element in determining a gun's age, was distorted by bluing.

Several times I went with Charlie to purchase guns from individuals. One occasion was from a former Texas Ranger. As we went through the small talk that preceded doing business, the man began talking about his horse, which he recently had to put down. As he spoke of the horse, tears came to his eyes and he choked up. So did I, because I knew too well the heartache accompanying the loss of an exceptional animal. When we were driving home, Charlie said, "Can you believe the way he talked about that horse? For a minute, I thought he was so worked up I might not get the gun."

I replied, "Yes, I can. It was more than a horse to him. It was a companion and a colleague." Charlie just shook his head from side to side.

Another gun purchase resulted in my getting a recipe for what would become my signature eggnog. The former gun owner, Mr. Lucky, died and left instructions with his widow for it to be sold to Charlie. As we exchanged pleasantries with Mrs. Lucky, she asked if we would like some eggnog. Though it was June, she said she made a large batch every Christmas so she could enjoy and serve it throughout the year. We accepted and she returned with two frosted silver punch cups filled with the concoction. My first sip told me this was no ordinary eggnog because within minutes I was feeling a substantial buzz. Charlie finished his cup and asked for more. I asked Mrs. Lucky for her recipe, which she was happy to give me. Glancing at it I saw it contained a mixture of rum, brandy, and bourbon. For years I referred to it as Mrs. Lucky's eggnog, but given its effect on guests, I changed the name to Mrs. Lucky's Kick Your Ass Eggnog.

Charlie was anxious about my meeting his mentor, H. G., who was very critical of the women Charlie married after divorcing Audrey, his first wife. To Charlie's surprise, H. G. and I hit it off, and I looked forward to entertaining him in our new home. He had been at the ranch several days when he arrived at the house one morning without Charlie.

"What a surprise!" I exclaimed.

"I wanted to talk to you alone."

"Is that good or bad?" I asked, leading him toward the living room.

"It could be very good for you," he said. "I'd prefer to talk in the gun room."

We walked into the gun room and I motioned toward one of the couches.

Mrs. Lucky's Kick Your Ass Eggnog

12 egg yolks (save the whites)

1 pound confectioners' sugar

2 cups dark rum, brandy, bourbon, or rye

2–4 cups of liquor of choice (Depending on which liquorIusedabove,Ithenchooseoneoftheothers)

2 quarts whipping cream

1 cup peach brandy (I prefer 1/4 to 1/2 cup peach brandy and regular brandy to make a cup)

8–12 egg whites

Beat egg yolks until light in color.

Gradually add sugar and stir to mix.

Add 2 cups of liquor and let stand covered for 1 hour, if you are in a hurry. If you have time, let stand overnight.

This completes the making of the "nog."

To the nog add the remainder of liquor and cream.

Cover the mixture and refrigerate for 3 hours.

Beateggwhitesuntilstiffbutnotdry.Foldintomixture.

Serve with nutmeg if desired.

This freezes very well and will last several months, if you can exercise restraint. I've never had it last beyond January.

He sat down. "How are you enjoying being mistress of the Y.O.?"

"It's certainly different. I've entered a whole new world."

"I can imagine. How long do you think it's going to last?"

"How long will what last?"

"Your marriage. You don't honestly think you're going to be the last Mrs. Charles Schreiner III do you?"

"I have every intention of being just that."

"You're his fourth wife in less than eight years. You're young enough to be his daughter, and you have little in common. You don't belong on this godforsaken ranch in the middle of nowhere. I'm surprised you've stood it this long. What kind of life is this for a vivacious young woman?"

I was stunned. I looked at H. G. trying to decide if this was a joke or a test of my loyalty to Charlie. "Why are you saying these things? Aren't you his friend?"

"I am his friend, and I want to be your friend too. I'm concerned about what will happen to you when this marriage ends, which it will. I don't know what kind of agreement you have or what your price was to marry him, but whatever it was, I can assure you it was too cheap. But it's not too late to change that. Three's a dirty old man and that's the best bargaining tool you have. Every time you screw him you should get something in return. The most valuable thing he has isn't this ranch. It's his guns. You should ask for one every time you have sex." H. G. walked over to one of the gun cases. "Come here so I can show you which ones to get."

I followed H. G. as he walked around the gun room, pointing to various guns, recalling when he sold them to Charlie, and why they were valuable. As he did this, he wrote down the serial numbers. I followed in a mute daze, bewildered and angered by his words. He handed me the sheet of paper. "When you leave Charlie, let me know how to reach you. I want to stay in touch." He patted my arm, said he would see at lunch, and left the house.

I went upstairs trying to sort out my thoughts and decide how and when to tell Charlie. It seemed only a few minutes before Charlie bounded into the room. "Ready for lunch?" he asked.

"I need to talk to you," I blurted out, and I recounted my conversation with H. G., showing Charlie the serial numbers H. G. gave me.

Charlie was dumbfounded. "I don't understand why he would do that. What's his motive? Did he think you wouldn't tell me?"

"He seemed to think I married you only for money and would be his willing accomplice."

"I don't know what to do."

"I think we should confront him together."

"No. I want to do it alone and I want to do it now."

Charlie was gone over two hours. As soon as I heard his car crest the hill, I went downstairs and met him at the front door. "What did he say?"

"He denied the conversation. Said you made it up to drive a wedge in our friendship."

I was flabbergasted. "Let's go see him together. I want to confront him."

"He's left the ranch."

"You believe me, don't you? You saw the paper with the serial numbers. It wasn't my writing."

"I don't know who to believe."

How could Charlie think I was lying? Did he not trust me? I wanted to get away from the ranch and sort things out. Hastily I packed and left for San Antonio, where I spent the next three days swimming laps in the Menger pool. As I swam, the pieces of the puzzle fell into place. H. G. had tutored Charlie in how to purchase guns that would increase in value. Every gun on the list H. G. gave me was sold to Charlie by H. G. He hoped to use me to get them back and sell them again at much higher prices. The most hurtful aspect of the sordid event was Charlie not knowing who to believe. Just as choosing my longhorns eroded my trust in Charlie, this incident indicated the lack of trust was reciprocated. I decided to return to the ranch, never mention the incident again, and hope Charlie would follow suit.

Forty-three years later, I learned the rest of the story. One of the people I talked with when writing this memoir was Richard Shea, a gun collector friend of Charlie's. Richard and his wife arrived at the ranch the evening the incident occurred. The next morning Charlie told Richard he needed his help. They got into Three's car and went to the saddle shed. H. G. had an expensive custom-made saddle he kept at the ranch. Charlie tied it to the back of his car and headed toward the front gate going as fast as the road allowed. Once there he turned and drove back to the Chuckwagon at the same speed, still dragging the saddle. There he untied the saddle, gave it to a ranch employee, and told him to send it to H. G. with postage due. Richard told me Charlie never explained his actions, but after that Richard noticed H. G. and Three avoided each other at gun shows. I wondered why Charlie didn't tell me about this when I returned to the ranch? It would have assuaged my fear he didn't trust me. Unfortunately, Charlie made a habit of not telling those close to him things he should.

I decided that if Charlie and I took a trip to a place of interest to both of us it might help repair the damage done by H. G. Since childhood, I dreamed of going to Africa. Charlie had not been there, and it seemed the perfect place to restore our badly bruised marriage. I proposed it to Charlie.

"No," he said. "No matter where I go, it's not as pretty as the Y.O., so I see no need to go there. If you want to go, get one of your friends to go with you." None of my friends could have afforded the time or money required for such a jaunt. It would be thirty-seven years before I finally went there, not once but twice.

A few weeks later a friend called and asked if I would like to accompany her on a trip to New York City and Washington, DC, to visit mutual friends. It wasn't Africa but it would suffice and allow me to see and do things that were of interest to me. I accepted immediately, certain Charlie would be glad to have some time without me. I was surprised when he chastised me for not getting his approval. I reminded him he had not sought my permission when he traveled to Las Vegas for the gun show or to New Mexico to hunt mule deer. He was still in a huff when I left and got even huffier when I called to tell him we were attending a World Series game between the Los Angeles Dodgers and New York Yankees. My traveling companion was friends with someone in the Yankees' front office who got us seats behind first base. Charlie's response was, "Goddamn it. I've always wanted to go to a World Series game. You don't even care about baseball and you're getting to go." As a conciliatory gesture, I returned to the ranch earlier than planned; however, it did little to placate him, and he sulked for days.

One of Charlie's recurring criticisms of me was my lack of interest in even the most basic culinary practices. I come by my aversion to cooking naturally. Neither my mother, her sister, nor their mother were cooks. I have no memory of my mother cooking or any special dish made by her. My mother's sister, in the final years of her life, let her cats sleep on the stove and in its oven because the pilot lights provided warmth.

At least once a month Charlie suggested I prepare our meals. At first I thought he was joking. "Why would I do that when we have Bertie?"

"Because occasionally I'd like for us to dine in the privacy of our home."

"What about mingling with guests during meals?"

"I can mingle with the guests before or after we dine," he countered.

"I could bring food from the Chuckwagon."

"Wouldn't you like to cook a meal for your husband?"

Mary Helen, Tiffany, and the author, Christmas 1978.

"No. I don't like to cook. You knew that from the first time you opened my refrigerator in Austin."

And so it went. Which was why, when I suggested inviting his sons for Christmas Eve dinner, he was amazed and erroneously assumed I was finally becoming domesticated. What he never found out was Bertie offered to prepare Christmas dinner for us. I never would have proposed such a dinner if I had to do the cooking.

As our first year of marriage drew to a close, I was realizing the idealized vision I concocted of living on a ranch and being Charlie's partner in projects was a fantasy. That was the role of his sons. My role was to be a gracious hostess and tour guide but not an integral part of ranch decisions or planning. When he was courting me, Charlie admired my "well-stocked mind." That mind was bored and yearning for cultural events and intellectual stimulation. There was no one on the ranch with whom I could discuss the books I read or current events, much less intimacies about my boredom. Visitors to the ranch only wanted to talk about hunting, the history of the ranch, or Charlie's guns. The remoteness of the ranch made it impossible to receive a daily newspaper. This was before internet or satellites, and radio and television reception was intermittent and often nonexistent. When the primary election was held in May, I spent the evening driving around the ranch trying to get radio reception to learn if the candidate I had worked for was winning. I never succeeded and didn't learn my candidate lost until two days later.

Most worrisome was the realization that I would never come first with Charlie. His first love always was and always would be the fifty thousand acres of scrub oak, cactus, longhorns, deer, and rattlesnakes comprising the Y.O. Ranch. I was completely dependent on him for every aspect of my life. What would happen if he died? I envisioned a scenario of this happening when I was in my fifties, hadn't worked for years, had limited financial resources, and would be facing growing old in precarious circumstances with no safety net. I tried to broach this with Charlie by suggesting he get a life insurance policy with me as beneficiary. He replied it was too costly at his age and with his heart problems. What if we purchased a house together in Austin or San Antonio that would be mine if he died? Absolutely not. Would he give me some land on the Y.O. where we could build a house that would be mine? That was the craziest idea he ever heard. We had a perfectly good house. I reminded him that under the prenup I could stay only two years after he died. He replied the boys loved me and would let me stay as long as I wanted. What was wrong with me? He had no intention of dying anytime soon.

I remembered the words of a friend when I told him I was marrying Charlie. "You realize you're going to be trapped in a fifty thousand-acre high-fenced cage, don't you?" His prediction was coming true, and I needed to find a way to be less dependent on Charlie.

As Charlie and I lay in bed one night, I said, "I think I'll apply to teach part-time at Schreiner College."

"Where in hell did you come up with that idea? Not only *no*, but *hell no*! Do you know what people would think if you did that? They'd think I couldn't support my wife and all kinds of rumors would start. I don't want to hear another word about it!"

"So much for my brilliant idea," I thought.

CHAPTER 22

"In the sex war thoughtlessness is the weapon of the male,

vindictiveness of the female."

CYRIL CONNOLLY

The Good, the Bad,
and the Ugly

IN JANUARY 1979, THE GOVERNOR appointed my friend, confidant, and attorney, Jim Nugent, to the Texas Railroad Commission. The Railroad Commission was established in 1891 to regulate the railroads in Texas, but after oil was discovered, its primary function became regulating the oil and gas industry. Unlike being a member of the Texas House of Representatives, the Railroad Commission was a full-time job, and Nugent and his wife were moving to Austin.

Nugent's swearing in on January 4 in Kerrville was followed by a reception. Charlie and I attended, but Charlie left after the swearing in for a meeting in San Antonio. After congratulating Nugent, I found myself talking with the head of one of the teachers' organizations. She mentioned they were looking for a lobbyist. I told her I was interested. She asked if I could be in Austin the next day to meet with the executive committee. I could. Charlie and I were to meet at the Menger Hotel the next afternoon to celebrate our first wedding anniversary, and I could go to Austin first, meet with the board, and then drive to San Antonio.

I drove to Austin the next morning, interviewed, and was hired immediately by the executive committee. The legislature wasn't convening for another two weeks, and little major legislative business occurred during the first six weeks of the session. This gave me time to decide whether to rent an apartment or stay at a hotel when I needed to be in Austin. On the drive to San Antonio, I mulled over when to tell Charlie about my new job.

When I arrived at the Menger, Charlie had a bottle of champagne waiting. Our evening together was reminiscent of when he was wooing me. We stayed in bed until noon the next day discussing how to celebrate the ranch's centennial in 1980. I kept waiting for Charlie to give me an anniversary gift. Our first anniversary seemed the perfect time for him to give me a proper wedding ring. But no gift was forthcoming, and finally I asked if he ever planned to give me a wedding ring. A horrible fight ensued, and I threw down my gauntlet of the lobbying job. I could tell it surprised and angered him. He left the hotel. Returning several hours later, he threw a small velvet box on the bed and left again. Inside was a diamond wedding band. Charlie did not return to the hotel, and I drove to the ranch the next morning. Charlie did not reappear for several days, and when he did, I acted as though nothing had happened.

The following weekend, Charlie told me guests were coming to the house for drinks before dinner. He did not tell me their names, but one of them turned out to be the movie star Ben Johnson. For years I admired him as an actor, especially in his Academy Award-winning role as Sam the Lion in *The Last Picture Show*. When I gave Ben and his wife, Carol, a tour of the house, both were friendly and asked a lot of questions about various objects. Many of the art pieces with horses caught their eye, especially my bronze *Widowmaker*. I told them about my horse wreck, and Ben said he did not know anyone who rode or worked with horses who hadn't had at least one accident. He smiled and said, "You're not a real cowboy until a horse has given you a broken bone or two. Most of us have had several but we always get back on, don't we?"

I nodded and asked if he always wanted to be in movies.

"No, ma'am. It was pure accident. The ranch I was working on leased some horses to a movie. It was my job to get the horses to the movie set, take care of them, and get them back to the ranch. When I got to the set, they asked me if I'd like to be a stuntman. I asked what they wanted me to do and it was mainly just chasing around on a galloping horse. I could do that. The ranch was paying me fifteen dollars a week wrangling, and the movie was going to pay me that a day. I may be a lot of things but dumb isn't one of them. It was my start in movies. I was perfectly happy being a stuntman, but then John Ford asked me if I'd be interested in signing a contract, and that got me into the acting. I have to say, it's been very good to me."

Ben said this in a soft drawl, looking me in the eye, genuinely humble. Carol, his wife of fifty-four years, was equally interesting and told me about growing up on a horse ranch in Arizona. As I recall, she had performed in rodeos. Later, as I sat listening to conversations about hunting and guns, Ben came and sat beside me on the couch. "You really don't enjoy all this do you?" he asked.

"Is it obvious? I thought I had on my having a wonderful time face," I replied, smiling.

"Carol says I'm good at reading people. I want to thank you for your hospitality," Ben said, extending his hand. "I wish you all the best."

The next day was the first meeting of the Y.O. Centennial Committee. Charlie asked a variety of his friends to be on the committee, and the first meeting was a brainstorming session about everything from whether the party should be formal to what type of food to serve. Charlie wanted everything about the celebration to be as distinctive as the Y.O. As ideas flew, most agreed it should be a formal affair with "black tie and boots." Moving on to what the menu should be, ideas ranged from barbecue to steaks to exotic game.

Several days later Charlie Four approached me about lobbying for the Y.O. A bill setting a hunting season for exotics had been introduced. Many ranches throughout Texas depended on exotics for year-round cash flow because there was no hunting season on them. Four said he would pay me for my services, something I was not expecting but happy to accept. "Perhaps," I thought, "this will be my role for the ranch."

When I mentioned this to Three, he did not see it that way. "I don't understand why you want to go galivanting off to Austin."

"I want to use my brain for something other than giving tours of the ranch and your house. Just because I'm lobbying doesn't mean I won't spend most of my time on the ranch. Lobbying gives me something that is mine, just like the Y.O. is yours."

"For the life of me, I don't understand why you aren't happy just being my wife. Is it asking too much?"

"Yes it is. As you've told me on numerous occasions, I'm smart. And ambitious. And bored by repetition. I like to be learning and doing new things. I need to keep up my political connections in case something happens to you."

"Nothing is going to happen to me."

So it went throughout January. The usual outcome was Charlie disappearing for several days. In the coming year, whenever Charlie and I disagreed, he would leave the ranch. At the time, I thought his behavior was unique to our relationship, but I learned he did this with all his wives. Throughout our marriage, a quote by journalist Mignon McLaughlin often crossed my mind: "Many beautiful women have been made happy by their own beauty, but no intelligent woman has been made happy by her own intelligence." I felt I was living proof of its truth.

Of all the men I have had relationships with, Charlie was the only one who never encouraged me to pursue my ambitions. Though he was quick to praise my intelligence, he did not urge my putting it to use in ways that would give me a sense of accomplishment. One of my friends sent me a T-shirt that said, "Behind every successful woman is a man who tried to stop her." Whenever Charlie and I disagreed, I would wear it to the Chuckwagon for lunch much to the amusement of everyone except him. Charlie found ways to retaliate in kind. After one of our bouts, we were in Kerrville when Charlie stopped at the meat processing company used by the Y.O. Several minutes later he returned to the car with a package wrapped in brown paper. He handed it to me saying, "This reminded me of you." I opened it to find a butcher knife. I looked at him quizzically. "It's to go with your sharp tongue," he said.

On February 1, one month into our second year of marriage, Charlie called from an undisclosed location and told me he wanted us to separate. I was stunned and told him it was the most idiotic thing I ever heard and asked him to come home so we could do the thing he most dreaded—talk. A week later he arrived at the ranch at midnight with three of his gun collector friends. He entertained them for the next several days, and I noticed he was no longer wearing his wedding ring. Once we were alone, I told him I saw no reason to separate. I believed we could work out our problems and have a better marriage, but I knew we could not do it by ourselves. I believed if we found a good counselor, he or she could help us find a way to resolve our differences. I knew if we separated Charlie would immediately begin searching for a new love interest, assuming he hadn't already found one. His missing wedding ring made me suspect he had.

There was another family crisis during this time. I never knew the particulars because Charlie refused to tell me, but his son, Walter, was in some kind of trouble. I heard rumors from hunting guides that Walter was involved in selling drugs. I also overheard several of Charlie's phone conversations discussing "how to get rid of this problem" and "payoffs." Years later, one of the hunting guides told me Three sent him and another ranch employee to deliver a large amount of cash to someone in South Texas.

In early spring, Charlie held a reunion of former Y.O. Ranch employees. The reunion was to show appreciation to those who helped make the ranch what it was and allow them to share their stories about the ranch. Charlie was planning to have a book written for the centennial and hoped some of their stories would merit inclusion.

While talking with one of the wives who lived on the ranch in the 1920s and '30s, I asked if she remembered Myrtle.

"Oh my, yes. We were living here when Mr. Walter brought her home. Everybody was shocked when he showed up with a bride. And, a very pretty one. She was a lot younger than Mr. Walter. She told me she met him when he got in her taxi up in New York City. They started talking and when he found out she was from Texas, he asked her to go to dinner with him. She said he just swept her off her feet and two weeks later they got married."

"She was driving a taxi?" I exclaimed.

"Yes. She told me all kinds of funny stories about New York and some of the passengers she had."

"Did she ever tell you why she was in New York?"

"No. I didn't ask."

When I told Charlie the story, he was as astounded by it as I. Regrettably, we would learn no more about this period in Myrtle's life.

Another link to Myrtle's past was Birdie Pie, Myrtle's cook in the 1940s and '50s. During the reunion, Charlie and I gave Birdie Pie a personal tour of the house, and she was delighted to see so many of Myrtle's possessions in our home. She told me about the dinner parties Myrtle gave at the ranch and how she and Myrtle prepared the meals together. Thirty minutes before the guests arrived, Myrtle would change into an elegant dress and greet her guests with a cool demeanor that belied the frantic pace at which she and Birdie Pie spent the afternoon.

Birdie Pie was most impressed by how quickly and efficiently Myrtle could field dress a deer. Field dressing involves removing the internal organs of the deer and must be done as soon as possible after the deer is killed to prevent bacteria from growing in the body. It is a gory and messy process requiring a very sharp knife and strong stomach. In addition to protecting the meat, it greatly lessens the weight of the animal if the hunter has to carry it any distance. Birdie Pie did not know where Myrtle learned the skill, but none of the ranch employees could best her.

Several times during the reunion, Charlie came up to me grinning and said, "This is one of the best ideas I ever had! I should have done it years ago."

A few weeks after the reunion, a letter arrived for Charlie from someone named Pauline Hasson who lived in Pasadena, California. Dian now gave me Three's personal correspondence because he never bothered opening his mail. As I read the letter, the writer said she hadn't heard from him since Myrtle's death. I showed Charlie the letter and asked who she was.

"I haven't thought about Pauline in years!" Charlie exclaimed. He told me Pauline worked for Myrtle during the 1930s, first as his nanny and later as Myrtle's personal maid, cook, and housekeeper. The letter deserved a response, and knowing Charlie would never get around to it, I wrote Pauline, introducing myself and bringing her up to date on Charlie and the ranch. That began a friendship that lasted until she died in 1998. We finally met in 1982 when I was in California visiting a friend. She had me over for dinner and filled in some of the gaps in Myrtle's history, but she also created new ones.

In the early 1930s Pauline responded to an ad for a nanny placed by Myrtle in the San Antonio newspaper. The interview took place in Myrtle and Walter's suite at the St. Anthony Hotel in San Antonio. Pauline said Myrtle was formal and polite in explaining her expectations and told Pauline she would live on the Y.O. and travel back and forth to San Antonio with them. Walter, or Mr. Walter as Pauline referred to him, came in during their interview. When Myrtle introduced them, Mr. Walter took off his hat, a courtesy white men seldom extended to Black women. After she was hired, Pauline was equally impressed with Myrtle's dressing down the hotel's manager when she learned the doorman made Pauline use the "colored" door when taking Charlie to Travis Park across the street. Pauline never knew how Myrtle learned of the incident, but she called the hotel's manager to her suite, and with Pauline present told him in no uncertain terms if her son and his nanny could not come and go through the hotel's front door then the Schreiners would move to another hotel. From then on, Pauline and Charlie used the hotel's front door.

Pauline was working for the Schreiners when Walter died in 1933. She remembered the night well. Myrtle was at the hospital with Walter, and Pauline and Charlie were at the St. Anthony Hotel. She did not remember

The author with Pauline Hasson, July 1994.

the time it occurred, but she and Charlie were awakened by a noise Pauline described as a door being shaken as if someone were trying to open it. She got up, checked all the doors, and called Myrtle's name but there was no response. Pauline went back to bed and was awakened early the next morning by Myrtle, who told her Walter had died. Pauline explained the door shaking as "Mr. Walter coming to tell Charlie goodbye."

In the late 1930s, Myrtle decided she, Pauline, and Charlie would go to California for a visit and Myrtle would drive them in her car. Pauline's most distinctive memories of the trip were places where the road was only boards laid over sand. If a driver should veer off the boards, they would be stuck and hold up the traffic behind them. Pauline said, "Miss Myrtle never once went off those boards."

Charlie had told me about living in Los Angeles as a child and attending school with Mickey Rooney, Judy Garland, and Shirley Temple. He did not know why Myrtle was there or remember how long they stayed. Pauline said she thought Myrtle moved there because she was dating "one of those movie stars." Pauline could not remember his name, but I wondered if it was the handsome mystery man in a photograph I found inscribed "To my little friend Charlie" with an illegible signature. While in California, they lived in a suite at the Beverly Hills Hotel and Myrtle gave parties that movie stars attended. When Myrtle returned to Texas, Pauline stayed in

California. Pauline said after experiencing the less restrictive laws and attitudes of California toward African Americans, she could never return to Jim Crow-era Texas. She had also met a gentleman who would become her husband.

In 1996 Pauline wrote to tell me her health was failing. I continued writing and sending her cards but seldom heard back. When I did not receive a Christmas card in 1997, I feared the worst. It was confirmed when a letter arrived from her niece telling me Pauline had died. I was touched that Pauline had included my name on the list of those she wanted notified of her death.

My two lobbying jobs turned out to be short-lived. The chairmen of the committees to which the bills were referred assured me the bills would "never see the light of day," political speak for never make it out of committee. I was once more left to my own resources to stay busy on the ranch. When Charlie attended the Las Vegas gun show, I decided to use the time to clean his office. Charlie's office made Einstein's, which I had seen in photographs, look orderly. There was a path leading from the door to his desk and the rest of the space was filled with stacks of books, files, quirts, spurs, bridles, antlers, and unopened mail dating back several decades. As I worked through the stacks, I found unopened Christmas cards, uncashed checks, and invitations to everything from balls to weddings to birthday parties. I also found an unopened letter revealing why Charlie did not let me accompany him to the previous year's gun show. Written in a feminine hand the previous February, it thanked Charlie for taking her to dinner to personally tell her he was recently married. She said she would remember him fondly. I wondered if he was renewing their relationship now.

Lupe left for his annual trip to Mexico in late January, and I was quickly overwhelmed by the impossibility of all that was required to keep up with the house and the yard while also playing hostess. My mother came to my rescue. She worked for the Houston Police Department and their offices were cleaned by jail trustees. One of them, Paul Ward, had made a favorable impression on everyone from the chief of police to my mother. Paul had been arrested numerous times, always for the same offenses of public intoxication, vagrancy, and loitering. He was being released the next week, and the chief would be happy to write a letter of recommendation. Charlie was aghast at the thought of a "criminal" cleaning our house. I replied that Paul came highly recommended by the Houston chief of police and I had already sent money for him to take the bus to Kerrville.

When I met Paul at the bus station and saw his wide, broken-toothed smile, I knew he was a threat to no one but himself. On the drive to the ranch, he told me he served in World War II, was many years divorced, and had children but lost track of them years before. He said he could do everything from gardening to minor repairs to cleaning. Within a week, Paul had the house in order and was working on the yard. Charlie was impressed and showed it by moving a trailer behind the house for Paul to live in. Paul was thrilled to be part of the Y.O., telling everyone he planned to work there the rest of his life. Two of the Y.O. dogs adopted Paul and accompanied him everywhere, riding in the back of his pickup and sleeping on the porch of his trailer.

In March of 1979, the Texas and Southwestern Cattle Raisers Association held its annual convention in Houston. I looked forward to it because this gave me an opportunity to visit friends and family in Houston. The convention was held at the downtown Marriott Hotel. As Charlie and I waited for the elevator for the welcome reception, I looked over the balcony and saw below a sea of Stetsons, mostly light gray with an occasional contrast of brown or black. We got on the elevator with Dolph Briscoe, the former governor, and his wife, Janey. The night before Charlie and I attended the musical *The Best Little Whorehouse in Texas*. I had seen it in New York and was certain Charlie would find it entertaining because he knew several of the characters depicted in it, e.g., the Texas governor and the sheriff who closed the whorehouse.

The musical was based on a true story. It was common knowledge in Texas there was a whorehouse called the Chicken Ranch outside of La Grange, Texas. Allegedly it was so named because during the 1930s, Depression-era patrons would sometimes pay with chickens. Because it caused no problems and the owner/madam supported local merchants and charities, law enforcement allowed its existence. In 1973, a Houston television reporter, Marvin Zindler, did an exposé on the Chicken Ranch. The story caused such an outcry that then-Governor Dolph Briscoe was forced to close it. After a few months it reopened, and once more Zindler resumed his quest to permanently shut it down, this time succeeding. The closing did not sit well with Jim Flournoy, the sheriff of Fayette County where the Chicken Ranch was located. He was angry Zindler had stuck his nose into affairs that fell under Flournoy's jurisdiction. When Zindler showed up in La Grange to do a follow-up story, fisticuffs ensued, with the sheriff attempting to pull Zindler out of his car through its window. In the melee, the sheriff grabbed Zindler's well-known and extravagantly coiffed mane of white hair, only to have it come off in his hand. Zindler managed to retrieve his toupee, but only after the sheriff vigorously stomped on it.

Texas journalist Larry King wrote a story about the closing of the Chicken Ranch that appeared in *Texas Monthly* and *Playboy* magazines. The article led to a book, which led to a Broadway musical and a movie. It was also the basis of the ZZ Top song "La Grange." When Charlie and I got on the elevator with former Governor Briscoe, Charlie turned to him and said, "Good to see you again, governor. We saw you last night in the whorehouse and you were great." We arrived at our destination and exited with no further explanation.

Whenever Charlie was on the ranch, there was a constant flow of guests through the house, and he invited them to join us for cocktails before and after dinner. I was finding that I did not care to spend my evenings listening to stories about hunting, guns, or the Schreiner family. I would play gracious hostess for before-dinner drinks but not after dinner. This became another point of contention between Charlie and me. The usual discussion went something like this.

Charlie: "Goddamn it, why won't you entertain our guests? You can charm the quills off a porcupine when you have a mind to. Is it asking too much?"

Me: "I don't care to waste my evenings listening to conversations I have no interest in. I'd rather be reading. I'm there for cocktails before dinner. I'm damned if I'm going to give up my entire evening."

The only time I spent alone with Charlie was when we were in bed, and usually we were asleep, though we still had passionate interludes.

One of the more interesting ranch and house tours I gave during this time was for a group of European journalists from the World Press Institute. Being journalists, they asked many questions about the Schreiners and the ranch and, to my surprise, about me. When they learned of my background, they expressed amazement at how I could go from being in politics to leading "this kind of life." I told them it was proving more difficult than I expected.

During this time Mary Helen and I developed a closer friendship when we decided to tackle cleaning the attics of the lodge and Chuckwagon. As we worked, we discussed our feelings of insecurity about living on the ranch. I was surprised when Mary Helen told me she feared Charlie Four would die from the stress of running the ranch. If he did, she was afraid his brothers would bring their mother, Audrey, to live on the ranch. Audrey had been asking her sons to do this for several years. When Charlie Three's

Walter Schreiner with Y.O. Linda, the Y.O.'s $20,000 heifer.

mother, Myrtle, died, Charlie was embroiled in divorcing Audrey. Myrtle was prescient enough to leave her portion of the ranch to her grandsons so that it would not become part of the divorce settlement. Thus, all or one of the sons could legitimately have his mother live on the ranch.

Mary Helen told me she and Four had the same disagreements as Three and I about the ranch taking precedence over their personal lives. After our conversation, I felt vindicated about having the fears I did about my future. It also made me wonder if Audrey, coming to the Y.O. as a young bride, felt those same insecurities.

One day Jim Nugent called and cryptically said, "When's the last time you counted your longhorns?"

"Why?"

"I have it on good authority. It's not unusual for longhorns out there to disappear never to be seen again. Especially calves."

"What are you talking about?"

"Just heed my advice and get an accounting of your cows within the next couple of weeks, especially those which recently calved. And, make it a regular practice to check on them."

Nugent's words struck terror in my heart because I knew my longhorns were valuable. Records had been set at a recent longhorn sale held by Red and Charlene McCombs. A Y.O. heifer named Linda sold for $20,000, the

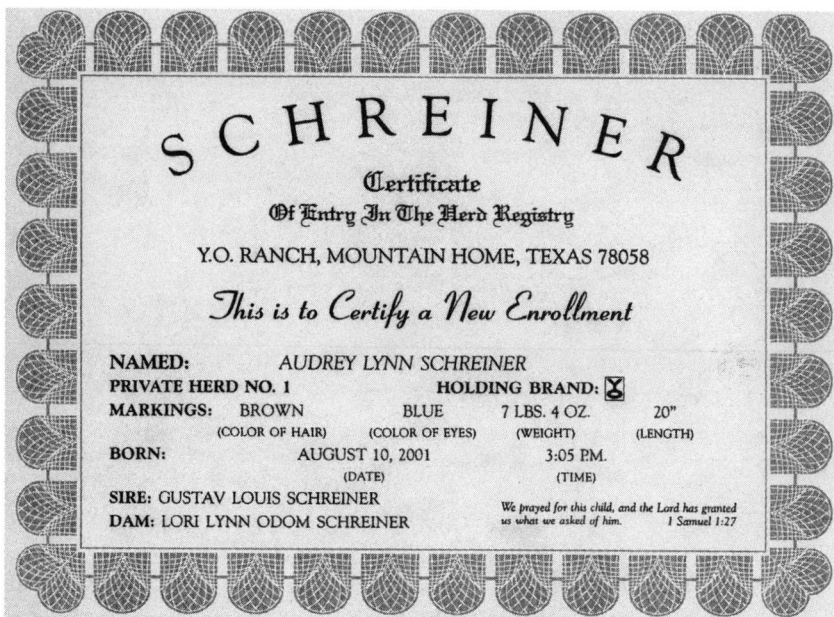

SCHREINER

Certificate
Of Entry In The Herd Registry

Y.O. RANCH, MOUNTAIN HOME, TEXAS 78058

This is to Certify a New Enrollment

NAMED: *AUDREY LYNN SCHREINER*
PRIVATE HERD NO. 1   HOLDING BRAND: ⊠
MARKINGS: BROWN   BLUE   7 LBS. 4 OZ.   20"
          (COLOR OF HAIR)   (COLOR OF EYES)   (WEIGHT)   (LENGTH)
BORN: AUGUST 10, 2001   3:05 P.M.
              (DATE)   (TIME)
SIRE: GUSTAV LOUIS SCHREINER
DAM: LORI LYNN ODOM SCHREINER   *We prayed for this child, and the Lord has granted*
                                        us what we asked of him.   *1 Samuel 1:27*

The birth announcement for Audrey Schreiner, daughter of Lori and Gus Schreiner.

highest price ever paid for a longhorn heifer. Charlie's second son, Walter, who was in charge of the Y.O.'s longhorns, was dating a woman named Linda at the time. Mary Helen and I suspected the heifer was named for her. I commented to Mary Helen that songwriters and poets wrote songs and poems to their lovers, but cowboys named livestock for them.

Another example of juxtaposing human and animal characteristics is the birth announcement that Charlie Three's third son, Gus, and his wife, Lori, sent for their first child.

The average price per cow at a Y.O. sale was $3,442, setting a record for an average price. Between calving and buying cows at sales, the ten cows Charlie originally gave me had grown to forty, with many due to calve soon. Based on the average from the McCombs' sale, my longhorns were dollars on the hoof that, given the fractious relationship between Charlie and me, could suddenly disappear.

CHAPTER 23

"There seems to be a kind of order in the universe,

in the movement of the stars and the turning of the earth and the

changing of the seasons, and even in the cycle of human life. But

human life itself is almost pure chaos."

KATHERINE ANNE PORTER

Long Hard Times

IN MAY, THE Y.O. HOSTED the annual meeting of the South Texas Longhorn Association, one of the regional associations of the national association founded by Charlie. There was a director position open on its board and when the floor was opened for nominations, I heard my name. I was stunned but also proud to be so honored. Then I heard another motion to unanimously elect me. The motion carried and I was blushing as I accepted. When the meeting adjourned, I tried to find Charlie, but he had disappeared. The sale would start soon, and because I was assisting Walter in handing out awards, I drove to the sale tent. The sale went well, and I was thrilled when one of my heifers sold to Red McCombs. I went back to the house to change for the after-sale party and dinner. Charlie arrived a few minutes later.

"Aren't you going to congratulate the first woman director?" I asked, beaming.

He looked at me with a fierce gaze, put his face close to mine, and spat out, "That position should have gone to one of my sons, not to my wife! You've only owned longhorns a little over a year. You don't deserve an honor like that. I want you to resign and recommend Walter or Charlie Four replace you."

I could smell the alcohol on his breath and see his face was flushed, both indicators of having drunk too much. I should have walked away because I knew no good would come from replying. But, like Alice in Wonderland, I can give myself good advice but not take it. Thus I replied,

"You son of a bitch! I will do no such thing. I was the one they nominated and elected. Fuck you, Charlie, and the horse you rode in on and all the horses behind it." In my journal I wrote, "We fought viciously; III [Three] drunk, mean, cruel." I retreated to my dressing room and locked the door. I had to regain my composure if I was going to play the gracious hostess that evening. I tried breathing deeply to no effect. Once I heard Charlie stomping down the stairs, I went to the upstairs bar and mixed what was becoming my drink of choice, gin on the rocks.

Leaving the house, I spied Three's oxcart in my rearview mirror and my anger surged again. I put my car in reverse and hit the accelerator. To my great surprise, when I hit the oxcart it did not budge. I tried again. The oxcart remained in place. After five attempts, all I had to show for my efforts was a dent in my trunk, but ramming the cart helped assuage my anger. Three made a point of avoiding me all evening and did not come back to the house that night. The next day he apologized and left the ranch for a week.

When he returned, Three asked if I knew how his oxcart became tilted. I took full credit, bracing myself for his anger. Instead he broke into laugher. "Did you really think your car could turn over a one hundred-year-old oxcart? That cart was built to last forever. You could run into it all day and never hurt it. Is that why your car has a dent in the trunk? I should have been able to figure that out."

I kept the dent in my trunk for several years and whenever someone asked about it, I told the story. Some years later, I had my car repainted. When I picked it up, the manager told me I must have forgotten to tell him to repair the dent, so he did it for no charge. He was so proud of his customer service, I did not have the heart to tell him that dent had a special place in my heart.

In early June, Mary Helen announced she was pregnant again. The baby was due in December or January. Three was delighted at the prospect of a centennial baby, telling Mary Helen to keep her legs crossed so the baby would not be born until January. He told me he hoped the baby would be born on January 6, his birthday. It didn't surprise me that once more Charlie assumed the baby would be a boy. I refrained from making a bet regarding its sex.

Three announced he was going to San Angelo and Dallas and did not know when he would return. I was tired of staying at the ranch alone and in no mood to go to Austin, since wherever I went I was overcome with sorrow remembering having gone there with Charlie. When I mentioned this to Mary Helen, she offered me the use of her family's condominium at Padre Island, which I gladly accepted. Ms. and I spent the next five days there. Albert Schweitzer said, "There are two means of refuge from the miseries of life: music and cats." If you don't have music, a cat suffices, though Ms. made it clear she would have preferred to stay at the ranch.

Being away from the ranch, I was able to think more clearly about the events of the past year. I had been seeing a marriage counselor by myself. Charlie grudgingly attended the first session and announced, "I am fifty-two years old. I don't hate my mother or father or grandfather or any of my relatives. I like myself just the way I am and I'm not going to change." He put on his battered hat and left, never to return.

I now realized my childhood dream of living on a ranch did not fit the reality or expectations for the woman I had become. I wanted to achieve success based on my capabilities and not because of my last name. I had envisioned a role on the ranch that would use my intelligence and skills. Charlie wanted a traditional wife, and it wasn't me. I needed to move on. Returning to the ranch, I went to the Chuckwagon to get my mail. Pulling into the parking lot, I saw Three lowering the Y.O. flag to half-staff. "Oh no," I thought. "There's been an accident." I pulled up beside the flagpole and asked, "Who died?"

"John Wayne," Three replied.

"Thank goodness. I was afraid it was someone at the ranch." Three scowled at me and walked into the Chuckwagon. I followed him into his office and closed the door. "We need to talk," I said. Before he could find an excuse not to, I said, "The past week has given me a chance to think. I was foolish hoping we could make our marriage work. Neither of us is going to change or accept the other for what we are. I'm ready to talk about a divorce so I can move on with my life."

Charlie was shocked. "That's the last thing I expected to hear from you."

"I'll start looking for a place in Austin so I can move as soon as possible."

"I'm not going to throw you out of the house. Take your time. Stay as long as you want."

"Where will I sleep?"

"In our bedroom, of course. Just because we're getting a divorce doesn't mean we can't still be friends." Charlie grinned. "Once we're divorced, you'll be free to do whatever you please, and I won't have to worry about your actions or lack of them as my wife. I know you don't believe it, but I do want to remain your friend."

"What you want is to keep bedding me," I replied and flounced from his office.

Through all of this, Charlie and I continued going places together and occasionally sleeping together. Charlie knew that many of the events he attended would interest me, and he enjoyed baffling people as he squired me around, which is how we came to attend the US Open Polo Championship in San Antonio. Polo is not a sport generally associated with Texas, but it has been played in the state since at least the early 1870s. That was when Capt. Glynn Tourquant, a former officer in the British Coldstream Guards, started the Texas Polo Club in San Antonio.

The championship game was being held at the recently opened Retama Polo Club built by Texas oilman Stephen Gose, who was one of the players for the Retama team. It was the largest polo center in the world with sixteen polo fields and four hundred horse stalls covering six hundred acres. When we arrived at the event, I was delighted to see Kerry McCan, whom I met when I attended my first Cattle Raisers Association event with Charlie. When Kerry discovered this was my first polo match, he led me to a table, ordered drinks, and explained the game to me. Kerry began playing polo while attending Yale and continued playing until his body and his wife told him it was time to quit. He said it was the most exhilarating sport he ever played or watched. Each team has four players, and the game is divided into four seven-minute chukkers. The players use several horses in the course of the match, which is one of the reasons the sport is called a "rich man's game." Most players have at least six ponies. The field is 160 yards wide and three football fields long. There is a goal at each end and the players use a mallet to strike a small plastic ball down the field and through the goal to score.

Kerry told me that Gose had managed to recruit Guillermo Gracida Jr., from Mexico, for the Retama team. Gracida held numerous polo records and could be a deciding factor for the Retama team. He would go on to be selected as "Player of the Centennial Era" in 1990 and inducted into the National Polo Hall of Fame in 1997, a unique honor for an active player. As soon as the game started, the skill of the horses and players enthralled me. I could not imagine staying on a galloping horse while hitting a small ball and being pursued by other players. It was one of the most thrilling sports I have ever seen, made better by the Retama Club winning 6–5.

I saw many of those attending the match several weeks later when Charlie and I attended the Texas and Southwestern Cattle Raisers Association directors' meeting in Corpus Christi. One of the events was a bus tour of the King Ranch. As we drove around, Charlie pointed to a pump jack and said, "None of this would be possible if it weren't for that. After Captain King's wife, Henrietta, died in the 1920s, they were hit with $3 million in estate taxes. They were about to go under when what was then Humble Oil came calling offering oil and gas leases. Bob Kleberg was running the ranch then and he got Humble to give him a loan that took care of the taxes. The loan was easily repaid once oil was discovered."

"Any chance of oil being found on the Y.O.?" I asked.

"Unfortunately, no. We've had some leases but nothing ever comes of them. I try not to think of how much easier our lives would be if the ranch had oil and running water."

Driving back to the Y.O., Charlie asked what I planned to do about my longhorns.

"I really hadn't thought about it."

"The ranch will be glad to buy them from you. How many do you have now?"

"With the latest calf crop it should be around sixty."

"Let me talk to Walter and see what he thinks is a fair offer."

A caustic comment came to mind, but I kept the safety on my tongue. The next day, Charlie told me the Y.O. would pay $30,000 for all of my longhorns. "You're kidding!" I exclaimed.

"It's pure profit for you. You've paid no fees for grazing or breeding."

"Charlie, do you think I'm stupid? I've been to the sales. I know what cows are selling for. Even if they sold at the lowest sale average, it would be double your offer."

"And, you'd have to pay to haul them to the sale and a consignment fee."

"Be that as it may, I respectfully decline your offer."

"Then the ranch will start charging you a monthly grazing fee."

"Our prenup specifically says I can keep them on the Y.O. for up to three years after we divorce. You've already reneged on our contract once so it wouldn't surprise me if you did it again, but I will fight you in court over it. I will get them off the ranch as soon as I can, but until then I'm not paying a cent."

We drove the rest of the way in silence, each of us percolating at a low boil. My birthday was the next week. I did not want to spend it at the ranch or with Three and evidently he felt the same because he told me he planned to ignore it just to prove how little he cared for me. If he thought I was going to be upset, he was wrong. I knew exactly where I would go to celebrate and with whom I would share my birthday cake and my bed.

CHAPTER 24

"If you made a list of reasons why any couple got married,

and another list of the reasons for their divorce,

you'd have a hell of a lot of overlapping."

MIGNON MCLAUGHLIN

Difficult Days and Turbulent Nights

A NEW HOTEL, THE PLAZA NACIONAL, opened in downtown San Antonio in the spring of 1979. Charlie and I attended the opening, which included spending the night at the hotel for a ridiculously low price. I was immediately charmed by its low-key elegance, and I liked that it didn't recall my painful memories of Charlie and the Menger. I made a reservation and then called my former lover, John M., to see if he was available to help celebrate my birthday. John, ever the smart-ass, replied, "I assume your husband won't be joining us, Mrs. Schreiner." John arrived Friday afternoon with several bottles of champagne and took me to dinner at a favorite San Antonio restaurant.

John and I met during the 1977 legislative session when he worked as an aide for one of the representatives. We became lovers and remained so until Charlie arrived on the scene. John was the polar opposite of Charlie in every way. John was as far to the left politically as Charlie was to the right. During the sixties and seventies, John marched in many of the protests against the Vietnam War and for civil rights and spent several nights in jail. John had attended Charlie's and my wedding reception and the birthday party I gave myself at the ranch the previous year. Whenever I visited Austin, we would have lunch or dinner. He delighted in giving me a hard time about my life with Charlie and its contradiction to my liberal views. It was John who warned me the Y.O. would be a "fifty thousand-acre high-fenced cage," a prophecy that had come true.

When I moved to the Y.O., John told me if I did not already do so, I should keep a journal. Throughout my life I have been a sporadic journal keeper, but I took his advice to heart, recording daily activities and thoughts. I also kept a file with notes on conversations I heard and information shared with me about subjects related to ranching. Both were invaluable resources for this memoir. One time when I was making a journal entry, Charlie asked, "What are you doing? You're always writing something down."

"Writing in my journal."

"Why?"

"I'm having lots of interesting experiences. Someday I may write a book." Throughout the last year of our marriage, whenever Charlie saw me writing he would say, "I know how you're going to get even. With your damn book! What are you going to call it?"

"Eight Miles to the Front Gate."

"Damn good title!" he said.

When I called the ranch on Monday to see if I had any messages, Button told me Nugent wanted me to call him as soon as possible. When I did, he told me Charlie had called saying he was filing for divorce and would like Nugent to meet with us to work out a settlement. In typical Nugent fashion, he did not ask if I was available but told me to be at his office in Austin on Friday morning. I decided to go back to the ranch, and to my surprise, Charlie showed up shortly after I arrived. He was in a good mood and said we might as well ride to Austin together on Thursday, which we did, spending the night at Charlie's hotel of choice in Austin, the historic Driskill.

The next morning, we'd hardly sat down in Nugent's office before he began lecturing us on how imprudent our divorce was. Nugent said he had spoken with Charlie's attorney, and they agreed if Charlie "blew it" with me, he would probably never succeed at marriage. Nugent proposed we separate for three months and try to work things out. I retorted if we did, Charlie would start seeing other women, if he hadn't already done so. Charlie countered if I could settle down and be happy being his wife everything would be fine. I rebutted being his wife provided no intellectual stimulation.

Nugent stood up, glared at us, and said, "Put away your daggers. It seems I was wrong, and this isn't going to work, so let's get down to business. When was the last time you had marital relations? We'll use it as the date of separation."

Charlie looked down at his hands. I looked out the window.

"Well?" Nugent asked.

"Charlie?" I said.

Charlie, looking sheepish, stuttered, "Last night."

"Good God Almighty!" Nugent exclaimed. "Are you telling me you're having sex but want a divorce? That's the craziest thing I've ever heard. I'm not discussing this anymore. Get the hell out. Both of you."

Charlie and I sheepishly left Nugent's office.

We returned to the ranch and within twenty-four hours Charlie left again with no word of when he would return. At the time, I assumed Charlie Four or other ranch employees may have known his whereabouts but would learn they did not. That night I was lying in bed reading when the phone rang. It was almost midnight, and I assumed it was Charlie. Instead, a strange male voice said, "Is this Mrs. Charles Schreiner III?" I confirmed it was, and the voice identified himself as a Texas Ranger who had some papers for me.

"What kind of papers?"

There was a long silence. "Divorce papers. I'm sorry, ma'am. I thought you were expecting these. Guess I was misinformed."

I was too shocked to reply. The Ranger said he was thirty minutes away from the Y.O. and asked whether he should he come to the house or meet me at the front gate.

"I'll meet you at the front gate."

He hung up, and I stood staring into space. Why hadn't Charlie told me rather than surprise me? I wanted to call Nugent, but it was too late. I had to emotionally pull myself together, dress, and drive to the front gate. I stopped in the kitchen and pulled a six pack of beer from the refrigerator. Thankfully drinking and driving was allowed on the ranch. I consumed two beers driving the eight miles and got there before the Ranger arrived. I parked my car, opened the front gate, and sat on the porch of the Game Warden's Cabin awaiting his arrival. As I waited, I thought about the last time a Texas Ranger crossed my path when Bevo was stolen by Texas A&M. Most people never even meet a Texas Ranger much less have two life events bringing them face-to-face with one. I was halfway through my third beer when I heard a motor and saw headlights piercing the darkness. I walked out to the road and motioned for the driver to park next to my car.

The Ranger got out and introduced himself. I asked if he would like a beer.

"Because I'm not on duty but doing this as a personal favor, I think I would," he answered.

It was a moonless night, and we were awed by the number of stars. We walked away from the Game Warden's Cabin and into the road trying to find constellations and planets. Finally, the Ranger said he best do what he came for, went to his car, and returned with the divorce papers. He handed them to me, and I asked if he would like another beer. He declined, saying it had been a pleasure meeting me, even under such circumstances.

I drank another beer and drove slowly back to the house. I wondered how many times I'd driven this road during the past two years, getting out to open and close the front gate in rain, blistering sun, gusting north winds, and swirls of dust? How many people and animals had traveled this road? Captain Schreiner, Charlie's parents, astronauts, politicians, writers, actors, artists, longhorns, horseback cowboys, the first exotic animals to arrive on the ranch, and most recently the giraffes. I remembered the first time I drove the road with Charlie and my awe at seeing the animals and ranch for the first time. In some ways it was hard to believe all I had experienced during the last two years.

I should not have been surprised about Charlie filing for divorce. Once he made up his mind to do something, he did not vacillate. But he should have had the courtesy to tell me he had done so or ask me if I preferred to be the one to file. It would have been the gentlemanly thing to do. The next morning, I called Nugent, told him what had happened, and asked his recommendation for an attorney. "You don't need to spend money on an attorney," he said. "You can represent yourself. I'll guide you through it. When are you moving off the ranch?"

"As soon as I can find a place in Austin. Three told me I can stay as long as I want, but I'd prefer not to."

"I agree. Have you started looking?"

"No, and I won't be able to for several weeks because I have other obligations. The annual longhorn convention is in Colorado Springs next week. As a regional director, I need to attend. Charlie and I are driving there together."

"Please don't tell me you're going to share a room."

"I think so."

Nugent snorted. "This is the most outrageous divorce I've ever been involved in. Call me when you get back to the ranch." He hung up.

There was a cocktail party the first night of the convention. I did not realize how much Charlie had to drink until we returned to our room. One positive aspect of Three's drinking was he would tell me things he never would when sober. We were no sooner in the room than he said, "I've come to the conclusion you're just too damned smart for me. There's just one man I know who's smart enough to take you on."

"Who would that be?"

"James E. Nugent."

"Mr. Nugent?! Are you crazy?"

"I'm going to talk to him about it."

"You're drunk, Charlie. Take off your boots and go to sleep."

"Not until you promise me something."

"What's that?"

"That you won't kill me or make the divorce so unpleasant it affects my health." After his heart attack several years before, Charlie lived in fear of another but did little to prevent it with exercise and diet.

"Why would you think such a thing? Are you thinking of harming me?"

"No, but I have a feeling you've thought about harming me."

It was true. After a particularly savage fight, I contemplated blowing out Charlie's brains. I knew where he kept a loaded pistol and envisioned getting it, holding it to his head as he slept, and pulling the trigger. As these thoughts went through my mind, I understood why he feared for his life when he and Audrey broke up. If he could drive me to contemplate killing him after a year and a half of marriage, I could imagine the wrath he aroused in Audrey after twenty years.

"You have nothing to fear from me, Charlie," I said. "I'm not going to ruin my life by killing you."

"Well, I'm glad to hear that. If that's the case, then after we're divorced I'd like to arrange for your services." With that he passed out.

I sat there trying to make sense of his drunken ramblings and decided to disregard everything he said.

At his attorney's insistence, when we returned from the convention, Charlie moved down to one of the cabins. He put a sign on the door saying, "Three's Dog House." Rusty contributed a drawing of a woebegone dog with "CSIII" on its collar. During this time, I often thought of the lines from a favorite childhood poem, "The Gingham Dog and the Calico Cat," by Eugene Field: "But the truth about the cat and pup, is this: They ate each other up!" Charlie and I seemed intent on doing just that.

The next time I saw Nugent I told him of Charlie's comments about having some type of arrangement after we divorced. "The sooner you get out of there the better for you and Charlie," Nugent said. "I'm going to tell you something I've thought for some time. That ranch isn't going to make it into the next generation. Charlie's attorney and I have tried for years to get him to incorporate the ranch, but Charlie doesn't like being reminded he's going to die or being concerned about what happens once he's gone. He's still paying off the estate taxes from his mother's death, and his boys will be doing the same when he dies if he doesn't get off his duff and do something to prevent it. He's in hock up to his nose hairs to Schreiner Bank and the Federal Land Bank." Nugent shook his head again. "Find a place in Austin and get the hell out of there as soon as possible. Do not let him convince you otherwise."

That evening when I walked into the Chuckwagon, Bertie pulled me aside to tell me Mrs. Lyndon Johnson, a.k.a. Lady Bird, would be visiting the ranch the next day. Mrs. Johnson had never been to the Y.O., even though by Texas standards, the LBJ Ranch was a close neighbor being only sixty miles away. She would arrive at noon for lunch, and then Three would give her a tour. Had Charlie deliberately not told me? He knew the high regard I had for Mrs. Johnson and that I would not want to miss the opportunity to spend an afternoon with her. "I'll fix him," I thought.

When I walked into the Chuckwagon at eleven-thirty the next morning, the look on Three's face was a combination of surprise and disappointment. "Don't worry," I said. "I'll behave. I assume you will do the same."

Mrs. Johnson arrived promptly at eleven thirty with a friend, her grandson, Lyn Nugent, one of his friends, and two Secret Service agents. Charlie welcomed them and introduced me. Then Charlie introduced her to Bertie, whose beans Mrs. Johnson would rave about whenever I saw her in the future. After a leisurely lunch, we left on a ranch tour in Charlie's new Suburban. Because the Suburban was new, his driving was more circumspect than when he was driving the Bronco; however, he could not restrain his mischievous nature and chased Junior, the ostrich, across the pasture to demonstrate to the former first lady that Junior could run forty-five miles an hour. Lyn Nugent and the Secret Service agents enjoyed the pursuit more than Mrs. Johnson, who braced herself against the door and dashboard. The Secret Service agents exchanged looks of amusement at Mrs. Johnson's discomfort.

We drove into the pasture where the longhorn steers were, but none were in sight. Charlie took a sack of range cubes from the back of the Suburban and began calling them. In a few minutes they came trotting over a

A letter received
from Lady Bird
Johnson after
her visit to the
Y.O. Ranch.

September 11, 1979   *Stonewall, Texas*

Dear Mr. and Mrs. Schreiner, ~~Charlie and Norma~~

Saturday still lingers dreamlike in my mind! My
visit to your Ranch was an experience I adored,
as did my friend, Olga Bredt, and my grandson, Lyn,
and his friend.

The three giraffes - running with such fluid grace -
were sheer poetry -- walking proudly thousands of
miles from their natural homeland, eating the tops
of the hackberry trees (I like their choice, but
soon you'll have to plant more unless they switch
to mesquite!). The oryx, elands, and especially
the combative ostrich also dance across my memory
when I think of our very special tour.

Charlie, your house is a true museum with your
marvelous collection of artifacts of the old west,
the log ranch houses -- the whole setup. I
particularly enjoyed the extraordinarily spectacular
"great hall" filled with the dramatic range of
impressive trophies. Lunch was all my favorite
fare -- as anybody could tell!

It was a fascinating day in substance and spirit --
the best part of which was seeing you once more,
meeting you - Norma - your four handsome sons and
their ladies, and of course, your granddaughter,
Tiffany. I wonder if she knows what a queen she is!

With my deepfelt gratitude and warmest wishes to you
and your family,

Sincerely,

Lady Bird Johnson

hill. Charlie invited Lyn and his friend to help feed them, which delighted
the boys. The Secret Service agents took their turn as well, thoroughly
enjoying the moment. Mrs. Johnson, her friend, and I observed from the
car. As we watched, I answered Mrs. Johnson's questions about the longhorns. Our next stop was Charlie's house where, to my surprise, Charlie
deferred to me to give the tour saying, "Norma gets all the credit for the
inside of the house. I only designed it." Throughout the tour I would

ask Charlie to explain the architectural pieces he incorporated into the design. Charlie gave the tour of his gun room, which impressed the Secret Service agents, especially the Gatling gun. Mrs. Johnson sent us the most eloquent and sincere thank you note I have ever received.

After the former first lady and her entourage left, Charlie and I sat in the living room debriefing her visit, laughing and complimenting each other on our roles. He told me he wanted to help me any way he could and wanted to remain friends. For the first time in months, we were able to talk to one another rationally. We ended the evening in bed. As Three held me he said, "Now that things are better between us, it's going to be hard to go through with the divorce." I pretended to be asleep. Over the previous months, I'd seen the unpredictability of Charlie's moods and how quickly he could change his mind.

Charlie wanted a wife but only on his terms. He loved his sons, but in the time we were together I never heard him say "I love you" to them, or they to him. He wanted grandchildren but had little to do with Tiffany. He built his dream house on the land he loved but spent little time there. He pursued guns, trophy animals, Western art, and women with dogged fervor but took little pleasure in them once acquired. Nugent's words came back to me, "For Charlie, the thrill is in the hunt." Now I understood. His ranch was an accumulation of things he had pursued and acquired. Yet none of his possessions brought him permanent happiness, nor had any of his wives. I'd been a fool to think it would be different with me.

CHAPTER 25

"I wonder among all the tangles of this mortal coil, which one contains tighter knots to undo, and consequently suggests more tugging, and pain, and diversified elements of misery than the marriage tie."

EDITH WHARTON

The Worst of Times

THE OCTOBER 1979 ISSUE of *Austin Homes and Gardens* featured the ranch and Charlie's house as its cover story. Kay Howard, who helped decorate the house, was responsible for this. She and her photographer boyfriend, Ron Dorsey, were at the ranch several times during the spring taking photographs of the house and ranch. Ron's photographs of the house captured its diversity and uniqueness. When Kay wrote the article, she had no idea of the tenuous nature of our marriage, thus it read as if we were the picture of bliss. We received phone calls and letters from many friends, relatives, and previous visitors to the ranch complimenting the article.

When Charlie and I returned to the ranch from the annual longhorn sale in Lawton, Oklahoma, Paul, our housekeeper, told me he had not seen Ms. in two days. My sixth sense, which seldom failed me, was telling me something had happened to her. I try not to anthropomorphize animals, but they are capable of sensing human emotions and understanding some words. After I was served with the divorce papers, I told Ms. we would soon leave the ranch. Was this her way of telling me she was staying? I spent the next week walking the airstrip and the road running beside the house calling her. As the days passed, I tried to accept she was gone but continued hoping she would stroll in with feline nonchalance. It was Ms. who kept me going as my relationship with Charlie deteriorated. More than once suicide crossed my mind, but when it did, my concern over what would happen to Ms. stopped me. I could not leave her fate to Charlie.

As I agonized over Ms., I learned one of my calves was missing. I asked Three about it and he said Walter told him it was probably dead. "A likely story," I thought. I decided to call Jimmy De Lesdernier (Jimmy Dee), the inspector for the Texas and Southwestern Cattle Raisers Association. I told Jimmy Dee about the missing calf and that I would like him to investigate. Given Nugent's previous warning about keeping up with my longhorns, I wanted to be on record in the event others went missing. Jimmy Dee said he would come out the next day.

When Jimmy Dee walked into the Chuckwagon at lunch, Charlie asked, "What are you doing here?"

"Well, pard [one of Jimmy's nicknames for Three], I'm here to investigate a missing calf."

"What?" Three said. "I'm not aware any of our calves are missing."

"It's one of Miss Norma's."

Three's face turned red. He threw his napkin on his plate, took Jimmy Dee by the arm, and steered him into the office area. A few minutes later, Jimmy Dee came out and told me Three was calling a meeting in his gun room at one o'clock. I invited Jimmy Dee to have lunch with us, which he did. Promptly at one o'clock Jimmy Dee, Three, Walter, and I assembled in the gun room. I had two guests at the ranch, and Three insisted they attend because he didn't want them thinking he was a cattle thief. Jimmy Dee began by asking Three and Walter about my missing calf. Before Walter could answer, Three went into a rant about the audacity of my calling him a cattle thief, impugning his good name and the reputation of the Y.O. Walter said it was not unusual for a calf to become ill and die with no trace ever being found. Jimmy Dee concluded by telling Three to separate out my cows and calves and move them into a separate, smaller pasture close to headquarters so I could keep track of them. Jimmy Dee told me to do a weekly check and let him know if others went missing.

I walked Jimmy Dee to his truck and thanked him. He said, "I understand your cat has gone missing too. I wish there was something I could do to help find her. If it's any consolation, Three told me he hated that it happened now because he knows how much she meant to you." My eyes filled with tears and I wondered, "Why can't Three say those words to me?"

Several days later, I was sitting on the patio overlooking Deer Park and smelled the stench of a decaying animal. I followed my nose, looked over the fence, and saw Ms.'s decomposing body. It was almost dark, so I would have to wait until morning to retrieve her. I spent the night pacing, crying, and trying to decide what I wanted to leave with her body. In the past I buried my pets with a favorite toy, but this time I wanted something that would remain with her and become part of the ranch just as she would.

When Paul arrived the next morning, I was waiting in front of the house. Carefully we made our way through agarita, cactus, and rocks to where Ms. was lying. I looked for clues about what caused her death, but there were none. Paul scooped up her body and put it in the box we brought. We took her back to the house and Paul dug her grave. As I placed her in it, I took my Y.O. ring, kissed it, and placed it between her paws. Walking away from the grave, I heard a guttural meow, the sound Ms. made when she was bringing me her latest kill. Caught off guard I turned, expecting to see her. "She's telling me this is where she wants to be," I thought, "and adding her voice to those I've heard in the pastures."

One of the few friends I told about burying my ring with Ms. was my first husband, R. C. Ever after, when one of my cats died, he would ask, "Did they rate having a diamond ring buried with them?"

In mid-October Charlie received the first draft of the history of the Y.O., which he'd commissioned as part of the Y.O.'s centennial. Joe Frantz, a noted history professor at the University of Texas, was writing it. Charlie handed it to me saying he wanted me to be the first to read it. I found it very sympathetic to Three's first wife, Audrey, with many quotes from her. This was ironic since Frantz had recently left his wife of forty years and was rumored to be having an affair with his graduate assistant. I returned the draft to Charlie and said, "I'll reserve comment until you read it." When he finished it, he was madder than a wet hen and called Frantz asking for a rewrite. Frantz refused, saying to do so impugned his integrity as a historian and writer. Charlie told Frantz he would find someone else to do the book. With the centennial occurring in mid-April, it was going to be a short deadline to get it written and published.

I don't know how Charlie found Neal Barrett Jr. to replace Frantz. Barrett had written numerous books in the genres of fantasy, science fiction, mystery, and historical fiction. When Barrett interviewed me, all of my comments were laudatory, and most are quoted in the book, *Long Days and Short Nights: A Century of Texas Ranching on the YO 1880–1980*. The closest I came to being negative was when Barrett asked me what faults Charlie had. My answer was, "Charlie has a pretty traditional way of showing his emotions—or not showing them. Sometimes he gets uncomfortable when people get too emotional around him." This was the epitome of understatement.

Charlie left the ranch in mid-November for his annual mule deer hunt in New Mexico. He would be gone for Thanksgiving, so I invited my friend Kathy, her two daughters, and my occasional lover, John M., to the ranch. I made sure John had his own room and presumed he would be seen as Kathy's date. After lunch, I took my guests on a tour of the ranch. For supper, I served leftovers at Three's house. I tried to convince John to spend the night with me, but fearing Charlie would make an unannounced entrance, John returned to his room.

Throughout December Charlie bought back several items he had given me. I was more than happy to sell him my half of the horseshoe collection, several guns, and the saddle I was riding when my horse wreck occurred. When he made an offer for the eagle, I said, "Where I go, so goes my eagle." The eagle and I would finally part company in 2019, but it remained in the Schreiner family. Gus, Charlie's third son, purchased it from me. One of the things Charlie insisted on doing whenever he gave me something was to give me a handwritten receipt for it on a page from a yellow legal pad. When he first started doing this, I thought it unnecessary, but now I was glad. He also tried to buy the title of my book, *Eight Miles from the Front Gate*. I refused but feared he would use it anyway. To his credit, he did not.

Reaching an agreement on grazing rights for my longhorns was the major impediment to finalizing our divorce. Charlie was unwavering in his refusal to abide by the terms of our prenup and give me grazing rights. Nugent told me to hang tough on this point. One other contentious point was that I wanted a photograph of me in the centennial book. I was the one who assembled most of the photographs for the book and to whom Neal Barrett, the author, often turned when he had questions about chronology, family members, or where to go for other information. Charlie said my name would appear in the acknowledgements and that was enough. "The only wife who will have her photograph in the book is Audrey because she's the mother of my children. It's the same reason I named a pasture for her." This statement confirmed what I suspected but never said. For a female of any species to earn Charlie's respect, she had to breed.

Each of us acted equally bad during this time. There were many skirmishes, major battles, and trench warfare. I cringe recalling when Three gave me his attorney's latest draft of the settlement in the parking lot of the Headliners Club in Austin. I tore it up and drove off, throwing its scraps out the window. Three retaliated by having me deposed. His attorney and a court reporter came to the house, and I spent two hours answering each question as Nugent had instructed, saying, "I refuse to answer without my attorney present." After the deposition was over, Three's attorney asked if I would give him and the court reporter a tour of the house. I made the transition from defiant plaintiff to gracious tour guide and obliged.

I've often been told I was a great actress, and never was it truer than during this time. I modeled my behavior on one of my role models, Jacqueline Kennedy Onassis, who maintained her stoic privacy throughout her marriages to two difficult men. I knew from my parents' bitter divorce that there are two sides to most stories, and people do not like to take sides. My most difficult times were when those who knew Charlie and I were divorcing would tell me how much they regretted things not working out, or when they would ask me to stay in touch with them after I left the ranch. These gestures of kindness touched me so deeply all I could do was nod in affirmation. If I spoke, I would have started sobbing.

No one knows better than me what a strong-willed, obstinate, difficult, and insufferable person I can be. Sometimes I even dislike me. Being obsequious, which I equate with manipulative, is not among my traits. My father was the first man to reprove me for being difficult. When I misbehaved, he scolded me with the words of HENRY WADSWORTH LONGFELLOW:

> There was a little girl,
> Who had a little curl,
> Right in the middle of her forehead.
> When she was good,
> She was very good indeed,
> But when she was bad she was horrid.

I have always been attracted to alpha males with whom I lock horns as each of us tries to control the other. A previous lover delights in telling me he understands why men want to marry me, and, though he still loves me, he is glad he resisted. Another man said I was best viewed from afar. My current partner says I am the most difficult woman he has ever been involved with. Marilyn Monroe said, "I'm selfish, impatient, and a little insecure. I make mistakes. I am out of control and at times hard to handle.

But if you can't handle me at my worst, then you sure as hell don't deserve me at my best." I'll let that stand as my rebuttal.

Recounting the events of 1979, I have not acknowledged the emotional toll they took on me. Whenever Charlie left with no goodbye or indication when he would return, I spent the day in bed, incapacitated by sorrow and depression. I reproached myself for not putting the time to better use but lacked the physical and mental energy to do so. During this time, I recorded despair and anger on almost every page of my journal. The entry for October 9, 1979, is an indication of my mental state, "Cried, planted crocus at Ms.'s grave, wrote letters and cried some more. It has been a bad day for keeping my composure, yet I've accomplished a good bit. I am so sad, sometimes, I do not think I will live through it." If you added together all the times in my life I have cried, they would pale in comparison to how often I cried during 1979. I came to a new understanding of what heartache means, because my heart would literally ache as I sobbed remembering the fun and laughter Charlie and I shared in the early days of our relationship. Several people commented on how unhappy I looked when I let my guard down. I now recognize and have seen this look on other women trapped in difficult marriages.

My anguish came from disappointment that the idealized life and relationship I envisioned with Charlie never materialized. I chided myself for thinking I would be the perfect wife for him. How could I have been so arrogant and ignorant of my own needs to achieve happiness? I assumed Charlie would give me an active role on the ranch, but that would never occur, and I was foolish to think otherwise. One night as I lay in bed sobbing, I thought, "Someday you won't love Charlie and will have a fulfilling life." That, together with something Mary Helen said, became my refuge when I thought it impossible to keep going. When I told Mary Helen about the divorce, she said, "I'm not sorry for you. You'll do fine and be better off. I'm sorry for us and the ranch." As I moved on with my life, achieving success in the corporate and academic worlds, I often remembered her words and how prophetic they were.

Our divorce was granted on December 18, 1979. We were married less than two years. I was in Houston when Charlie's attorney called to tell me the divorce was final. I decided to keep Schreiner as my last name because my gut told me Charlie and I were not done yet. The next day I drove to Austin and signed a lease for an apartment. The end of December, I was hired by the Travis County Democratic Party to set up polling places for its primary election. At last, my life seemed to be falling into place, and I was looking forward to rather than dreading the future. I remembered one of my father's favorite Psalms, "Weeping may endure for a night, but joy cometh in the morning."

On Christmas Eve, Mary Helen and Four hosted Three, his sons, and me for dinner and exchanging gifts. I gave Mary Helen a cross-stitch quilt I made for the new baby whose arrival was imminent. I gave Three a lithograph of a horse bucking off its rider. Across the bottom I wrote a favorite quote from D. H. Lawrence's *Women in Love*. "And woman is the same as horses: two wills act in opposition inside her. With one will she wants to subject herself utterly. With the other she wants to bolt and pitch her rider to perdition."

Charlie read it and said, "Truer words were never spoken."

CHAPTER 26

"The night is passed and the day lies open before us. Let us rejoice in the gift of this new day."

THE BOOK OF COMMON PRAYER

Starting Over

MY LAST DAY LIVING ON THE Y.O. was January 13, 1980. As I was getting into my car to drive off the ranch, for what I thought would be the last time, Charlie approached and gave me a book. Why he felt the need to do this I have no idea. The book was a bound edition of the March 1845 *American Review: A Whig Journal of Politics, Literature, Art and Science*. Several days later I perused it wondering if there was a hidden message in its contents. If there was, I didn't find it, just as in cleaning out his storage barns I never found Charlie's Rosebud.

Because my apartment would not be ready until February, Charlie Four told me I could stay at the Onion Creek Ranch in Buda, twenty miles south of Austin. Onion Creek was a four thousand-acre hunting ranch recently leased by the Y.O. from its original owner, Cecil Ruby. Ruby was a boyhood friend of Lyndon Johnson, who often visited Ruby's ranch and had a room named for him in the Onion Creek Lodge. I was with Three and Four when they toured the ranch prior to leasing it. Both were impressed by the quality of the game—turkey, quail, axis, and whitetail deer. The most memorable aspect of the ranch was a three-story hunting blind with an elevator for those either unable or unwilling to walk up the stairs.

Onion Creek Lodge had several bedrooms as well as a den, kitchen, and dining room. I had the lodge to myself as well as the services of the cook who lived on the ranch. One night I hosted a dinner party for Austin friends. Among those attending was my roommate from the University of Texas, Brenda Bell. After dinner we moved into the den for drinks and conversation. After a trip to the restroom, Brenda came up to me and whispered, "You may want to go in the kitchen. There's some old cowboy in there picking at the food." When I did, I discovered Charlie, who was indeed picking at the brisket and could pass for an "old cowboy" in his usual unpretentious attire and bedraggled hat. I knew what he was up to. He thought by showing up unannounced he could spend the night with me. He did spend the night, but it was by himself in the LBJ Room.

The Y.O.'s centennial year granted Charlie Three's wish when his first grandson, Charles Bowmer Schreiner V, was born on January 17, 1980. Much to Three's displeasure, the newest member of the Schreiner family was given Mary Helen's maiden name for his middle name. Joy turned to apprehension when, within minutes of his birth, the doctors discovered the baby had a severe problem with his mitral valve. Over the next year, Mary Helen and Charlie Four would consult numerous doctors and live in Boston several months so Baby Charlie could be treated at Boston Children's Hospital, renowned for its pediatric care. I asked Charlie Four how Three reacted to his grandson's illness. Four said when Three found out the baby was ill, he had no interest in him. "Sounds familiar," I thought, remembering how he treated me when I had my horse wreck. Was it because Three did not know how to show his concern, was embarrassed to do so, or considered the baby "handicapped"?

On the evening of April 11, the Y.O. centennial weekend began with several hundred guests attending a barbecue at the Y.O. Lodge and the pavilion behind it. On my way to the party, I stopped at Charlie Four and Mary Helen's to meet Baby Charlie. He was cooing and acting like a typical three-month-old, but Mary Helen told me he would be having surgery once he was older. Not wanting to pry, I asked no questions and told her I would keep them in my prayers. Her eyes filled with tears as she thanked me.

Three started the centennial festivities by riding Ranger, a longhorn steer, into the Y.O. Lodge. It was a pleasant spring evening with a south-easterly breeze providing perfect temperatures for dining and dancing in the open-air pavilion. When the band began playing "Waltz Across Texas," I found Three and asked him to dance with me. I could tell he was uncomfortable at the prospect. "What's the matter, Charlie? You want to sleep with me but won't dance with me?" He sheepishly grinned, took me in his arms, and we danced a few bars before he excused himself saying, "I need to greet my guests."

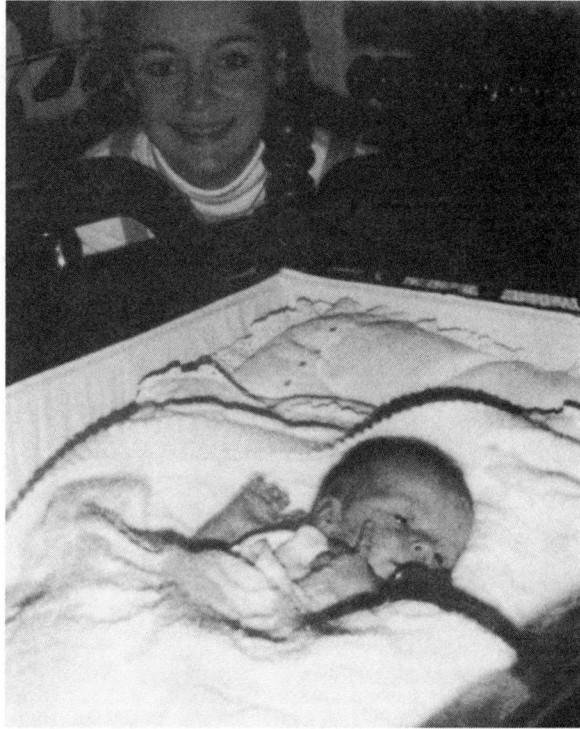

Mary Helen Schreiner with three-month-old Charles Bowmer Schreiner V.

In celebration of the one hundredth anniversary of the ranch, the Texas Historical Commission recognized the ranch with a historical marker, and Charlie Three had numerous centennial items created including a commemorative six-shooter, limited edition bronzes, a belt buckle, saddle, hat, and spurs. *Long Days and Short Nights: A Century of Texas Ranching on the YO 1880–1980*, was published in a regular edition and a limited cowhide-bound edition with the Y.O. brand prominently imprinted on the front. Charlie Four told me over ten thousand invitations were sent for the Saturday night party. He understated the obvious when he said, "It got a little out of hand." Fortunately, only around 4,500 attended.

The ranch was an hour's drive from Kerrville, where most of the guests were staying. Knowing there would be a traffic jam getting into the ranch, I left Kerrville at five o'clock. Several miles from the front gate I joined the procession of cars inching their way into the ranch. Texas Highway Patrol and Kerr County Sheriff's Office officers were stationed along the highway directing traffic. After guests showed their invitation at the front gate, each person received a bronze of the Y.O. brand. Getting to the Y.O. Lodge took almost an hour as cars inched along the rutted caliche road.

A bronze by Clay Dahlberg and a six shooter with an engraving by Frank Hendricks for the Y.O. centennial in 1980.

Charles Schreiner III riding his prize longhorn steer through the Y.O. Lodge during the centennial celebration of the Y.O. Ranch, 1980. Photo by Wendy Watriss for the New York Times. © Collection of Wendy Watriss and Fred Baldwin.

The firing of Charlie's Gatling gun officially started the party—and what a party it was! Charlie, in gray tuxedo and boots, again rode into the lodge on Ranger. Attendees included politicians, the ambassador from Jordan, the US marshal of Dodge City, Kansas, professional sports figures, television stars, and Texans from all levels of society.

An hour into the celebration, Mother Nature crashed the party when a cold front arrived with wind gusts growing increasingly colder and whipping the multiple food tents set up outside the Y.O. Lodge. Catering staff and cowboys scurried around finding rocks large enough to anchor the tents securely. Thunder and lightning followed, joined by a cold driving rain. Once the rain stopped, sleet began. Through it all, guests laughed, ate, drank, and made merry. Guests arriving later in the evening had an advantage over those of us arriving early because they had donned long underwear under their party attire. Many a flimsy evening gown covered T-shirts and long johns. A variety of coats were retrieved from vehicles and ran the gamut from furs to hunting jackets. Women in expensive shoes stepped lightly around mud puddles, hoisting their designer gowns and occasionally being carried across by gallant escorts. Several women exchanged their heels for sturdy waterproof rain boots. Fortunately, my shoes were black, so I gave up trying to avoid the puddles and walked through them.

The food tents represented each of the countries from which the animals on the Y.O. came, featuring dishes unique to that country and game dishes featuring those animals. After midnight there were ostrich egg omelets, menudo, and chili. Separate tents had dance floors where guests could dance to music ranging from big band to country and western.

For me, the evening passed in a blur of seeing old friends, making sure my mother and aunt were safely ensconced in the Y.O. Lodge with a good view for people watching, occasionally dancing, and finally gathering about thirty of my friends into the Longhorn Room, where we had a party within a party telling stories and rehashing all we had seen and done during the evening. At 2:00 a.m., we walked outside, where a gently falling snow had turned the ranch into a winter wonderland. I decided all good things must end and rounded up my brothers, both of whom were having a grand time with new friends they made at the party, and headed back to Kerrville. The snow continued falling, and it was challenging to keep my eyes on the road and not be mesmerized by the minute flakes swirling down. The cowboy breakfast planned for Sunday morning in the South Home pasture was wisely canceled. When I returned to Austin,

The centennial party invitation.

*In Celebration
of the First Hundred Years.*

*The descendents of
Captain Charles Schreiner
and the people of the Y.O. Ranch
cordially invite you to join us
for our Centennial Celebration.*

*The Evening of April 12, 1980
Seven O'Clock
At the Y.O. Ranch*

*R.S.V.P.   Black Tie and Boots
(Card Enclosed)*

Please show invitation at Gate

The menu for the centennial party.

Centennial Menu
Y.O. Ranch Exotic and Native Game

INDIA
Axis Deer & Blackbuck Antelope
Curry
Served with Rice
and Condiments
Pappadoms

EUROPEAN
Corsican Ram & Wild Boar
Stuffed Dolmas
Shish Kebob
Pilaf
Roasted Wild Boar

ORIENTAL
Sika Deer
Terriyaki
Stir fried with vegetables
Filled Oriental Pancakes
with Plum Sauce
Egg Rolls

MEXICAN
Venison Tacos Al Carbon
Javalina Gorditas
Cabrito
Handmade Corn and Flour
Tortillas
Condiments and Sauce

AFRICAN
Eland
Charcoal Broiled
Assorted Rolls and Sauces
Exotic Fresh Fruit and Nuts

TEXAS
Smoked Wild Turkey
White Tail Picadillo
Fried Rattlesnake
Mesquite Roasted Texas Longhorn

SERVED AFTER MIDNIGHT
Ostrich Egg Omelets
Menudo   Chili

I had a T-shirt made for Charlie Four that said, "Ski Gobblers Knob." The party was covered by newspapers, magazines, and television stations across the United States as the quintessential Texas-sized party.

I returned to the ranch in May for the Y.O. Ranch Centennial Longhorn Sale. I sold half of my cows, most bought by Red McCombs or Lloyd Brinkman for considerably more than the $30,000 Charlie and Walter offered me for my entire herd. With some of the money, I purchased a home in Austin. That summer I achieved a lifetime goal when I was hired by Austin Community College as an adjunct professor to teach courses in US government and Texas politics. It started a second career that gave me more job satisfaction than any of my more lucrative careers.

Throughout the fall I worked on a fundraising dinner honoring Robert Strauss to be held in Washington, DC, on December 9, 1980. Strauss was a major player in the Democratic Party, beginning his political career working in Lyndon Johnson's first congressional campaign in 1937. He was chairman of the Democratic National Committee (DNC) from 1972 to 1977, ambassador to Russia under President George H. W. Bush, and US trade representative and special envoy to the Middle East for President Jimmy Carter. The fundraiser was to endow a chair in Strauss's name at the University of Texas Southwestern Medical Center. Strauss was quick with a quip and one of my favorites is, "You can fool some of the people all of the time, and those are the ones you need to concentrate on."

I arrived in the nation's capital on Friday before the Strauss event the following Tuesday. Several events were scheduled for those of us working on the dinner. On Saturday morning, we toured the White House, and on Sunday afternoon attended a matinee of Charles Dickens's *A Christmas Carol* at Ford's Theater, followed by a party with the cast. The theater had been restored to look much as it did on the evening of April 14, 1865, when John Wilkes Booth jumped to the stage shouting, "Sic Semper Tyrannis!" after assassinating Lincoln. There was a special area in the theater displaying information on the assassination, the capture of Booth, and the gun used in the assassination, which I immediately recognized, thanks to Charlie, as a Colt single-action.

On Monday, December 8, I was so busy working on preparations for the next evening's black-tie dinner there was no time for anything else. It was around two in the morning when I fell into bed exhausted. When I awoke to the radio on December 9, it was to the news of John Lennon's death by an assassin. The first thing I thought was, "This is a joke and it isn't funny." As I listened to the announcer repeating the events of the previous evening, the reality finally registered. Just as with President Kennedy's assassination, it was hard to believe death could randomly strike down someone in their prime. The Beatles and their music were a defining part of my youth. I wanted to grieve, but it would have to wait until I returned to Austin.

The dinner was attended by, in the words of Ambassador Strauss, "a montage of America," and included President and Mrs. Carter, Vice President and Mrs. Mondale, the Speaker of the House, numerous senators, Vice President-elect George H. W. and Mrs. Bush, and many corporate and industrial leaders. Though President Carter had been defeated by Ronald Reagan in November, the conviviality between the members of the two political parties was good-natured kidding and generous praise of one another and the democratic system's peaceful transition of power. Lady Bird Johnson was there, wearing several strands of opera length pearls that took my breath away. I made a point of speaking to her, and she immediately took both of my hands in hers exclaiming, "Oh, Norma, I shall never forget that magical day at the Y.O., not to mention Bertie's delicious beans." When I passed Senator Edward Kennedy on the stairs, I was struck by his good looks and understood his reputation as a ladies' man.

On returning to Austin, I held my own tribute for John Lennon. By the light of my fireplace and candles, I spent a night listening to his albums and those of the Beatles while drinking too many snifters of brandy. I awoke the next morning with a horrific hangover. It had been a good year for me. I was pleased with my new life and though Charlie and the Y.O. regularly haunted my dreams, I was reestablishing myself in Austin, starting a new career teaching, and leaving behind the tumultuous, precarious existence I had on the Y.O.

CHAPTER 27

"The love that I knew is living again and

nothing else matters, we're together again."

BUCK OWENS

Together Again

THE BLEAKNESS OF THE DAY matched the occasion. The overcast skies threatened rain but it never arrived. A small group of mourners sat and stood under the tent. On the front row were the grieving parents and grandparents. Mary Helen asked me to sit with the family, but I felt it would be an intrusion.

I remembered my father talking about how difficult it was to perform a child's funeral because there were no words adequate to comfort the parents. Such was evident now as Mary Helen's body shook with sobs and Charlie Four embraced her. Charles Bowmer Schreiner V died in his mother's arms at a doctor's office on January 2, 1981, his mother's birthday and fourteen days short of his first birthday. The funeral and burial were at her parents' ranch sixty-five miles northwest of Austin.

After the service, the mourners moved into the house. I noticed my mother talking with an attractive blond woman I assumed was Audrey since she was sitting with the family during the service. My mother and Audrey met the previous year after Gus was in an accident, suffered a serious concussion, and was flown to Houston for treatment. When I told my mother, she went to see him and consequently met Audrey. Not wanting to interrupt, I went to my car to retrieve the bouquet of flowers I brought for Baby Charlie's grave. After placing it on the grave, I looked up and was surprised to see Three. Motioning to my flowers he said, "I know Mary

Helen and Charlie will appreciate that. I don't know why this happened to those two kids. They haven't done anything to deserve it." Years later, I would tell Charlie Four about his father's remark and asked if Three ever expressed those sentiments to him. It came as no surprise when Four said, "No."

"Have you spoken to Audrey?" I asked, knowing their relationship after the divorce was contentious. One Mother's Day when Three and I were married, he decided to call Audrey and thank her for bearing him four sons and being such a good mother to them. When he told me of his plan, I could tell he was doing it with a combination of mischief and sincerity. Audrey must have felt the same because her reply was, "Go to Hell!"

Charlie looked down and begin shuffling his feet. "When I said hello, do you know what she said? 'You son of a bitch, don't you dare speak to me.'"

"And how did you reply?"

"I tipped my hat and said, 'It's good seeing you too, Audrey.' But that's beside the point. I'm on my way to San Antonio and was wondering if we could meet for dinner tomorrow night."

"Why?" I asked.

"It would give us a chance to catch up and I know how much you like the Argyle, so I thought I'd take you there."

"How thoughtful of you, but if you expect me to pay for my dinner by sleeping with you, think again."

"I'll see you at seven," he replied, and walked away.

When I arrived at the Argyle the next evening, the waiter welcomed me saying, "Mrs. Schreiner, it's so good seeing you. I was just telling Mr. Schreiner how much we've missed you. I've given you and Mr. Schreiner a special table."

Charlie rose as I approached, thanked the waiter, and kissed me on the cheek. We ordered drinks and he began asking questions about what I had been doing during the past year. I told him about purchasing my house and the teaching position. "What about you?" I asked.

After a few remarks about longhorn sales and a new gun he purchased, he commenced telling me about a woman he'd recently broken up with. I tried to keep a straight face when Charlie told me she was a member of PETA (People for the Ethical Treatment of Animals), and he'd attended several of their meetings with her. I remembered the times Charlie railed against the stupidity of the organization and its members. Numerous sarcastic remarks crossed my mind, but I restrained myself. She lived in Austin, was married, and even though she professed her love for Charlie, would not ask her husband for a divorce. Charlie decided to take matters into his own hands and in his words, "call out" her husband.

Charlie phoned the husband at his office and invited him to meet for drinks at the Night Hawk restaurant, saying he had a proposition the husband might be interested in pursuing. Charlie came armed with a pistol, and for backup, Jimmy Dee—his friend and the cattle inspector—who was also armed and sitting at another table. The husband arrived and Charlie, to the husband's astonishment, professed his love for the man's wife and that he wanted to marry her. Charlie recommended the husband do the gentlemanly thing and give her a divorce. Once the husband regained his composure, he told Charlie he would do no such thing. He loved his wife and was not divorcing her. He rose and left the restaurant. Later in the evening, Charlie received an outraged call from the wife, who ended their relationship.

"Can you believe it?" Charlie asked. "I was doing the honorable thing by calling him out. I thought she would appreciate what I did. I swear, I don't understand women."

I sat quietly, trying to suppress a guffaw. "Of course, she's angry. Did you really think she wouldn't be?"

"I honestly didn't. I've been trying to call her, but she won't take my calls. I want to apologize and try to make it up to her."

It seemed obvious to me she wanted to have her cake and eat it too. "Accept the fact it's over and move on. If she ends up breaking up with her husband, she'll be back in touch. I am not going to counsel you on your love life. Let's move on to a more pleasant subject."

We spent the rest of the dinner with Three telling me about his projects at the ranch and attempting to get me to talk about my love life. I sidestepped the subject, telling him I was seeing several men, which I was. He acted surprised when I told him having been married to him was proving an impediment to dating. Many of the men I went out with told me there was no way they could compete with Charles Schreiner III and the Y.O. Ranch.

"What do you tell them?" he asked.

"They shouldn't underestimate themselves."

Three chuckled.

Driving back to Austin, I kept laughing at Charlie's calling out his lover's husband. He was as determined in pursuing women as he was in divorcing them.

Several months later, Kay Howard, my interior designer friend, and

I decided to open an interior design and home furnishings shop incorporating the concept we used in decorating Charlie's house of bringing together dissimilar elements to create an elegant whole. Kay had recently designed two lines of furniture, and having a shop would be the ideal way to display the pieces. We named our shop the Crystal Coyote, and Kay designed the logo, a sitting coyote howling at a full moon rising behind it. After developing a business plan and finding several investors, we set an opening date in April of 1982.

We wanted to carry cowhide rugs and use them to upholster furniture. Charlie had a source for them, and I called him to get it. When I told him about the shop, he agreed to give me the information on the condition he could be one of our investors. He told me he was planning to build a hotel in Kerrville, an idea I remembered him mentioning when we were married. He wanted Kay to assist with the interior design. As an investor, Charlie now had an excuse to call me regularly. It did not take long before he was courting me with the same fervor and intensity as the first time. I made a point of not always being available when Charlie asked me out and continued seeing other men. I still found Charlie attractive, and he obviously felt the same about me. It was difficult to resist his invitations, such as accompanying him to Brownsville, Texas, to pick up a horse mannequin for his gun room to display his vintage saddle collection. The mannequin was life-size, which meant we were pulling a horse trailer to accommodate it.

Brownsville is on the Gulf Coast in South Texas, adjacent to the Mexican border town of Matamoros. Driving down, Charlie reminded me Brownsville had the dubious distinction of being the site of the last battle of the Civil War, the Battle of Palmito Ranch on May 13, 1865, a month after the war ended. The Confederate forces, led by Col. John (Rip) Ford, won. Before the war, Ford was head of a company of scouts for the Texas Rangers. That was when he earned his nickname, Rip, because when he submitted his company's casualty lists, he would always write, "rest in peace" beside each name. Charlie admired Ford and owned one of his guns.

On Saturday night we crossed the border to have dinner with a friend of Charlie's who lived in Matamoros. The house was an adobe hacienda filled with Mexican antiques. One in particular impressed me. The mantle in the living room was a six-foot-long, two-foot-thick piece of wood with Spanish words carved into it. I asked Charlie's friend to translate them.

"'You will never regret having kept your secrets. Tell them and you will.' The mantle was my grandfather's, who left it to my father. I have followed its advice throughout my life and never regretted it." I too have followed it. Until writing this memoir.

On Sunday morning we loaded the faux horse into the trailer and headed back to the Y.O. Driving through Ingram, we saw Charlie Four's car outside Mary Helen's gift shop, and Charlie stopped. As soon as we walked into the shop, Three took his son by the arm and said, "I want to show you the horse I just bought." Charlie Four was trying to develop a quarter horse division at the ranch, which Three was less than enthusiastic about. Three opened the back of the horse trailer and proudly pointed at the horse. "The good thing about my horse is he won't cost me anything because he doesn't require feed and can't get sick or die."

The success of the Y.O.'s centennial party led to the forming of the Y.O. Social Club, which hosted an annual party at the ranch mimicking, on a smaller scale, the centennial party. Joining required an annual membership fee and a fee to attend the party. Rather than black tie and boots, the dress was "cowboy chic." The first party was held in September 1981 and was as successful as the centennial party.

In addition to teaching, I had several political consulting jobs for candidates running in the May 1982 primary. One was helping Ann Richards, who would later be elected governor of Texas, in her first statewide race for state treasurer. I arranged a luncheon with Ann, Charlie, and the president of Schreiner Bank in hopes they would support her. The luncheon was cordial, and Ann left with a contribution and their support.

I was also helping Jim Hightower, who was running for state agriculture commissioner. I donated one of my longhorn bulls to Jim for him to auction in a fundraising effort using the slogan, "No More Bull if You Vote for Hightower." Charlie was, no surprise, supporting Hightower's opponent; getting the bull off the Y.O. involved coordinating with Charlie Four and Walter, so I could move the bull while Three was away. The bull was not keen on leaving the Y.O., and, as the cowboys were attempting to load him, he wedged his head between two partitions in the pen. After much pushing and shoving—and one cowboy literally standing on one of the bull's horns and jumping up and down—the bull was extricated and glad to seek shelter in the trailer. Three did not find out about my donation until after the bull was sold and a friend who read about it in a newspaper called to needle him.

One day Charlie asked me what I did with my Y.O. ring. Regrettably, I told him I buried it with Ms. I explained my reason. I wanted to leave something on the ranch that meant as much to me as she did.

Cowboys attempting to extricate the author's recalcitrant bull from his predicament. Photograph by Ron Dorsey.

"Harrumph," was his reply. Several months later, Charlie and I went to Maui for a banking convention. On the flight over, Charlie proudly told me he found Ms.'s grave and dug up the ring. A combination of rage and sorrow overwhelmed me. I said nothing and retreated to the restroom where for the next thirty minutes I sobbed. It astounded me Charlie would do such a thing and boast about it. I knew better than to attempt to discuss it with him, so I pulled myself together and went back to my seat. I asked him to return the ring to me. "I can't," he replied. "It was stolen." By now I knew Charlie's capacity for duplicity, and my gut told me he was lying. The next time I was at the ranch, I spent a morning searching for it at the house to no avail.

Charlie's friend Richard Shea provided me with the rest of the story when I was writing this memoir. Richard and his wife were at Charlie's house one day and Charlie was telling them about the ring and my burying it with Ms. "I want that ring back," Charlie said. "Let's see if we can find where she buried the cat." They walked around the yard searching. According to Richard, his wife found a place which she thought might be a grave and they began digging. They found what was left of Ms. and the ring.

I asked Richard if he knew what Charlie did with the ring. "He gave it to Gary Ann," Richard replied. I knew she was someone Charlie dated occasionally. When Richard told me this, the first thing to cross my mind was, "Of course he did; it's exactly what he would do." When I hung up the phone, I felt as I did on the plane to Maui. I was overcome by a sense of intense loss and overwhelming sadness. I was surprised that forty years later I could still be so wounded by Charlie's thoughtlessness.

Charlie and I returned from Maui only a few weeks before the opening of the Crystal Coyote. I put out a press release for our opening, which garnered mention in the Austin newspaper and led to an article about the shop in *Texas Homes Magazine* and *USA Today*. *Texas Homes* called the shop "a treasure trove of Texas chic," saying, "The inspired notion of elevating the ordinary to exceptional, of making dramatic design declarations by combining the most unlikely elements makes the Crystal Coyote as much an instructive exhibit in lifestyle as an extraordinary treasure trove of both class and curios. The attitude is youthful yet refined; the look is unforgettable."

These two articles resulted in phone calls from around the state ordering pieces of furniture, cowhides, and our Zapotec woven rugs and throw pillows. It also led to a phone call I almost dismissed as a prank. It was my habit to use Sunday mornings to relax, read the newspaper, and not work on anything, no matter how pressing. When my phone rang at ten o'clock one Sunday morning, I debated whether to answer the call. Against my better judgment I did. A hoarse, gravelly voice that sounded vaguely familiar asked, "Is this Miz Norma Schreiner?"

"Yes," I replied.

"This is Willie Nelson."

My friend, Rusty Cox, was famous for doing impersonations, often leaving messages for me in the voices of Daffy Duck, James Stewart, John Wayne, and others. "Rusty, I am not amused. I'm trying to spend a quiet morning."

"No ma'am, this isn't Rusty, whoever he is. This is Willie Nelson. My wife was wondering if there was any way she could come over to your shop this afternoon and order a few things." I still was not convinced it was really Willie Nelson but decided to play along for the moment. "When would be a convenient time, and could you tell me what items she's interested in?"

"Just a minute. I'll let you talk to her."

The next voice introduced herself as Connie Nelson. All the items she wanted to order, from furniture to a king-size Zapotec bedspread, were custom-made. I told her Kay would meet her at the shop at one o'clock.

Kay Howard, left, and the author in ad for the Crystal Coyote. Photograph by Ron Dorsey.

Kay found Connie charming and inquisitive about the shop and Kay's designs. It turned out to be one of the largest custom orders we received. Kay and I laughed about how I could have blown the entire order had I persisted in thinking it was Rusty and followed my impulse to hang up.

Another major project followed close on the heels of the Nelson purchase. Two entrepreneurs had purchased the Stockyards Hotel in Fort Worth, Texas, and were restoring it. The hotel opened in 1907, and the new owners wanted the décor to emphasize Texas and the importance of the longhorn in the history of Texas and Fort Worth. After reading about our shop, they thought Kay's furniture and aesthetic awareness of all things Texas made her perfect for the job. In addition to designing much of the furniture for the hotel, Kay also created English woven Axminster carpet with a longhorn skull for the stairs and hallway. In 2018, I stayed at the hotel and the carpet was still there, looking as good as it did on opening night in 1984.

Cleverly, Kay used old saddles for bar stools in the hotel's saloon, Booger Red's. "Booger" is a cowboy term describing an outlaw bucking horse that cannot be ridden. Booger Red was a cowboy who, in the early 1900s, was famous for being able to ride any wild horse. The hotel was the perfect venue for Kay's unique talents as well as giving the Crystal Coyote more publicity and visibility. Once completed, the hotel was granted a Texas historical marker and a Historic Hotels of America plaque.

In late August 1982, Charlie and I spent the weekend in San Antonio. Charlie had always talked of taking me to the Mexican *charreada*, the Mexican forerunner of rodeos. It started in the sixteenth century in Spanish colonial Mexico and was held at the end of the cattle roundup. The San Antonio charreada is sponsored by the San Antonio Charro Association and, following tradition, is held only on Sunday afternoons. Teams of charros, the forefather of the American cowboy, compete in a series of events based on skills needed for ranch work. Unlike a rodeo, points in a charreada are awarded for style and personal carriage, as well as skill.

The charreada began with a grand entry of the cowboys, who were dazzling—and no doubt sweltering in the August heat—in their embroidered leather suits and sombreros. To ensure historical accuracy, charros follow strict regulations for their clothing and saddles, often spending thousands of dollars for the entire assemblage. Some of the events, such as roping and bronc and bull riding, were familiar from American rodeos. Others were a mystery. Fortunately, I had Charlie explaining each event's significance.

Coleadero, or steer tailing, is one of the oldest traditions of the charreada. A mounted charro races after a running steer, grabs its tail, and wraps it around the steer's leg to trip the animal. The steer instinctively wanders back to the herd after it falls, which allowed a nineteenth century charro to keep his herd together without having to dismount or use his lasso. For the modern charro, points are granted for technique, speed, and the roll of the steer. Just as in the old days, there are no cash awards. The prize is the respect of fellow competitors.

The *escaramuza*, or skirmish, honors the contributions of women during the Mexican Revolution. A team of eight horseback women perform a high-speed, synchronized routine set to music. The women ride sidesaddle in colorful dresses with full skirts and layers of crinolines underneath. This is referred to as "Adelita attire." It is a graceful, beautiful, and moving event as riders in their brilliantly colored costumes perform intricate maneuvers.

The final charro event is the *paso de la muerte*, or pass of death. A charro riding bareback leaps from his horse onto an unbroken mare and rides her to a stop using only her mane for support. If he falls, the charro risks being trampled by the mare or his mounted teammates who are following at a gallop.

When we returned to the hotel, I prepared to cool down in the pool while Charlie took a nap. As I was leaving the room, Charlie called me over to the bed, took my hand, and said, "I want you to promise me something." I sat down on the bed. "Let's agree neither of us will become involved in a relationship with anyone else until we've discussed it with each other."

I was struck by the strangeness of this request. "Why would you ask that?"

"Because I keep hoping we can get back together."

"We have gotten back together, Charlie. Surely you don't mean marriage. I think we've proven that doesn't work."

"I'm hoping you'll get your fill of having a career and decide to settle down with me on the ranch. I want a wife, and of all the women I've met you're the best in every way."

"Oh, Charlie," I said, shaking my head. "Have your forgotten neither of us have changed? We only make each other miserable when we're married." I bent down and kissed him on each cheek and his forehead.

"Lie down beside me for a minute," he said, patting the bed. I did. "I know you're right, but I don't want to lose you again and I don't want to grow old alone." His voice was poignant. Within minutes he was asleep.

Being in my mid-thirties with so much of life before me, I did not understand this yearning, nor did I realize Charlie was revealing to me a fear that would drive him for the rest of his life. Several of his friends confirmed this when I talked with them for this book. Each mentioned Charlie making similar remarks to them when they questioned him about why he was so relentless in his pursuit of women, often marrying the wrong woman. It also helped explain Charlie Four's comment about the seven to eight years his father ignored the ranch while chasing women and what it cost the ranch financially. As I write this at an age never reached by Charlie Three, I understand his desperation. One of author Graham Greene's characters expressed this same yearning: "In the end there is no desire so deep as the simple desire for companionship."

CHAPTER 28

"An' here I sit so patiently waiting to find out what price, you have

to pay to get out of going through all these things twice."

BOB DYLAN

Fool Me Twice

THE Y.O. SOCIAL CLUB was holding its second annual party on Saturday, September 11, 1982. Charlie asked the Crystal Coyote to decorate the Y.O. Lodge and Pavilion for the party. Kay and I arrived at the ranch on Wednesday afternoon bringing with us lariat wreaths adorned with flowers and antlers designed exclusively for the party. I spent most of the next day in the live oak trees around the lodge stringing lights. My time with Charlie was limited. When we went to bed at night I found it curious he never tried to make love, assuming it was because he was as tired as I. One night I rolled over and put my arm around him. Usually, he would respond by patting it, but this night I felt his body tensing. I asked him if anything was wrong, to which he replied, "I'm just tired."

The night before the Social Club party, there was a smaller gathering around the newly completed swimming pool. I could not help noting the irony of Charlie completing the pool once I was gone. Guests gathered around the pool and Charlie christened it with a bottle of champagne. Then he announced the engagement of his second son, Walter, to Teri Richburg. The engagement came as a surprise to me, and I wondered why Three had not mentioned it.

At the party was former movie star George Montgomery, who starred in B-grade Western movies in the 1950s. Charlie met him at a gun show earlier in the year. When Charlie mentioned it, I told him how I watched Montgomery at Saturday matinees in El Campo, Texas. Several months later Charlie presented me with an autographed copy of Montgomery's autobiography. Charlie must have told him of my memories because in his inscription, he mentioned my being one of his loyal fans from El Campo. Montgomery was still a nice-looking man and several times throughout the evening, he made a point of finding me and talking with me. After we exhausted every possible topic of conversation, I made a point of disappearing when I saw him approaching. Later I would wonder if, to assuage his conscience, Charlie asked Montgomery to pursue me.

The Y.O. Social Club party the next night was the usual mix of guests from near and far, an abundance of good food, and liquor flowing like a flooded low-water crossing. Charlie and I never spent much time together at Y.O. parties. We would enter the party together and then go our separate ways. My mother came for the party as did several friends from Austin, including Bill Head, a man I dated occasionally. As a joke, Bill brought Charlie a copy of Mao Zedong's *Little Red Book* in Spanish. He jokingly told Charlie that he'd brought enough to distribute to the employees on the ranch. Charlie replied, "I've already got a land redistribution program. It's called my ex-wives."

As the night slipped away, I realized it was midnight and I hadn't seen Charlie for several hours. This was unusual since our paths usually crossed several times in the course of an evening. I looked for him in and around the Y.O. Lodge to no avail. I wondered if he had gone back to the house. It would be highly unusual, but perhaps he was not feeling well. We came to the party in separate cars, so I drove back to the house. As I entered, Lupe met me, and I asked him if Charlie was there. He said no. This was becoming stranger and stranger, and my sixth sense was telling me something was rotten at the Y.O. I returned to the lodge and resumed my search. I realized I had not looked at the pool, though it seemed highly unlikely Charlie would be there because he preferred being in the thick of things. I entered the pool area and saw Charlie sitting on the other side talking to a woman. My intuition told me this was not a casual conversation. I headed in their direction. Charlie rose and started toward me. We met halfway. Raising his hands defensively, Charlie said, "It's not what you think. Don't go jumping to conclusions."

"And just what am I thinking?" I asked as I tried to get around him so I could introduce myself.

"That she's my date."

"That hadn't crossed my mind, but since you raise the question, is she?"

"No. She's someone I met recently and invited to the party. She doesn't know anyone so I'm just being friendly."

"Then introduce us."

"That wouldn't be wise."

"Why?" I asked.

After several seconds, Charlie stuttered, "She doesn't know about us."

His answer told me all I needed to know. "Give me the keys to the gas pumps so I'll have enough gas to get home."

"I'll meet you at the gas pumps," he said.

As Charlie pumped the gas, I said nothing. I was angry, hurt, confused, and wanted to escape from the ranch as quickly as possible. Only a few weeks before, he was asking me not to commit to anyone else and saying he hoped we could get back together. How could he have the audacity to say such things and bring someone else to the party? When would I learn, no matter what he might say, he was not one to keep his word, or at least not with me? I drove back to the house and got my things. As I told Lupe goodbye, he pressed a small box into my hand saying, *"Buena suerte* [good luck]." I realized Lupe knew something I didn't.

It was two thirty in the morning when I left the ranch. Ordinarily I would have dreaded making the three-hour drive in the dead of night, knowing the increased odds of deer and other wild creatures crossing the roads. But I was too caught up in my own thoughts to worry about it. Charlie's aloofness toward me and lack of physical intimacy during the last few days was now explained. Was he already seeing the woman when we were in San Antonio only a few weeks before? If so, why didn't he tell me? I turned on the radio hoping it would provide a distraction. It was difficult finding a station, but I found one playing gospel music and hymns, all of which were familiar from my childhood as a Baptist preacher's daughter. I forced myself to sing along, astounding myself with how well I remembered the words.

Once home, I went to bed but could not sleep. At nine o'clock my phone rang. I hoped it would be Charlie but it was Mary Helen calling to ask what happened. I told her I would explain later. I wondered if Charlie would call. My gut told me he wouldn't, and as usual, my gut was right. That evening I opened the box Lupe gave me as I was leaving the ranch. In it was a rabbit's foot. I wondered what made him give it to me and suspected he knew I would not be returning to the ranch. I treasured and kept it for thirty-five years. When I traveled to Mongolia to ride horseback across the steppes, I took it with me for luck and tucked it into a pocket each morning before we rode. To my great regret, I lost it on one of those rides.

The woman I saw with Charlie at the pool was Lynn Peñafiel. Originally from Australia, she lived in Mexico for many years and was married to a wealthy Mexican businessman who divorced her. She came to Kerrville to visit a friend and met Charlie at a dinner party. Thirty years later, I would become friends with the woman who gave the dinner party and through her learn details of Charlie and Lynn's meeting, marriage, and divorce. Lynn moved into Charlie's house the week after the Y.O. Social Club party, and they married at the house on November 22, 1982.

On December 22, one month after Charlie married Lynn, my phone rang. When I answered, a familiar voice said, "How are you, Ms. Cude?" It was Charlie referring to me by my last name when we met. I could tell he was nervous, and I was not going to put him at ease. "Hello, Charlie," I said in a frigid and hostile tone.

After hemming and hawing for several minutes, he said, "I'm in Austin and was wondering if we might have dinner tonight?"

Taken aback, all I could think of to say was, "Is your wife with you?"

"Hell, no. I need to talk to you, and what I have to say is none of her business."

"Whatever you have to say to me can be said on the phone."

"I know we didn't part under the best circumstances, but I was hoping you'd let me apologize over dinner."

"Mr. Schreiner," I said, "I'm starting to think you want to sleep with me. Am I right?"

Charlie cleared his throat. "Anything's possible, isn't it?"

"Well, Charlie, there's just one problem."

"What's that?"

"I don't fuck married men. Unless they're married to me." I hung up the phone.

The following February, the Crystal Coyote had a booth at the Travis County Livestock Show and Rodeo. One night as I was closing it, I heard someone say, "When you're through there would you like to have a drink?" I turned and saw Charlie, eyes twinkling and mustache twitching.

"Where's your wife?" I replied.

"Obviously, she's not here or I wouldn't be asking."

I sighed and stood arms akimbo, pursing my lips.

"I promise I'll behave," Charlie said. "I just want to talk."

We walked to one of the bars outside the rodeo arena and found a table. "Before you say a word," I said, "I am not fucking you."

Charlie smiled. "I always did like your way with words. I was hoping you'd forgive me for how things ended between us."

"Forgive? Maybe. Forget? Never."

Whatever else we talked about I do not remember. When we parted, Charlie tipped his hat and said, "I wish you all the best. I sincerely mean it. You are one hell of a woman."

Following his established pattern, less than two years after marrying Lynn, his fifth wife, Charlie filed for divorce. There had been no prenuptial agreement. Charlie offered her a monetary settlement, but she refused, took the case to court, and threw Charlie's Gatling gun in the Guadalupe River. The judge awarded her less than Charlie's initial offer. In 1991, Lynn married Belton Kleberg (B. K.) Johnson, the great-grandson of Capt. Richard King, founder of the King Ranch. They remained married until Lynn died of cancer in 1994.

At some point, Charlie, with his penchant for nicknames, began referring to Lynn as Taco Bell. It remains the name used by family members when talking about her. Jimmy Dee told me Three had two nicknames for me. Jimmy came up with one of them, "The Thoroughbred," because, he said, I had all of a thoroughbred's characteristics: intelligent, athletic, spirited, and hard to handle. Rusty gave me another nickname Three sometimes used, "the former Ms. Normer." It is a name still used by many of those who knew me during that time in my life.

CHAPTER 29

"Give me a man with a future and a woman with a past."

OSCAR WILDE

A Brown-Eyed Handsome Man

IN AUGUST 1983 there was an article in the Austin newspaper about a video dating service, the forerunner of internet dating sites. I decided to give myself a membership as a birthday gift that year. I was not looking for a permanent relationship. I had come to the conclusion my cats and I would grow old together, but it would be nice to have someone I could enjoy going to dinner with and taking to political events. As I looked through a notebook with photos and short bios of available men, a handsome visage caught my eye. He gave his profession as "soldier," and he was stationed at Fort Hood, ninety miles northwest of Austin. He was thirty-six and never married. After watching his video, I wanted to meet him. He seemed serious and straightlaced and I remember thinking, "He needs someone to loosen him up, and I'm just the girl to do it."

We met on a Sunday afternoon for coffee, which extended into having dinner and making a date to meet again. What I most remember about our meeting were his eyes and his arms. He had beautiful brown eyes and muscular arms the likes of which I had not seen since my first husband, R. C. As we were saying goodbye, I looked at his arms and thought, "I want those arms to hold me."

Dean Schmelling was born in San Francisco and grew up in Sacramento, California. After getting his bachelor's degree in art with a minor in cinema, he joined the army, not with the intent of having a military career but to support himself until he figured out what came next in his life. When we met, he had been in the army ten years. As life often does, it threw him a curve ball. He enjoyed the army, its discipline, rigorous training, challenges, and travel. Two years after enlisting, Dean attended the US Army's Officer Candidate School followed by Army Ranger training. Because Dean was new to Texas, he had never heard of Charles Schreiner III or the Y.O. Ranch. We were a clean slate to each other and as our relationship became more serious, he told me, "Our pasts are behind us. All that matters is our future."

Dean accompanied me to political events where I introduced him to political figures including Lady Bird Johnson, Ann Richards, and Molly Ivins. He introduced me to the military, taking me to battalion balls, change of command ceremonies, an open house hosted by Fort Hood's commanding general, and hail and farewells. I learned a new language because the military uses acronyms as readily as civilians use adjectives. Even the letters of the alphabet had words for the letters they depicted. A is alpha, B is bravo, C is Charlie, and all the way to zulu for Z. Time is told by a twenty-four-hour clock, and when Dean told me he would pick me up at 1900 hours, I learned he meant 7:00 p.m. "Zero dark thirty" means any time after nightfall. XO is not hugs and kisses but the executive officer, and the "old man" is the commander of a military group be he in his twenties or sixties. I learned the ranks from private up to the five levels of general and the insignias for each.

After dating six months, we moved into a charming one hundred-year-old rock house sitting in the middle of two hundred acres on a hilltop outside of Salado, Texas, which is equal distance between Austin and Fort Hood. Shortly after moving to Salado, Dean and I were at an antiques show in Austin when I saw Charlie across the room. He had not seen me and I debated whether to approach him. I turned to Dean and moving my head in Charlie's direction said, "There's Charlie."

"I'd like to meet him," Dean said.

Charlie was studying an old Texas map when I walked up beside him. He looked up, a smile spread across his face, and he hugged me. Introductions were exchanged followed by stilted conversation. Charlie asked Dean where he was from and what he did. When Dean told him, Charlie said, "Get Norma to bring you to the ranch."

"Thanks, but I think we'll pass," I said quickly, bringing the conversation to a close.

My friends liked Dean but were concerned about my ability to adapt to the military. One thing they did not know was I was bored with politics and the Austin scene. I did not want to be fifty years old, sitting in the

Quorum Club, and buying drinks for an egocentric politician as he bored me with stories of how important he was. I was ready to start a new career and had been attempting to do so in Austin to no avail. Thanks to selling my herd of longhorns, I had more savings than most of my friends, but I was tired of living with the wolf loitering outside my door, wondering when my next political job would appear.

Most important, I loved Dean and did not relish the idea of him moving on without me. I like to think I learn from at least some of my mistakes and knew from my marriage to R. C. the toll distance takes on a relationship. I had been single long enough to know Dean was an exceptional man in his integrity, intellect, thrift, and loyalty. He exemplified the definition of an officer and a gentleman. I knew beyond a doubt, I would never have to worry about him being unfaithful, lying, or not keeping his word.

One afternoon I answered the phone and heard Charlie's voice stuttering a greeting. He was calling to ask if I would attend the Texas Longhorn Breeders Association's convention to help him get his slate of candidates elected as directors. I told him I wasn't available. He was insistent, keeping me on the phone pleading his case. My refusals became more adamant, and finally I said, "I am not going to change my mind. Goodbye, Charlie," and hung up. It was the last time we spoke.

On December 17, 1984, Dean and I were married in the Texas Supreme Court chamber by my friend, Justice William Kilgarlin. When I told Dean I would marry him, it was with one caveat: he would have to agree to retire in Texas. I would leave Texas but only if I knew someday I would return. To cover all my bases, on our wedding night, I made him promise that should I die while living out of the state, he would not inter my bones in foreign soil but take my ashes back to Texas. He promised he would. It was a promise I knew he would keep.

The following June we moved to Leavenworth, Kansas, where I would have my best teaching experience and start a career in human resources. Shortly after we moved, I was hired to teach for the University of St. Mary in Leavenworth. This job presented a new challenge because I would be teaching political science courses at the Kansas Correctional Institute for Women and the US Disciplinary Barracks (DB in military speak), the military's only maximum-security prison. My classes at each prison were very different and also very rewarding. Several friends expressed concern about my teaching an all-male class at the DB. At the orientation for new instructors, I learned those in the program worked hard to be accepted, and one word from me about inappropriate behavior would lead to their

A brown-eyed handsome man, Dean Schmelling, and the author, 1985.

permanent dismissal from the program. At both prisons, students had to receive a grade of C or better to remain in the program.

I was terrified my first night of classes at the disciplinary barracks, but by the time the class ended I was completely at ease. The students were engaged, asking questions and participating at a level I never experienced before or since. On the last night of class, we had a discussion of what had been studied, their impressions, concerns, and questions. Toward the end of the class, one of the students said, "I am speaking on behalf of the class when I tell you the thing we most appreciated about you was you weren't scared of us." I debated how to respond and then decided to answer honestly. "Actually, I was terrified the first night, but by the end of the class, I was over it." The student replied, "Because you discovered we were people too."

To my surprise, I had a difficult time establishing rapport with my students at the women's prison. My preconception was that since I was a woman there would be an immediate bond between us, but there wasn't. I attribute this to our coming from such different life circumstances. It was midsemester before they would arrive early, participate in class, or stay after class to ask questions. Those two classes were the best I ever taught in terms of student participation, cogent student questions, and desire to achieve not just acceptable but exceptional grades. In both classes, the lowest grade was a B, and the majority made an A.

Our second year in Kansas, I was hired by Eastern Airlines to be their employment representative for the western United States, beginning a career that would culminate twenty-three years later when I retired as head of employee relations for an international corporation.

In the spring of 1989, Dean learned his next assignment would be in Honolulu, Hawaii. Dean loved to say most wives would welcome the chance to live in Hawaii but not his wife. I had been to Hawaii twice with Charlie, and the islands did not cast a spell on me as they did with so many visitors. In researching Hawaii, I realized trips back to Texas would be infrequent. Hawaii is the most remote island chain in the world, sitting in the middle of the world's largest ocean. A nonstop flight from Honolulu to Dallas was eight hours and four time zones away.

In an attempt to give me a proper Texas fix before we moved, Dean suggested we spend a week in Texas at a location of my choosing. Because my heart's home is the Hill Country, I rented a picturesque limestone house on a bluff overlooking the Medina River outside of Bandera, Texas. Bandera is less than thirty minutes from Kerrville, and Dean and I visited several of my friends there. After listening to our conversations about the Y.O., Dean said he wanted to visit the ranch. I called the ranch and made arrangements for a tour and lunch at the Chuckwagon. I was relieved to learn Charlie Three would not be there.

It was my first time back at the ranch since my abrupt departure from the Y.O. Social Club party in September 1982. We had lunch in the Chuckwagon, where I visited with many dear friends. Dean was gracious and charming, feigning interest as stories were told about my days on the ranch. Bertie, the cook, took me aside and whispered, "You done good, Norma, and if anyone deserves it, you do."

Charlie Four insisted we sign the guest register in the Chuckwagon. Knowing Three read it regularly, in the comment section I wrote, "A nice place to visit but I wouldn't want to live here." Surprisingly, the only emotion I felt was happiness at seeing so many of those with whom I shared that brief period of my life.

As we drove off the ranch, Dean commented, "Don't they realize this kind of life is over? They're living in the past." At the time it struck me as a strange remark because the usual reaction to the ranch was wonder and fascination for the life it represented. Twenty-five years later I would realize how prescient he was.

CHAPTER 30

"Our lives are full of surprises, for none of us has followed

a specific ambition toward a specific goal. Instead, we have

learned from interruptions and improvised from the materials

that came to hand, reshaping and reinterpreting.

As a result, all of us have lived with high levels of ambiguity."

MARY CATHERINE BATGESON

A Winding Road
Back to the Y.O. Ranch

I WAS IN THE BEDROOM at Charlie's house, leaning against the wall. Charlie was standing in front of me, his hands placed against the wall on either side of my head. His eyes were twinkling and he was smiling his roguish smile. "Letting you get away was the biggest mistake I ever made. I'll never find another woman like you, and you'll never find another man like me. We deserve each other."

My heart was racing as I anticipated his kiss. I was elated and giddy as I put my arms around him and drew him to me. Just as our lips were meeting, I remembered. I was married to Dean! What was I thinking? I yearned to go back to Charlie, but it would be unconscionable to leave Dean. Why did this have to happen now? Why couldn't it have happened before Dean and I married?

Slowly I awoke from the dream but remained so immersed in it, I was certain it was reality. I struggled to become fully conscious and realize Dean was sleeping soundly beside me, and we were living in Hawaii. This was not the first time I had such a dream. They always took me by surprise, leaving me wondering what recent event had unlocked that door of my subconscious. The dreams varied but always took place at the Y.O., sometimes at Charlie's house and sometimes at the Y.O. Lodge or Chuckwagon. Sometimes only Charlie and I were in the dream. Sometimes his sons and ranch employees were there. Sometimes Charlie was married to someone else and sometimes I was. Sometimes I was married to Charlie and Dean, and our *ménage à trois* was living happily on the Y.O. In some of the dreams, I was trying to convince Charlie to come back to me, and he was refusing. In others he was wooing me unsuccessfully. In one dream I was trying to leave the ranch. The horse trailer was packed with all my belongings, but Charlie's Bronco was blocking the front gate, refusing to let it pass. Charlie carried me into the Game Warden's Cabin and tried to convince me not to leave. Each time on awakening, I wondered if I would ever be free of them.

I rolled over and put my arm around Dean, trying to pull myself back into reality. We had been living in Hawaii almost a year. I was adapting to Hawaii and finding the aloha spirit and blend of cultures fascinating. Some members of the military and their spouses complained about native Hawaiians being rude, but I never found it to be the case. Many Hawaiians had the same antipathy toward military people. On several occasions Hawaiians told me I was one of the "nicest haoles" they ever met. *Haole* is the Hawaiian word for white people. I think my rearing as a minister's daughter was instrumental in this. The two scriptures I tried to follow were the golden rule and "whatever one sows, that will he also reap."

I try to learn the history and culture of the places I live. Soon after arriving in Hawaii, I took a course in the Hawaiian language at the Bishop Museum so I could correctly pronounce words like *kapiolani, kulaniakea, mauka,* and *kine*. Once I learned all syllables in Hawaiian end in a vowel, it became easier to break down the words and do a passable job of pronouncing them. I also took classes to learn the history of the islands. Like Texas, Hawaii was once a sovereign nation, which entitled it, like Texas, to fly its flag at the same height as the US flag. Like Texans, Hawaiians have great pride in their history and allegiance to their state.

The blending of the numerous cultures produces a variety of cuisines, music, and a polyglot language found nowhere else in the United States. My favorite experience in this regard was when Dean and I attended a party for one of his coworkers recently promoted to colonel. She was of Japanese ancestry, and her mother, who was reared in Japan, and I were talking. She asked me, "Have we met before?" When I told her we had not, she said, "I apologize for asking, but all white people look alike to me." Rather than being insulted, I tried not to burst into laughter remembering all the times I heard "white people" make the same statement about those of Asian ancestry.

We had been in Hawaii less than a year when the Schreiners once more entered my life. A friend sent me an article from the May 27, 1990, *Fort Worth Star-Telegram*. Under the headline "In a Hill Country town, the name of the game is antagonism," were two articles written by Barry Shlachter. The article titled "Normally quiet Kerrville split over tribute to family," was about renaming the five hundred-acre Kerrville State Recreational Area. Charlie's cousin was spearheading an effort to change the name to Kerrville-Schreiner State Park because the land was once owned by the Schreiners. The reporter interviewed a member of the family from whom the Schreiners obtained the land. They opposed including Schreiner in the name because the Schreiners owned the land only a month before selling it. She said when her grandfather died in 1934, her family had to pay off a debt to Schreiner Store. The five hundred acres, which eventually became the park, were deeded to the store as payment. She stated, "These were . . . Depression times. They were strictly doing business and that's how they acquired land because everybody owed the Schreiners." Ultimately, the park's name was changed to Kerrville-Schreiner State Park in spite of a nonbinding referendum in which 1,517 Kerrville residents voted against the name change and 206 supported it.

The other article by Shlachter was titled "Schreiner clan's roots deep, far-reaching in hometown." It gave a brief history of Captain Charles Schreiner and the prominent role he played in the Hill Country. The article stated, "Customers were given credit and those . . . who couldn't repay sometimes lost their property to the Schreiners, who became among the biggest landowners in the Hill Country." The article continued, "Before his death in 1927, the entrepreneur [Captain Schreiner] . . . was named captain of a local militia, accumulated more than $6 million in assets and 566,000 acres of land—nearly the size of Rhode Island and including the historic Y.O. Ranch. . . . A philanthropist and local booster, he bought a private hospital and gave it to the city, provided the land for a veterans hospital, started what is now Schreiner College, funded a school for Hispanic children, paid a $25,000 cash bonus to lure a railroad to town, underwrote local roadbuilding, owned the water company and served 30 years as county treasurer and clerk." A local businessman who wanted to remain anonymous said, "In the past, they were a heck of a force. It's quite obvious their influence is diminished. It doesn't take a mental giant to figure that out."

The most shocking news to me was the failure of Schreiner Bank because of "poor lending and underwriting standards as well as inadequate internal policies and procedures." The article went on to say the Schreiners had sold their interest in the "money losing" Y.O. Hotel, and there would be an auction of the game trophies, guns, saddles, and other memorabilia decorating the hotel in September. Louie Schreiner, Charlie's youngest son, said, "The real blow was building the hotel in the first place. We put our own money in it, millions." Charlie Four later told me that to pay off the hotel debt, parts of the Y.O. and the eight hundred-acre Bear Creek were sold. I remembered the day Three took me to Bear Creek, driving through the creek bed under cypress trees filled with white egrets. It was unadulterated Hill Country beauty any Texan would sell his soul to own. Charlie put the land in a trust for his sons to protect it while they were young. The trust did not protect it once they were adults, and unfortunately it had to be sold.

In June of 1992, I received a note from my friend and former business partner Kay Howard. She wrote, "Thought it might interest you to know that III asked a friend of mine to ask me if I'd seen you? That was just a few days after I had. III said of all his wives . . . you were the best."

A year later I was visiting my father in Houston, and he told me Charlie came by to see him. After our divorce, Charlie remained in touch with my father, going by to see him at least once a year. On this latest occasion, my father told me Charlie said, "Letting her get away was the biggest mistake I ever made. I've never found another woman like her." I wondered why, after so many years, Charlie would visit my father and tell him that? Did he think it might lead to me contacting him? There was a certain *schadenfreude* in knowing he had regrets but, as Mary Helen predicted, I had a better, fuller, more complete life without Charlie than I would have had as his wife. Knowing Charlie regretted losing me didn't provide the satisfaction I once imagined it would. As comedian Jo Brand said, "They say revenge is a dish best eaten cold but for most people, by the time it's ready to eat, they just don't fancy it."

Another Schreiner-related event was brought to my attention by friends who sent me a clipping from the September 14, 1993, *Kerrville Daily Times*. The headline was "Schreiner Bank directors sued." The article said the bank was declared insolvent "more than three years ago leaving the federal government with a $154 million tab." Now the FDIC was suing the bank's former directors, including Charlie, and the bank's president for unfair lending practices, negligence, breach of fiduciary duties, and other causes. The FDIC was requesting a jury trial in the lawsuit. The article by Mike Thomas stated, "Typically the lending scheme involved a systemic pattern of origination, renewal, extension, rollover and consolidation of loans, rubberstamp approval, no reduction in principal whatsoever and final charge off of unpaid loans." The directors used the bank as a cash cow, rolling over their old loans into new ones with no interest or penalties and seldom, if ever, making payments on the principal of the loans. I always suspected Charlie did this but never imagined it included the entire board. What an ignoble end for a family whose founder was known as "the father of the Hill Country" and whose personal fortune guaranteed the funds deposited in his bank until the late 1950s.

But Dean and I had only good news. After five years in Hawaii, Dean's next assignment would be in Texas!

CHAPTER 31

"Every happiness is the child of
a separation it did not think it could survive."

RAINER MARIA RILKE

Remembrance of Things Past

DEAN'S NEW ASSIGNMENT was commander of Camp Stanley, an Army base on the northwest outskirts of San Antonio. Since we were in Texas and he had promised to retire there, he decided to do so at the end of his assignment. I was hired as assistant director of human resources for a telecommunications company, so we decided we would stay in the San Antonio area. I found the perfect house northwest of Bandera, which was where we spent a week before moving to Hawaii. The house was on ten acres, and during the years we lived there we purchased an additional eighty acres around it.

We occasionally had lunch or dinner with Charlie Four and Mary Helen. In mid-March of 2001, Mary Helen asked me to join her for lunch at the Y.O. Bertie, the cook, had asked about me, and Mary Helen wanted to surprise her with my visit. We drove to the ranch on a perfect spring day, and the bluebonnets were so profuse they created a river of blue on the median and beside the road. It is a rite of spring in Texas to take family photographs in fields of bluebonnets, which are the state flower. Occasionally there would be a smattering of red Indian paintbrush or yellow black-eyed Susan. Every spring when this multihued visual feast appears, I send a prayer of gratitude to Lady Bird Johnson for her highway beautification efforts as first lady.

As we drove, Mary Helen told me the latest Schreiner news. Four was at loose ends trying to decide what to do with his life. He was only happy when he was on the ranch, but he did not want to live there. His youngest brother, Louie, was doing an excellent job running the ranch, but there was increasing contentiousness between the four brothers with Four and Louie aligning against Walter and Gus. The ranch partnership was set up so each brother had one vote with Three as the tiebreaker. I remembered Three saying he hoped all his sons would return to the ranch after college. Once more, answered prayers were causing more grief than happiness.

As we drove through the pastures, I recited my catechism of their names: Gilmer, West Feed, Blackbuck, South Home, and House Trap. The pastures wore spring coats of green grass. I had never seen the ranch looking so verdant. As soon as I walked into the Chuckwagon, Gus welcomed me with a bear hug. As he released me, Bertie, the best cook in Texas, was waiting with outstretched arms. Four and Mary Helen's three daughters greeted me next. It was hard to believe Tiffany, whom I last saw when she was five, was now twenty-two. All three girls were beautiful, charming, and self-confident. They took pleasure in recounting the many stories Mary Helen told them about when I lived on the ranch and our adventures cleaning out attics and dealing with prostitutes. Bertie filled me in on ranch gossip. Three was not in good health and still suffering from a hip replacement he had several years before. Walter, Charlie's second son, and his wife were expecting their third child. They had two daughters and were hoping for a boy who would be named Walter Richard Schreiner III. The baby's arrival was imminent. On a sad note, Bertie told me the male giraffe, part of the pair Charlie and I purchased, had recently died.

After lunch, Mary Helen and I drove to Three's house so she could drop off Christmas gifts for Three and his sixth wife. They weren't home but the front door was unlocked. I was reluctant to go in, remembering the times visitors entered the house unannounced when I was its mistress. Mary Helen assured me it would be okay though I remained doubtful. As I stepped inside the scent of cypress and burning oak embraced me, taking me back to my days on the ranch. Walking around the downstairs, I was surprised to see little changed from when I lived there. Every object on the walls was where I hung it. Tchotchkes on mantles and tables remained frozen where I had placed them twenty-three years before. Why hadn't the wives who followed me rearranged things? Would Charlie not let them, or were they simply not interested in doing so? Mary Helen left her gifts and asked me if I wanted to leave a note for Three. I replied, "No," but then something told me I should. I had a notepad in my car and wrote how lovely the ranch looked and how much I enjoyed seeing everyone. After some hesitation I closed saying, "The only disappointment was not getting to see you." I cannot remember if I signed it with love.

We left Three's house and drove to Charlie Four and Mary Helen's house. Their house was as they left it fourteen years before. Circa 1980s clothing still hung in closets; toys were still on shelves in the girls' room. China and crystal sat unused in a breakfront. As we sat at the dining room table talking, Mary Helen asked me how I could come back to the ranch and not be overwhelmed with sadness. I told her it was because, as she had predicted, I had found happiness and success in the life I'd had the past twenty years. When I started my life with Dean, I reinvented myself professionally and socially. In doing so, Charlie and the Y.O. were left behind, and few of my new acquaintances knew about that time in my life. I mentioned the irony of living in such close proximity to Kerrville and hearing rumors about the Schreiners when I was there shopping.

"What do you say?" she asked.

"Nothing. But I think to myself, 'If only you knew my relationship to the Schreiners.'"

Several weeks later, Mary Helen called to tell me Three was in the hospital and not doing well. I was not surprised based on what Bertie told me when I was at the ranch. I asked what was wrong, and she said there were complications after he had a procedure for his heart. I asked her to keep me advised on his condition.

The next Friday when I returned home after a business trip, Dean greeted me with, "Mary Helen called. Louie died."

"You mean Charlie," I said

"No. She said Louie. He had a heart attack."

I was stunned. Louie was only forty-one. I tried to call Mary Helen and Four, but their phones went to voice mail. I left messages for both.

I wondered if Three knew Louie was dead. If not, who would have the unenviable task of telling him? Would the news literally kill him? When I called Jim Nugent to tell him of Louie's death, he said, "If Three dies now, that family's going to have a huge mess on their hands sorting out and paying taxes on two estates."

"Did Three ever incorporate the ranch?" I asked.

"Not to my knowledge."

Louie's funeral was Tuesday, April 17, 2001, at First Presbyterian Church in Kerrville. An honor guard of Texas Highway Patrol officers stood in front of the church. As I walked into the sanctuary, I remembered the first time I'd come to this church for a speaking engagement as a lobbyist for the Equal Rights Amendment. Had someone told me twenty-four years later I would be here attending the funeral of my former stepson, I would have thought them insane.

The church was filled with mourners with only a few single seats available, one of which I took. The overflow was seated in the assembly hall, where the service would be broadcast. Resting on the closed casket were a spray of freshly picked wildflowers and Louie's battered cowboy hat, reminiscent of the one worn by his father. I remembered the first time Charlie told me about his sons. He said Louie had a special place in his heart because he was so good-natured and never let anything get him down. Three admired Louie's ability to make friends with everyone he met. That was obvious in the overflowing church. The most touching part of the service was the elegy given by Louie's brother-in-law; the two had been friends since third grade. Speaking directly to Louie's three sons, aged ten, eight, and six, he sobbed and told them never to forget how much their father loved them.

The casket was carried from the church by Louie's three brothers and his friends. His widow, Chrisie, and their sons followed. The boys had their pants tucked into boots with the Y.O. brand on the front. Louie was to be buried on the Y.O. next to his mother, Audrey Phillips Schreiner, who died at the age of fifty-nine in 1988. Audrey had told her sons of her desire to be buried at the ranch, and they granted her wish. I asked Charlie Four what Three said about it. Four said, "We didn't consult him. He was off somewhere. He definitely was not pleased. In fact, his displeasure may have been more about us not getting his advice and opinion, but it wasn't his decision to make." Mary Helen told me Audrey always felt her sons chose their father over her because all of them ended up working at the ranch. "No," I thought, "they chose the ranch, the mistress no flesh and blood woman could compete with."

The funeral procession was five miles long for the forty-five-minute drive to the ranch. The Highway Patrol shut down Interstate 10 from Kerrville to the Mountain Home exit to accommodate it. The drive was as beautiful as when Mary Helen and I made it a month before, but now the dominant flowers were Indian paintbrush, phlox and black-eyed Susan. Two horseback cowboys with hats over their hearts were on either side of the front gate. Along the eight miles of road into the ranch, diverse types of yellow wildflowers bloomed so profusely it appeared a bucket of yellow paint had been thrown across the pastures.

The day began as a warm and muggy spring day, but as we left the church a norther was arriving. By the time we arrived at the grave, gusty northerly winds were dropping temperatures into the forties. None of the mourners had dressed anticipating this drastic change. Because of the length of the funeral procession and the time it took for the last cars to arrive, early arrivals huddled around the open grave, seeking warmth by hugging themselves and each other. Men gallantly removed their coats and gave them to women.

The Mexican ranch employees formed an honor guard around the grave as the pallbearers brought the casket from the hearse. The minister announced he was doing an abbreviated version of the graveside service out of consideration for the shivering mourners. After the last prayer, he removed Louie's battered cowboy hat from the casket and handed it to his oldest son.

I was anxious to get out of the weather and to the Y.O. Lodge where lunch was being served but saw Walter talking with Red McCombs. I walked up to them, and Red hugged me commenting on what a sad day it was. After a few minutes, Walter excused himself saying, "I need to say goodbye to Louie." Red and I stopped talking as Walter walked away and stood, hat in hand, beside the grave for several minutes.

At the lodge, the Y.O. flag was at half-staff and whipping in the north wind. Inside the lodge, photographs of Louie from childhood to father-hood sat on tables. Mary Helen introduced me to Louie's wife, Chrisie, who was bearing up remarkably well. I knew from my mother's sudden death the blow an unexpected death deals the survivors. When I offered her my condolences, she took me in her arms and held onto me for a long time. When she released me, she said, "Charlie Three was so happy about your visiting the ranch. He told us he was so sorry he wasn't here, and if he'd known you were coming he wouldn't have missed it for the world."

There were so many in the crowd I had not seen in over twenty years—hunting guides, ranch hands, Schreiner cousins, and friends of Charlie Three. It was a joyous reunion juxtaposed with terrible sadness. As this was taking place, Charlie Three lay in the hospital unaware of his young-est son's death. The family left instructions no one was to be allowed to visit and the television not to be turned on. I asked Charlie Four when they were planning to tell Three. He replied, "Not until we absolutely have to. I'm afraid Dad will ask why Louie hasn't come to visit and my face will give me away." Fortunately, Charlie Four would be spared that heart-wrenching task.

CHAPTER 32

"Oh lay my spurs upon my breast, my rope and old saddle tree

And while the boys are lowering me to rest,

go turn my horses free."

TEDDY BLUE

The Last Roundup

ON THE DAY LOUIE DIED in Kerrville, Three was moved to intensive care in San Antonio and sent word to Charlie Four he wanted to see him. As Four was leaving for San Antonio, the Y.O.'s attorney called and told Four he needed to get to Kerrville as soon as possible because Louie was in the hospital, and it was serious. Four reached Kerrville a short time before Louie died. By the time he got to San Antonio, Three was unconscious. He never regained consciousness, and on April 22, doctors told the family Three would not live. Family members individually told him goodbye. Charlie Four was with him when he died.

The reason Three wanted to talk with his oldest son will never be known. Once more, Three failed to say what he needed to say to the person who needed to know it. Charlie Four told me, "One of the most important things [Three] neglected to tell me was I was . . . the trustee of his estate. If he'd done so, I would have insisted he give me or LAS [Louis Albert Schreiner] the hammer in all Y.O. partnership decisions. The way the partnership was left was gridlock, (2 against 2)."

On April 27, Three's service and burial were held on Gobblers Knob, his favorite place on the ranch. I was surprised because Three said he wanted to be buried beside his mother and father in Kerrville. I wondered if he changed his mind after Audrey was buried at the ranch or had his widow made the decision. A large tent had been erected, and as Dean and I walked toward it, the Y.O. cowboys rode by driving the longhorn steers.

Three's saddled dun horse was being led by one of the cowboys who broke off from the steers and proceeded to the newly dug grave. There he dismounted, removed the saddle and bridle from Three's horse, and placed them at the head of the grave. The cowboy removed his hat and stood at the grave for several minutes as the horse gently nudged him. Then he slapped the horse's flank, and it trotted away to graze with the steers. The steers were magnificent in their variety of colors and assortment of twisted horns. Tears began rolling down my cheeks as I remembered the fall evening when Charlie showed me the longhorns for the first time and taught me how to call them.

Former Y.O. cook Bertie was slowly making her way up the hill with the help of her son. We stopped and spoke to her, and she told me arthritis was taking a toll on her knees. Entering the tent was like walking back in time. Button, the official greeter of guests, looked exactly the same except his hair and beard were completely white. Rusty Cox, sometime employee of the Y.O., was sitting by hunting guide Haunch Alexander, who played mandolin as part of the Y.O. Band. In front of him was hunting guide and guitar player Tommy Thompson and his wife, Pam. Tommy had called me the previous Thanksgiving after learning from Charlie Four that I was living in Bandera. We ended our conversation saying, as people always do, we would get together soon, but neither of us imagined it would be like this.

Jimmy Dee, who investigated my cattle rustling complaint, still had his distinctive mustache, but it was now snow white and he was no longer the robust figure of a man I remembered. He tried to rise to meet me but could not, so I bent over and hugged him. There was a woman with him who told me Jimmy suffered a stroke on the day of Louie's funeral. I introduced Dean and as I was speaking, Jimmy began weeping. I bent over and kissed him on the forehead.

Mary Helen invited me to sit with the family, but I declined. Dean and I found a place to stand in the back of the tent, which gave us a better view than sitting. Looking out over the lush green pastures, I remembered the first time Charlie brought me to Gobblers Knob and gave me my Y.O. ring. Two other times stood out. One was during a spring thunderstorm, when we turned the back of his Suburban into a makeshift bed, and another when we lay on the ground and watched a full moon rise, illuminating the hills of the ranch.

The service was conducted by a Texas Ranger chaplain who spoke of Charlie's love of Western history and the Texas Rangers. He said the

Rangers considered Charlie one of their own, even if he was never officially sworn in. I smiled when he said each of those assembled had many stories they could tell about Charlie. He spoke of the devotion of Lupe Ortega, Charlie's housekeeper, who throughout Charlie's illness caught the bus to San Antonio to visit him.

A cowboy trio played and sang the first and second verses of "HOME ON THE RANGE." I remembered Charlie telling me the second verse was his favorite:

> "Where the air is so pure, the zephyrs so free,
> The breezes so balmy and light,
> That I would not exchange my home on the range
> For all of the cities so bright."

As Charlie's casket was carried to the grave, mariachis began singing "Adelita," the famous *corrido* that Charlie sang for me as we sat on the patio having lunch in Guadalajara. Thoughts of that weekend overwhelmed me, and I remembered Charlie saying he wanted it played at his funeral because the final stanza was so appropriate: "I beg you do not mourn for me." Tears started streaming down my cheeks. Dean put his arm around me, and I laid my head on his shoulder, struggling to regain my composure. The family accompanied Charlie's casket to the grave, and the service ended with a horseback cowboy reading a poem he had written about Charlie.

Mourners filed by the casket. Men removed their hats, many crossed themselves, and most touched the casket. I wanted to say my goodbye privately after everyone left. I saw Lupe standing under some live oak trees, and as I approached his face lit up. He had streaks of white in his hair but was still a handsome and distinguished-looking man. I knew it might make him uncomfortable, but I could not help hugging him, which he reciprocated, both of us pulling away with tears in our eyes. In a combination of English and Spanish, he said, "You are the best. Of all the wives, you are the best."

As we talked, I kept my hand on his arm, holding onto this physical link from my past. We conversed as we had when I lived on the ranch, Lupe in broken English and I in broken Spanish. We reminisced about my horse wreck and Ms. bringing me a half-dead rat. Charlie Four walked up and hugged me. I asked how he was doing.

"I was doing okay until those damn mariachis started playing. Then I completely lost it. I could see Three looking over his glasses with that twinkle in his eye, jiggling his foot and loving that song."

"Me too," I said, starting to tear up again.

I gave Lupe a final hug, walked to the casket, and placed my hand on it. I bent over and whispered my own elegy to Three, lines of a poem by EDNA ST. VINCENT MILLAY:

"Into the earth with you,
Be one with the dull, the indiscriminate dust.
A fragment of what you felt, of what you knew,
A formula, a phrase remains,—but the best is lost."

I stood quietly for several minutes and then bent and kissed the casket as tears trickled down my cheeks. Throughout the afternoon, Lupe kept a silent graveside vigil, the most poignant tribute of the day to Charlie Three.

The Y.O. flag in front of the lodge was again at half-staff. The crowd was scattered throughout the lodge and the pavilion behind it. Dean and I went through the serving line to get plates of barbecue. Jim Nugent was sitting alone at a table, and I asked if we could join him. "I would be honored," he said. "I sure would hate to be this family right now. Can you imagine having two estates to settle and the taxes they'll owe? I always told you the ranch wouldn't make it into the next generation. I fear this will be its death knell."

"Surely not," I said.

"It will take a miracle to hold it together. Over the past ten years they sold off as many acres as they could afford to and still keep the ranching and hunting business going. Even though I hated you and Charlie not working out, I'm glad you won't be stuck dealing with what comes next. Charlie Four will bear the brunt of it, and it won't be easy."

Rusty came up to our table, removed his hat, greeted everyone, and said to me, "There's someone who wants to meet you." I excused myself and followed him to a tall woman dressed in black. "Mrs. Schreiner meet Mrs. Schreiner," Rusty said as he smiled, bowed, and made a quick exit.

I looked quizzically at the woman who extended her hand and said, "I'm Sully. I was Charlie's third wife."

I almost said, "The menopausal wife," but caught myself.

"Charlie was a good egg," Sully said.

I agreed. As we talked, I learned she had not remarried and recently moved to San Antonio. She asked me about Charlie's house, had I lived in it with Charlie, where did Charlie and I marry, and if I had spoken to Charlie's widow.

The author's favorite photo of Charlie Three, September 1979.

To the last question I replied, "No, I think it would be too awkward for her."

"I agree, and besides, I came for Charlie, not for her. He was a good guy, and I owe him."

As Sully and I talked, I realized of Three's six wives, half of us attended his service—Sully, his widow, and me. Of the remaining three, two were dead, Audrey and Lynn, and no one knew if Patricia was dead or alive. Before leaving the ranch, I stopped at Louie's and then Charlie's graves to leave flowers at each. Standing at Three's grave and looking out across the Y.O., I had to admit this was the perfect place for him to be in perpetuity.

In addition to appearing in newspapers throughout Texas, Charlie's obituary appeared in numerous magazines and livestock publications. Several publications ran the obituaries for seventy-four-year-old Charlie and forty-one-year-old Louie side by side, a stark illustration of the randomness with which death chooses its victims. The obituaries of the *New York Times* and *Los Angeles Times* contained erroneous information. The *Los Angeles Times* obituary, written by Myrna Oliver, contained the most. It stated Charlie inherited the ranch in 1949 when in fact he inherited it on the death of his father, Walter, in 1933. It also implied the Y.O. was at one time five hundred thousand acres. Charlie Three's grandfather, Captain Schreiner, once had six hundred thousand acres, but only sixty thousand of that composed the Y.O. Ranch, which was what Captain Schreiner gave to his son Walter, Charlie's father. It incorrectly stated the ranch currently had 250,000 head of longhorns when the number was closer to five hundred. The Y.O. never could have supported that number of cattle, and Charlie must have spun in his grave at such an egregious error. The ratio of cows per acre in the Texas Hill Country is eighteen to twenty acres to support one cow.

The most blatant mistakes were found in this section: "Widowed in 1988, the thrice-married Schreiner lost one of his four sons, Louis, to a heart attack on Easter. He is survived by the other three, Charles IV (known as Charlie Four) Walter and Gus; and nine grandchildren, including 'Charlie Five.'" There were four major errors in those two sentences. Charlie was not a widower or "thrice married" but on his sixth wife when he died. Louis did not die on Easter, and Charlie Five (Baby Charlie) had been dead for twenty years.

The *New York Times* obituary stated, "Mr. Schreiner's wife, Audrey, a University of Texas cheerleader when he met her, died in 1988." Audrey was not a cheerleader, she and Charlie divorced in 1973, and Charlie married five more times.

In 2001, the *Texas Country Reporter* television show covered the funeral of Charles Schreiner III, https://youtu.be/xAAvgJioYUU?si=lgB-F1Y9Lt3AeQUG.

CHAPTER 33

"When sorrows come, they come not single spies.

But in battalions."

WILLIAM SHAKESPEARE

When Sorrows Come

"WHAT HAPPENED TO Three's gun collection?" I asked. Dean and I were having dinner with Four and Mary Helen, the first time we'd seen them since Three's funeral five years before.

"I had to sell it to pay taxes," Four replied

"If anything would make him spin in his grave that should," I thought. Three detested what he considered the overreach of government regulations. Several times I accompanied him when he personally delivered a check to the Internal Revenue Service for his mother's estate taxes. He would always give the building the middle finger salute as we drove away. He railed against any attempt at gun control because he believed it would be opening the door for allowing the government to take away his guns, which was exactly what happened to his guns, metaphorically speaking. When Three was interviewed for the book *Forever Texas* he said, "What with taxes and federal control on just about every aspect of a man's business, it's sad to think what generations of a family sacrificed to build a legacy for . . . can be severely jeopardized by sprouting special interest groups." Sadly, it wasn't the government but Three's fiscal irresponsibility and failure to plan ahead that took his gun collection and doomed the ranch.

Later, when Charlie Four and I were exchanging emails on his father, Four wrote me, "Three loved to start things, to wit the Longhorn Association and Exotic Wildlife Association, and build things; maintenance was not in his vocabulary. He did this project after project and maybe marriage after marriage." I agree. Three was a brilliant entrepreneur and, with Schreiner Bank to provide capital, exceptional at implementing ideas. But he was not one for follow-up. Charlie Four's comment made me realize that the way Three treated me during our marriage was likely a pattern established with his previous wives. He wanted to be married but either would not or could not carry out the emotional obligations and intimacies necessary for a successful marriage. I doubt he was much of a husband to any of his six wives. A friend summed it up best when she said, "Charlie often neglected his women but never his cows, guns, or whiskey."

Approximately seven hundred items from Three's gun collection were auctioned, including knives, rifles, guns, badges, documents, saddles, advertising signs, bronzes, and artwork. The auctioneer, John Gangel of Little John's Auction Service, said the articles "represented the premier assemblage of privately-owned Texas Ranger memorabilia. And there are few museums that even come close to what Charlie had." Guns and memorabilia from three Texas Rangers drew the greatest interest: Capt. Frank Hamer, who led the ambush that killed Bonnie and Clyde; Capt. W. W. Sterling, who worked with Frank Hamer in bringing order to Borger, Texas, during the oil boom and was appointed adjutant general of the Texas National Guard in the 1930s; and Manuel "Lone Wolf" Gonzaullas, who gained renown for bringing law and order to Texas oil fields and along the Mexico border. After retiring, Gonzaullas worked as a consultant for radio, movies, and television shows, most notably *Tales of the Texas Rangers*.

The selling of Three's gun collection was the opening act for the tragedies to come. In the early morning hours of April 11, 2009, the pavilion, which Three designed and built while we were married, caught fire, along with the Wells Fargo cabins adjoining it. The fire was spotted by guests staying in the cabins. Two volunteer fire departments fought the blaze, using over sixty thousand gallons of water from the ranch swimming pool. The fires were contained within several hours, but it took twelve hours for firefighters to put out the ceiling beams used in the pavilion. When Three built the pavilion, he used floor joists salvaged from the Schreiner Wool Warehouse for those beams. Cut at a mill that was in downtown Kerrville, they were twelve feet long and two feet wide. The Wells Fargo cabin, also built by Three, was made of hand-cut limestone blocks taken from a fence built in the late 1800s by Captain Schreiner for his Live Oak Ranch foreman, Robert Real. I called Charlie Four to express my condolences and ask him when the pavilion would be rebuilt. "It will depend on when we can afford it," he answered. I recoiled at his honesty, my first hint of the ranch's dire financial condition.

In October tragedy struck again when a ranch employee, twenty-seven-year-old Brandon Buchi, was gored to death by a barasingha deer being unloaded from a trailer. The deer stabbed Buchi in the side and thigh, and he bled to death before emergency medics could arrive. His widow filed a lawsuit against the individual ranch partners—Charlie Four, Walter, Gus, and Louie's widow—for negligence in failing to train employees on proper safety measures when performing such jobs. Charlie Four told me the widow received a six-figure settlement.

Dean and I had our own crisis to deal with that fall. Dean inherited from his father a prolapsed mitral valve. The mitral valve allows blood to flow to the left ventricle in the heart. Throughout his military career the prolapse caused no problems, but now he began having instances of rapid heartbeat, night sweats, and shortness of breath. Tests showed the prolapse had become worse, and the only solution was open heart surgery to repair or replace the valve. The only time Dean had been in the hospital was when he was born, and he was reluctant to have the surgery. The doctor told him that to maintain any quality of life, he must have the operation, and in December, he started the battery of tests required for the surgery.

On a personal level, I broke out of the corporate gulag where I had been doing time for fifteen years and retired. My success disproved the adage that to be successful you must love what you do. The company I began working for fifteen years earlier grew during my tenure from three locations with several thousand employees to an international corporation with over forty thousand employees. Throughout my tenure, I received promotions, and for the last three years, I was the head of employee relations for the entire company. As such, I was constantly in the hot seat dealing with lawsuits and legal issues, being deposed, testifying at trials, and managing efforts to prevent unionization of the company's work force. When I was promoted to the position, I was not happy about it. One of the executives, with whom I was friends, called to congratulate me and ask how I felt about the promotion. I bluntly replied, "I feel like I've been fucked and didn't even get kissed."

Dean always attributed my success to my "studied indifference to it." The best thing about the job was the people I worked with and the friendships I made that continue to endure. Even though it almost caused me an ulcer, my success gave me the ability to retire comfortably. Once retired, I returned to teaching as an adjunct professor of political science at Alamo Community College. Returning to the classroom confirmed that teaching gave me the intellectual stimulation and sense of accomplishment I never found in the corporate world.

The new year of 2010 began with the news that Rusty Cox, my friend and occasional Y.O. employee, had died of a heart attack. In March, Dean had open heart surgery at Brooke Army Medical Center at Fort Sam Houston in San Antonio. The human toll of the Iraq and Afghanistan wars was visible throughout the hospital. Young men and women with missing limbs, some on crutches and some in wheelchairs, filled the halls, lobby, and cafeteria. I could not look at them without wondering how many would be able to put their lives back together. It is easy to disassociate oneself from the human toll of military conflicts when viewing them from afar. Within those walls, the reality of the war met you coming and going. Each time I passed one of the soldiers, I uttered a silent prayer for their physical and mental recovery.

On May 1, Rusty's memorial service was held at the Y.O. Lodge, and his ashes were scattered on Gobblers Knob. I was struck by the irony of this given the contentious relationship between Rusty and Charlie Three. The service was attended by about two hundred people representing the many spectrums of Rusty's life—music, movies, art, and the Y.O. Ranch. I was surprised and happy to see Lupe there. I refrained from hugging him but held onto his hand for a long time as we exchanged greetings. One of the more memorable parts of the service was when the person conducting it spoke of Rusty's ability to woo the ladies. He asked any of those who had been a "lady friend" of Rusty's to come forward. Over ten women walked to the front of the room as the crowd applauded. I was standing beside a friend who turned to me and said, "I'm certainly not going up there. Are you?"

"Not on your life," I replied. I wondered how many more of the mourners preferred discretion to going public.

After the service, Charlie Four, Mary Helen, Dean, and I went to Three's house. His widow had moved out several years before, and the house had fallen on hard times. The mounted steer heads were coming apart, and one had a spider web strung from the tip of a horn to the steer's nose. Ceiling lights were burned out, and the upholstery on the furniture in the living room and upstairs parlor was badly faded and torn from sun damage. Furniture, artwork, and knickknacks remained where I hung or placed them thirty-three years before. In the kitchen cabinets, Myrtle's crystal and Aunt Mimi's monogrammed Sevres china sat where I placed them after bringing them from the storage barns. I wondered if the last time they were used was at the Christmas dinner Charlie and I hosted for his sons in 1978. The most poignant item was a dried flower arrangement in Charlie's bathroom that I arranged and placed there. The house reminded me of Miss Havisham's in Dickens's *Great Expectations*, destined never to move forward in time but remain as it was when Three and I lived there.

In mid-December, I had a phone call from former Y.O. cook Bertie Varner. She asked if I knew about Charlie Four. My heart raced as I answered, "No." He was in the hospital in San Antonio, extremely ill, and might not live. He had gone in for an issue with his heart, but something went wrong. That night I spoke to Mary Helen. She told me Charlie Four had heart surgery that had not gone well. He had been on a ventilator for three weeks, was running a fever, and had a yeast infection. No visitors were allowed except for immediate family. I asked who was running the ranch. She said that before the surgery, Charlie told Tessa, their second daughter, to take over if he was unable to resume his responsibilities. Tessa was in her late twenties, about the same age as her father when he took over as ranch manager. I smiled thinking how once more, a woman was stepping into the breach to keep the ranch going. Tessa was obviously cut from the same cloth as her great-grandmother Myrtle.

CHAPTER 34

"Well, the blues come to Texas lopin' like a mule."

BLIND LEMON JEFFERSON

The Blues Come to Texas

"Y.O. RANCH OWNERS embroiled in lawsuit" was the headline in the March 2, 2013, edition of the *Kerrville Daily Times*. The first sentence stated, "More than half the owners of a historic game ranch west of Kerrville want a court to dissolve the operation, citing negative cash flow, the impending maturity of loans and a deadlocked governing board." The article continued, "Five out of the seven claim unless the court intervenes immediately, the ranch won't have enough money to pay bills, employees, wildlife feed and many other items beyond March or April." My first impulse was to call Charlie Four who, after a long recuperation, had recovered from his heart surgery. Then I reconsidered. It was none of my business, and I correctly assumed those involved were under a gag order. No doubt there would be continuing coverage by newspapers. There was.

On March 7, 2013, the *San Antonio Express-News* ran a story headlined, "Kerrville has grown out of ranch's shadow." This article cited the positive things the Schreiner family had done for the community, e.g., the department store, bringing the first railroad to Kerrville, creating the town's first water and sewer systems, wiring the town for electricity, Schreiner College, and the many tourists and hunters who visited the Y.O. Ranch and stayed at the Y.O. Hotel. It went on to point out Schreiner Bank had failed, the hotel was now part of the Hilton chain, Schreiner's department store had been sold and ultimately closed, Schreiner College was now run by a board of trustees, and the Y.O. covered forty thousand acres, down from the original sixty thousand given to Charlie Three's father. The article said the Y.O. began coming apart after the death of Charlie Three, stating, "Charles Schreiner IV is listed as the ranch's senior partner. For ten years . . . family members allowed him to run the ranch. But stung by decisions in the past few years . . . some family members demanded last year to have board meetings to discuss business moves before they were made. That soured an already tense relationship between siblings, the source said." The article concluded, "While Kerrville owes its past to the Schreiners and the Y.O., residents here aren't worried about the future."

A month later the Schreiners were on the front page again. "Y.O. owner accused of stealing sheep" was the headline on the April 10, 2013, *Kerrville Daily Times*. Beneath the headline was a picture of Walter, who was jailed on April 5. Walter had been indicted by a Burnet County grand jury in June 2012 for writing a bad check to purchase sheep "with the intent to deprive the owner of the property." The indictment said there were insufficient funds to cover the check. The final paragraph of the article contained more startling news: "Gus Schreiner is involved in a lawsuit with . . . Broadway Bank, which alleged he deposited three stolen checks into accounts he opened for three businesses. The bank alleged he falsely claimed ownership of the businesses. The bank, in its suit, claims losses totaling $130,963.11."

"How terrible," I thought, "not just for Walter and Gus but for their wives and children.

The death knell for the ranch was sounded in the *San Antonio Express-News* on August 22, 2013, with the headline, "Y.O. Ranch up for sale for $85 million." The article stated the purchase price included twenty-nine thousand acres, five residences, a lodge, an adventure camp, and other perks. Not included but also for sale were the exotic animals and longhorns. Whoever bought the ranch could keep its name but not licensing rights for the Y.O. Ranch or use of the brand. A few days later, I saw an ad for the ranch in the glossy real estate magazine *Texas Farm and Ranch*. A color photograph of the interior of the Y.O. Lodge consumed half a page. Staring at it, I was transported back to that Sunday afternoon when Charlie switched on the lights and I saw it for the first time. Memories of so many happy events there swept through my mind. The party after Charlie and I married, the hunters sharing tales of their day's adventures, the Y.O. Trail Drive parties, parties before and after longhorn sales, and, of course, the unforgettable centennial party. My heart ached remembering what once was. I wanted to visit the ranch one last time before it sold. In a week, Dean was going to California to visit his family, which would provide the perfect time to do so. I called Charlie Four, and he made the arrangements for my visit.

I arrived at the Y.O.'s front gate around noon on a Sunday, just like the first time Three took me to the ranch. In the three years since I was there for Rusty's memorial service, the main road had deteriorated considerably, and it took almost forty-five minutes to reach the paved portion. As I drove by Deer Park, I noticed it was overgrown with tall grass, the high fence was sagging and in disrepair, and only the ghosts of animals who once roamed there haunted it. Driving by the Y.O. Lodge, I saw a large blue tarp over the roof. I assumed it was to keep out rain and wondered how long it had been there. I drove to the Chuckwagon where the key to Charlie's house had been left for me.

Driving up the steep incline to the house, I noticed a mass of weeds consuming what was once the cactus garden. Standing before the house, I was swept away by memories of all the hopes and expectations I envisioned the first time Three took me through it, and how few turned out as I expected.

I walked up the stone pathway and unlocked the front door. Entering the hallway, my first sensation was the familiar smell of the cypress paneling and oak fires. Closing my eyes, I inhaled deeply and thought, "this will be the last time I smell it." I remembered lines from the poem "Smoke in Our Hair" by Ofelia Zepeda: "Smoke, like memories, permeates our hair, our clothing, our layers of skin." The smell reminded me of the fall and winter evenings at Charlie's house, the lodge, and the Chuckwagon, and I was transported back to those golden hours and days of my first autumn on the Y.O. Now the house was a ghost of its former self, and I could almost hear it moaning in anguish at what it had become. Most of the furniture was gone, but the objects I hung on the walls remained. The grizzly bear Charlie shot in Alaska, previously a resident of the lodge, now stood sentry in the living room. Like the ranch, it was in a bedraggled state and missing one of its paws. I remembered the good times Charlie and I had in the house, our first smoke-filled night, entertaining guests and friends, and my solitary endless nights as our marriage unraveled when all I could do was cry.

I heard a car coming up the drive. Soon Gus's wife, Lori, walked into the living room. We hugged, and I saw her oldest daughter, Audrey, named after the first Mrs. Charles Schreiner III, accompanied her. They were on their way to see a recently born giraffe and thought I might like to accompany them. As we drove to the Africana pasture, I told Lori about going to the Oklahoma City Zoo with Charlie Three to purchase the first giraffes, and Three designing and building the Giraffe Hilton. I recounted their arrival under a full moon and everyone assembling to greet them with toasts of champagne. I realized that I was privy to information about the events occurring during my tenure that few others knew.

As we watched the baby giraffe, several Mexican employees who'd been around since Three and I were married drove into the pasture. I had forgotten how quickly word spread on the ranch. They greeted me with smiles and handshakes and kept saying over and over, *"Eres la mejor esposa"* (You are the best wife), and *"Estuviste en el rancho en los mejores tiempos"* (You were at the ranch in the best of times). As they said it, they would place a hand over their hearts. Fighting to keep my composure, I replied, *"Muchas gracias,"* over and over. They told me Lupe, Three's former housekeeper, came to the ranch once a month to spend the night. His daughter, with whom he lived in San Antonio, brought him. I told them to give him my best wishes and tell him I was sorry not to have seen him.

Lori took me back to Three's house, and I continued my pilgrimage through the rooms. Many of the closets had mildew in them, and windowpanes and light fixtures were broken. Pieces of Myrtle's coromandel screen were scattered across the garden room floor. The vault door to Charlie's gun room was locked, which was just as well because it was my least favorite room. I was starting up the stairs when I heard a voice calling, "Norma? Where are you?" It was Gus, Lori's husband and Charlie's third son. He came toward me with arms open, and I walked into his bear hug. We walked back to the living room, and I asked his feelings about selling the ranch.

"I hate it. I'd give anything not to do it, but we can't go on with things like they are. There's no other way. We just can't get along. I wish you had never left. If you and dad had stayed together, things would be different."

I smiled and said, "I doubt that Gus."

"No. It would have been. I know it would have been. Why did you divorce him?"

"I didn't divorce him. He divorced me, but it doesn't matter. It's over and done."

We talked of people and events, told stories about Three, and laughed at some of the antics and practical jokes of the hunting guides. Gus left, and I went upstairs. Several pieces of furniture remained in the upstairs parlor and master bedroom. I walked into what was once my closet and opened the chest of drawers to see what might be there. The only item was the framed collage of photographs I had assembled showing the building of the house. I took it out and ran my finger across the images of the pouring of the slab, the first limestone blocks being laid by Reyna, the Y.O. stonemason, the concrete beams for the gun room ceiling being put in place, and the soda fountain being moved into the living room. Once more my reverie was interrupted by someone calling my name. It was Audrey, and she was holding a copy of *Long Days and Short Nights*, the book published for the ranch's centennial. She said, "Would you autograph this?"

"I would be honored," I replied, signing my name above the photo of Three and me that he finally agreed could go into the book. I handed the book back to Audrey, hugged her, and told her I was touched she would want my autograph. "Dad says you'll always be a member of the family and you're his favorite stepmother," she said.

After she left, I walked over to Three's closet and opened the doors. His clothing was still hanging there. I hoped to see one of his signature red-and-white-checked shirts, which I had every intention of absconding with. I wanted a physical reminder of him. But there were none. I opened his dresser drawer and saw several folded sheets from yellow legal pads. This was how he kept his "to do" list. He would fold the paper into fourths, writing phone numbers and information on each fold and keeping it in his shirt pocket. I took two of the sheets, not bothering to look at them. What was written on them was immaterial. All I wanted was a physical remembrance.

The sun was casting long shadows, and I needed to leave soon if I wanted to be home before dark. There was one more task I needed to complete. I wanted to leave a personal item immured in Charlie's house. I tried to do that when I buried my Y.O. ring with Ms., but Charlie's digging it up and giving it to another woman nullified that. This time I wanted to make certain what I left would remain there. After secreting it away, I walked onto the patio and stood where Charlie and I were married. It was where I loved to stand in the early morning, watching and listening as the ranch came to life. Standing there I felt a presence, as if someone brushed by me. I heard a guttural meow.

Driving to the front gate, I recited my rosary of pasture names—the House Trap, South Home, Blackbuck, West Feed, and Gilmer. When I reached the Gilmer, longhorns were grazing along the road. I stopped and watched them until they grazed out of sight.

When I called Charlie Four to thank him, we reminisced about our time together at the ranch. I said, "Whenever I think of those days, I see them in a golden haze. At times it seemed magical. Even with the bad times, I wouldn't have missed them for the world."

"You're right. I'll always think of it as the ranch's best days." He hesitated and then said, "I was brought up by Three and Myrtle to run that ranch, and now there's no ranch for me to run."

For Three to have loved the Y.O. and his heritage as much as he did, there is no explanation for why he did not take the necessary steps to protect its legacy. Perhaps it would have been an impossible task.

CHAPTER 35

"As for man, his days are as grass: as a flower of the field,

so he flourisheth. For the wind passeth over it, and it is gone;

and the place thereof shall know it no more."

PSALM 103:15–16

This Too Shall Pass Away

"DID YOU KNOW Walter Schreiner is dead?" The voice on the phone was a friend who lived in Kerrville.

"What?!" I exclaimed, trying to comprehend the statement.

"I don't know the details, but he died last night."

"I need to call Four," I said and hung up. When Four answered I said, "Is Walter dead?"

"News travels fast."

"What happened?"

"He was driving back from Fredericksburg last night, went off the road, and overcorrected. His truck flipped and he was thrown out because the dumb shit wasn't wearing a seat belt. He died at the scene."

Though Walter and I were never close, I still felt the loss, especially for his wife and three children, especially the much longed for son, Walter Richard Schreiner III, born in 2001. Walter's funeral was held in an overflowing church on July 23, 2014, followed by his burial at the Y.O. Of Three's four handsome sons, only two remained.

The year, 2014, had started on a positive note. The oil company for which I did consulting placed me on retainer to develop and teach a leadership program. In February, the book *Kid Me Not*, to which I contributed an essay, was published and well received. But these good times were negated as Dean's health problems worsened. A month before Walter was killed, Dean suffered what the doctor termed a "small stroke." I wondered at this oxymoron because in my opinion no stroke is small, especially as I watched Dean's cognitive functions deteriorate and his short-term memory disappear. In September, he confessed he no longer had the strength or will to take care of our place, and we listed it for sale.

When I got out of bed the morning of October 17, I saw the light was on in my bathroom. Dean and I had separate bedrooms because his snoring made it impossible for me to sleep. I walked into the bathroom where Dean was splashing water on his face.

"I have the worst headache," he said, slurring his words.

"Get back in bed," I said, putting my arm around his waist and moving him toward his bedroom. As we got to the bed he collapsed. I called 911 and within ten minutes EMS arrived. I showed the two responders to the bedroom and one of them said, "Air Life is on the way." The EMS paramedic went through the litany that by then I knew by heart to assess whether a stroke had occurred. Smile, grasp my hand, speak to me. Dean could not respond. He was placed in the ambulance for the trip down the hill to the county road in front of our house where the helicopter had landed. As the ambulance pulled away, our dog Patches sat in the driveway barking farewell.

By the time I dressed and drove to the hospital, Dean was in surgery. An MRI revealed he had an intracranial hemorrhage (bleeding inside his brain), and surgery was necessary to stop it. As I sat in the waiting room with a thousand-yard stare, my mind blank, suddenly it felt as if something brushed by me. I remembered a comment from one of the wives whose husband was a firefighter on 9/11. He was in one of the towers when it collapsed. She said that as the dust from the tower enveloped her, she knew he was in it. That was how I felt. In that infinitesimal moment, I knew Dean's spirit passed me as he shuffled off his mortal coil.

A nurse came and said Dean was out of surgery. Walking into his room, I saw he was on a ventilator. The surgeon arrived, introduced himself, and told me the extensive bleeding in Dean's brain made his condition "dire." The bleeding was in areas involving motor skills, and if Dean lived he would be a paraplegic. The doctor's prognosis was Dean probably would not survive, but he wanted to wait twenty-four hours before making a final assessment. Then the surgeon said the kindest thing anyone could have said to me, "Go home. Hospitals are toxic places. They are noisy, cold, full of light, and uncomfortable. You need to be in familiar surroundings and in your own bed tonight even if you do not sleep a wink. You cannot do your husband any good staying here and you will be miserable. The nurses will take good care of him and call you if his condition changes."

Before leaving the hospital, I signed a do-not-resuscitate order. Through the years, Dean and I discussed that neither of us wanted to be kept alive by artificial means. Dean recalled his father being on a ventilator and the family being told he would need to be on one for the rest of his life. Dean's father was still conscious and made the decision himself, shaking his head in the negative when asked if that was his wish. Dean admired his father for having the courage to make that decision.

Driving out of San Antonio at seventy miles an hour in four lanes of traffic, the enormity of the situation overwhelmed me. I began shaking and then sobbing. I clutched the steering wheel and forced myself to concentrate on driving. I thought of Margaret Thatcher's words to President George H. W. Bush, "Don't go wobbly, George." As I drove I repeated those words over and over until I pulled into our front gate.

Two friends from Dallas arrived late that night. I appreciated their coming but did not think I needed babysitters. But once we went to bed, I was glad not to be in the house alone. Sleep was intermittent, and finally I got up at 4:30 a.m. and walked onto the back porch accompanied by Patches. As Patches sniffed around for raccoons, I looked up at the sky and saw first one and then two more shooting stars. I thought of Shakespeare's lines from *Romeo and Juliet*, "When he shall die, take him and cut him out in little stars, and he will make the face of heaven so fine that all the world will be in love with night and pay no worship to the garish sun." Dean always said I would make a great primitive given my superstitious nature and belief in dreams and signs. It was true. Seeing those shooting stars provided me serenity and acceptance that Dean was gone.

At two o'clock the next afternoon, I watched as the doctor examined Dean. He pinched Dean's arm and leg. There was no response. He ran a ballpoint pen up and down the sole of each foot. There was no reaction. When the doctor shone a light into Dean's lovely brown eyes, I could see the pupils were dilated to the point they almost obscured the irises. The doctor told me that Dean's condition remained the same as yesterday; the next step was mine, but I did not need to make a decision immediately. I could take as long as I needed.

"I've decided," I said. "Please take him off the ventilator." The surgeon left and another doctor arrived to oversee this process. This doctor took me aside and said, "It won't take long. I've been monitoring him throughout the night. He's not capable of breathing on his own."

I held Dean's hand as his heartbeat slowed and finally stopped. I smoothed his hair into place, raised his hand to my cheek, then kissed it. "I always thought you had the most beautiful eyes and hands," I said, placing it back on the bed. After thirty years of marriage, I was a widow.

▬▬▬▬▬▬▬

CHAPTER 36

"Fate returns us to the same stage and the same director

but hands us a different script."

THOMAS SAVAGE

▬▬▬▬▬▬▬

You Can't Go Home Again

ON OCTOBER 5, 2015, a large portion of the Y.O. Ranch was sold to two couples, Byron and Sandra Sadler and Lacy and Dorothy Harber. They purchased about one-fifth of the twenty-seven thousand acres that remained of the once sixty thousand-acre ranch. This included the headquarters area and approximately five thousand acres of the northwest portion of the ranch. Charlie Four retained ownership of the name Y.O. Ranch and the Y.O. brand, thus the portion purchased by the Sadlers and Harbers was renamed Y.O. Ranch Headquarters. On October 8, an article in the *San Antonio Express-News* stated, "Neglect has taken a toll on many of the ranch buildings," and quoted Byron Sadler saying, "It's kind of run-down." His wife went on to say, "We're going to invest several million dollars to bring it back to what it had been."

The article said the eight miles of road leading into the ranch had become so rough that tour buses could no longer drive on it, and the Sadlers were already beginning road repairs. It quoted the ranch's tourism director as saying bookings dropped off in 2013 after newspaper articles about the lawsuit between Charlie Three's sons and the arrests of Walter and Gus. It went on to say both Walter and Gus pled guilty and were placed on deferred adjudication probation. Gus also served seventy-five days in the Kerr County jail and paid $112,420 in restitution.

In the spring of 2016, I received a call from Haunch Alexander, one of

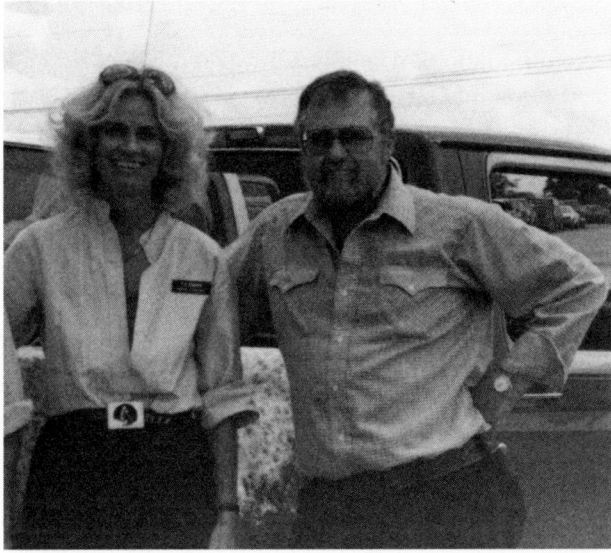

The author with Jerome (Haunch) Alexander, former Y.O. hunting guide, 1982.

the Y.O.'s former hunting guides who also played mandolin and guitar in the Y.O. Band. He was friends with the director of tourism at the Y.O. Ranch Headquarters. She invited Haunch to come see the improvements the new owners had made. He asked if I would like to accompany him, and I accepted.

As we pulled up to the Y.O.'s front gate, the changes were obvious. There was now an automatic gate opener, and with the push of a button the gate swung open. No more getting in and out of your vehicle in all types of weather to open and close the gate or having bits of gravel embedded in your shoes. Stretching before us was a widened paved road.

I looked at Haunch and said, "Can you believe this?"

"I wonder what Three would think about it?" Haunch asked. We both started laughing.

"I remember asking Charlie why he didn't pave the road," I said. "He told me one reason was the cost, but the other was because it created ambiance to remind city slickers they were on a real ranch, not a movie version of one."

With the new and improved road, we made it to the headquarters in less than fifteen minutes. We stopped at the lodge and went inside. It still looked much the same but most of the shoulder mounts on the walls were now African animals, which Haunch told me were the new owners' trophies. The ranch offices had been relocated from the Chuckwagon to the structure adjoining the lodge. It had originally been the home Myrtle built for Three and his first wife and was later converted by Charlie into guest accommodations. The interior was remodeled and bore little resemblance to the original structure. A two-story building stood where the pavilion once was and contained eighteen guest rooms. The log cabins had been spruced up with fresh ceilings, new plumbing fixtures, and new furnishings. The ranch had moved into the twenty-first century with Wi-Fi and satellite television. I remembered how removed from civilization it was when I lived there—the sporadic television and radio reception and no daily newspaper delivery.

We drove around Deer Park and Africana to see the animals. In addition to the exotic species Charlie Three brought to the ranch, new additions included llamas, a camel, wildebeest, a mini burro, nilgai, kudu, and Himalayan tahrs (a type of wild goat). Haunch asked if I wanted to go to Three's house. The house was now used for weddings and special events. I declined.

"Amazing what a few million dollars can do, isn't it?" I said to Haunch as we drove back to the front gate. My emotions vacillated. I was glad part of the ranch and the magnificent structures Charlie Three designed and built were being preserved. But the ranch was lacking the authenticity it had when the Schreiners owned it and it was a working ranch, an authenticity that no amount of money could replicate. There were no Mexican cowboys with their spurs jingling and their horses tossing their heads as they rode out to work cattle. The shearing barn no longer echoed with a cacophony of bleating sheep as shearers plied their trade. Nor were there cattle trailers and beat-up trucks in the Chuckwagon parking lot. There was no one with the distinctiveness of Button chomping on his cigar to welcome guests. Or Bertie's biscuits, chicken-fried steak, beans, and chocolate cake. Where were the equivalents of Butch, Rusty, Haunch, or Tommy Thompson to serenade guests, play practical jokes on one another, and tell tall tales?

Against grave odds the ranch survived, and like all survivors, it adapted and took on a new character. Guests visiting the ranch would never know what the ranch was like once upon a time. They would drive the eight miles of paved road into and out of the ranch in ease and comfort, oblivious to the difficult and time-consuming task it once was. They would have Wi-Fi to stay in touch with world events rather than driving around the ranch trying to find a place where there was radio reception. They would visit Gobblers Knob, but as far as they could see would not be part of the Y.O. They would hold parties and weddings at Three's house unaware of the history of its design and building, the architectural antiques

"I always get to where I'm going by walking away from where I've been."— Winnie the Pooh. The author at the 1979 Y.O. Trail Drive. Photograph by Ron Dorsey.

incorporated into the rooms, and the first wedding that occurred there on Charlie Three's birthday in 1978. Some might hear the soft meow of a cat or voices floating across the pastures above the live oak trees. But how could they know what it meant to be a part of this ranch and its history, or that those whose spirits returned here had the Y.O. brand engraved as deeply on their hearts as it once was on the hides of the ranch's animals?

When I left the Y.O. in 1980, I mistakenly assumed it was a closed chapter in my life; however, that was not to be. Over the next forty years, the ranch and the Schreiners remained a part of my life, making me realize that I also bore the Y.O. brand. When Charlie and I divorced, my mother wrote me a letter that I thought was maudlin and ridiculous. Now I realize she was right.

She wrote, "[Whoever lives in that house] should be taught to watch for a blonde long haired young lady and a grey brindle cat that will forever haunt the Y.O."

"All that anxiety and anger, those dubious good intentions,

those tangled lives, that blood. I can tell about it or I can bury it.

In the end, we'll all become stories.

Or else we'll become entities. Maybe it's the same."

MARGARET ATWOOD

IN EARLY 2022, the Y.O. Ranch Headquarters was sold again to three investors. What its future holds no one knows. At the time of this writing in early 2025, the ranch remains a hunting, special event, and guest ranch.

The era of large Texas ranches comprised of thousands of acres is over. Only a handful of those that contributed to the mythology of Texas and the cowboy are still owned by descendants of their founders. With the death of each generation, the ranches have been divided among more heirs; if left intact, family members' personalities have collided and quarrels resulted in the dissolution and sale of the ranch. The Waggoner Ranch in north-central Texas is an example. It was the second largest ranch in Texas with over 520,000 acres. In 2014, a district judge ordered the ranch be sold to end more than twenty years of litigation among family members. It was purchased by billionaire Stan Kroenke, who made his fortune in real estate.

The equally famous Four Sixes Ranch in North Texas was started in the early 1870s. Anne Burnett Marion, the great-granddaughter of Burk Burnett, who founded the ranch, specified in her will that the ranch of over 266,000 acres was to be sold upon her death. In 2021, it was purchased by a group of investors that included movie director and actor Taylor Sheridan, who made his name and fortune with the television series *Yellowstone*.

Sunset on the Y.O. Ranch. Photo by Ron Dorsey.

The two historic ranches remaining in the families of their founders are the King Ranch in South Texas, and the lesser-known Lambshead Ranch in north-central Texas. The fifty thousand-acre Lambshead Ranch is entirely owned by direct descendants of its founder, John Matthews, and by covenant cannot be sold outside the family. The King Ranch in South Texas is the best-known Texas ranch and the largest at 825,000 acres. Though still owned by family members, it has morphed into a professionally managed private corporation. It has properties throughout the world with interests in cattle ranching, feedlots, farming, citrus groves, and hunting. The ranch's Running W brand is found on leather goods, home furnishings, wine glasses, and Ford pickups. Such diversification epitomizes what is necessary for a large ranch to survive in the twenty-first century.

Thirty or so years ago, I read an article predicting the demise of large

Texas ranches. Reading those words pierced my heart, and I was certain it could never happen. Now, I have lived to see it, and I've acquired enough worldly wisdom to understand nothing lasts forever. I was able to live a small portion of my life as part of one of those ranches and become friends with the heirs of other historic ranches that, like the Y.O., no longer exist in their original form. I consider it one of the greatest gifts life has given me, and one for which I shall be forever grateful.

Appendix

Children of Captain Charles Armand Schreiner and Mary Magdelena Enderle Schreiner

Aime Charles Schreiner	1862–1935
Gustave Fritz Schreiner	1866–1962
Louis Albert Schreiner	1870–1970
Caroline Marie Schreiner Partee	1873–1947
Emilie Louise (Mimi) Schreiner Rigsy	1875–1971
Charles Schreiner	1876–1967
Walter Richard Schreiner	1877–1933
Frances Hellen Schreiner Jeffers	1881–1940

Children of Charles Schreiner III (6 Jan. 1927–22 Apr. 2001) and Audrey Phillips Schreiner (6 Sept. 1928–17 June 1988)

Charles Schreiner IV	17 Aug. 1951–
Walter Richard Schreiner Jr.	9 Jan. 1954–17 July 2014
Gustav (Gus) Louis Schreiner	21 July 1958–
Louis (Louie) Albert Schreiner II	4 Oct. 1959–13 Apr. 2001

Bibliography

Barrett, Neal Jr. *Long Days and Short Nights: A Century of Texas Ranching on the YO 1880–1980*. Mountain Home, TX: Y-O Press, 1980.

Batura, Sean. "YO Ranch owners embroiled in lawsuit. Plaintiffs seek breakup of 27,000 acres." *Kerrville Daily Times*, March 2–3, 2013, 1.

———. "Bank sues owner of YO Ranch. Schreiner, bank accuse each other of negligence over more than $130K in missing funds." *Kerrville Daily Times*, March 25, 2013, 1.

———. "Y.O. owner accused of stealing sheep." *Kerrville Daily Times*, April 10, 2013, 1.

———. "Widow settles with YO." *Kerrville Daily Times*, June 20, 2013, https://dailytimes.com/news/local/article_e9b9fa26-da27–11e2–8297-0019bb2963f4.html

———. "Schreiner facing felonies. Great-grandson of famous rancher accused of theft, money laundering." *Kerrville Daily Times*, August 26, 2014, 1.

Baulch, Joe R. "Schreiner, Gustave Frederick (1866–1962). In *Handbook of Texas Online* (Texas State Historical Association). Updated June 1, 1995. https://www.tshaonline.org/handbook/entries/schreiner-gustave-frederick.

Benham, Joseph. "A few more things for which we owe the Schreiners." *Kerrville Daily Times*, February 24, 2013.

Bernhard, Autumn. "Wild Ranching. Iconic ranch thriving under new ownership." *Texas Hill Country Culture*, November 2018, 23–26.

Bragg, Roy. "Kerrville has grown out of ranch's shadow." *San Antonio Express-News*. March 7, 2013, 1A.

Centennial Issue: The Y.O. Mountain Home, TX: Y-O Press, 1980.

Danini, Carmina. "Schreiner was Y.O. Ranch owner, Legendary spread once had more than a half-million acres." *San Antonio Express-News*, April 15, 2001.

Dobie, J. Frank. *The Longhorns*. New York: Bramhall House, 1941.

Emmett, Chris. *Texas Camel Tales, The U.S. Camel Corps in Texas*. Corpus Christi, TX: Copano Bay Press, 2012.

Ennis, Michael. "Three's Company." *Texas Monthly*. June 1980. 130–41.

"Exotic Deer Gores Man to Death." ABC 13 News. October 7, 2009, https://abc13.com/archive/7053336/.

Fehrenbach, T. R. Lone Star: *A History of Texas and the Texans*. New York: MacMillan Publishing Co., Inc., 1968.

Grinstead, J. E. "The House of Schreiner." *Grinstead's Magazine*, June 1920, 26–34. https://grinsteadslibrarian.wordpress.com/resources-from-schreiner-u/the-house-of-schreiner/.

Haley, J. Evetts. *Charles Schreiner General Merchandise: The Story of a Country Store*. Austin: Texas State Historical Association, 1944.

Holon, Gene. "Captain Charles Schreiner, the Father of the Hill Country." *The Southwestern Historical Quarterly, Texas State Historical Association* 48, no. 2 (October 1944): 145–68. https://www.jstor.org/stable/30237466.

———. "Schreiner, Charles Armand, (1838–1927)." In *Handbook of Texas Online* (Texas State Historical Association). Updated January 8, 2020. https://www.tshaonline.org/handbook/entries/schreiner-charles-armand.

Howard, Kay. "Home on the Y.O. High on a hill, the house overlooks the ranch." *Austin Homes & Gardens*. October 1979, 43–49.

———. "The Y.O.—Escape to the West." *Austin Homes & Gardens*. October 1979, 50–55.

Hunter, J. Marvin. "Captain Charles Schreiner, Pioneer." *Frontier Times Magazine*, vol. 5, no. 2. November 1927, 91. https://www.frontiertimesmagazine.com/blog/captain-charles-schreiner-pioneer.

"In Memoriam 1954–2014 Walter Schreiner." *Texas Longhorn Trails*. September 2014, 22.

"Kerr Ranch Hand Fatally Gored by Exotic Deer." *San Antonio Express-News*. October 7, 2009. https://www.mysanantonio.com/news/local_news/article/Kerr-ranch-hand-fatally-gored-by-exotic-deer-858138.php.

Kerrville Mountain Sun. "Norma Schreiner Named Director of Longhorns." May 30, 1979, 1.

Krane, Gene. "Going, Going, Gone." *Heritage, A Publication of the Texas Historical Foundation*. Spring 2003, 36.

Lynch, Dudley. *The Duke of Duval, The Life & Times of George B. Parr*. Waco: Texian Press, 1976.

MacCormack, Zeke. "Civil disputes dogged Schreiner before arrest." *San Antonio Express-News*, April 17, 2013. https://www.mysanantonio.com/news/local/article/civil-disputes-dogged-schreiner-before-arrest-4441327.php.

———. "For sale for $85 million: Storied, exotic YO Ranch." *San Antonio Express-News* and MYSA.com." August 23, 2013, 1.

———. "YO Ranch co-owner headed to jail after pleading guilty to theft." *San Antonio Express-News*, July 13, 2015. https://www.expressnews.com/news/local/article/YO-Ranch-co-owner-headed-to-jail-after-pleading-6382402.php#:~:text=KERRVILLE%20.

———. "Section of famed ranch changes hands." *San Antonio Express-News*, October 8, 2015, 1.

Martin, Douglas. "Charles Schreiner III, 74, Dies; Colorful Texas Rancher Fought to Save Longhorn." *New York Times*, April 29, 2001, 27.

Murf, Jim. "EWA Mourns Charlie III and Louie." *Exotic Wildlife*, vol. 11, no. 3. May/June 2001, 1.

Oliver, Myrna. "Charles Schreiner III; Rancher Helped Save the Texas Longhorn." *Los Angeles Times*, May 8, 2001. https://www.latimes.com/archives /la-xpm-2001-may-08-me-60852-story.html.

Sanders, George W. "Trail Drivers Save Texas from Ruin." *Up the Trail, Number of the Pioneer History, A Monthly Supplement of the Kerrville Times*, vol. 2, no. 8. August 1933, 1.

Schlachter, Barry. "In a Hill Country town, the name of the game is antagonism." *Fort Worth Star-Telegram*, May 27, 1990, 1.

———. "Schreiner clan's roots deep, far-reaching in hometown." *Fort Worth Star-Telegram*. May 27, 1990, 1.

Schreiner, Charlie III. "The YO Ranch and the Texas Legacy." In *Forever Texas: Texas History, The Way Those Who Lived It Wrote It*, edited by Mike Blakely and Mary Elizabeth Goldman, 191–93. New York: Tom Doherty Associates, 2000.

Schreiner, Charlie III, Audrey Schreiner, Robert Berryman, and Hal F. Matheny. *A Pictorial History of the Texas Rangers: "That Special Breed of Men."* Mountain Home, TX: Y-O Press, 1969.

Schreiner v. Schreiner, 502 S.W.2d 840 (1973). https://www.leagle.com/ decision/19731342502sw2d84011214.

"Schreiner, Louis Albert (1870–1970)." In *Handbook of Texas Online* (Texas State Historical Association). Updated February 19, 2019. https://www .tshaonline.org/handbook/entries/schreiner-louis-albert.

Taylor, Gary Lee. "Trial postponed for bank heads." *The Mountain Sun*, vol. 115, no. 12. January 11, 1995, 1.

Thomas, Mike W. "Schreiner Bank directors sued." *Kerrville Daily Times*, September 14, 1993, 1.

Williams, Docia Schultz. *The History and Mystery of the Menger Hotel*. Plano: Republic of Texas Press, 2000.

Van Winkle, Irene. "YO redux. Legendary ranch being revived, rejuvenated and remodeled." *West Kerr Current*. March 31, 2016, 1.

Wilson, Mark. "YO Ranch partner killed in crash." *San Antonio Express-News*, July 18, 2014.

Index

Photograph page numbers are italicized

About the Author

NORMA SCHREINER is a sixth-generation Texan. She was the fourth wife of Charles Schreiner III (Charlie Three or Three) and was involved with the Y.O. Ranch from 1977 to 1982. During this time the ranch was at its zenith and celebrated its centennial.

She was the first woman to be elected to a livestock board of directors—the South Texas Longhorn Association—and for this and her work on the Y.O. centennial was named a "Yellow Rose of Texas" by Texas Governor William Clements. She is currently a director of the Texas Historical Foundation and a lifetime member of the Texas Longhorn Breeders Association of America.

Her careers have included lobbyist and political consultant, adjunct professor of political science, owner of two small businesses, and corporate executive. She writes for newspapers and magazines. She contributed an essay, "An Old Soul," to *Kid Me Not: An Anthology of Child-free Women of the '60s Now in Their 60s*, edited by Aralyn Hughes. Her favorite pastime is traveling to see animals, and in this pursuit she has taken a horseback trek across Mongolia, hiked into the jungles of Africa to see mountain gorillas, visited snow monkeys in northern Japan, and visited the Arctic Circle and Antarctica. She volunteers at the Houston Zoo and with Wildlife Rescue and Rehabilitation in Kendalia, Texas. She lives in the Texas Hill Country with two cats and her fiancé, who is allergic to cats and horses.

A portion of the sales from this book will go to animal welfare organizations.